G. DEBORIN

Secrets of the Second World War

Progress Publishers

Moscow

Translated from the Russian by **Vic Schneierson**

Designed by **Yuri Markov**

Г. А. ДЕБОРИН

ТАЙНЫ ВТОРОЙ МИРОВОЙ ВОЙНЫ

На английском языке

First printing 1971

Printed in the Union of Soviet Socialist Republics

CONTENTS

4

FOREWORD

The Second World War (1939-1945) left a deep mark on the minds of all. It claimed a toll of more than 50 million lives.[1] Priceless treasures, the fruit of the labour and genius of many generations, were devoured by the flames. Terrible was the suffering of the peoples of Europe, Asia and Africa.

Not surprisingly, a quarter of a century after the war people still want to know the truth: how it originated, what forces were to blame, how it ended and whose were the martial feats that forged the victory. The world will never forget the men who defeated fascism. Their daring inspires poets and artists, and writers of books such as this one.

The title of this book, *Secrets of the Second World War*, was not selected merely to attract more readers. That is hardly needed. War books evoke a keen enough interest, no matter what their title. This author's motivation was anything but that.

It may appear to some that there were no secrets of the war. Could there indeed be secrets where tens of millions of people were involved? Yet secrecy often envelops the origins of war and many of the subsequent military developments. It will not be too much to say, in fact, that secrecy has been a satellite of the origin and course of war.

There are two kinds of wars—just, liberative, progressive ones, and wars unjust, aggressive and reactionary. Lenin wrote: "... there are just and unjust wars, progressive and reactionary wars, wars waged by advanced classes and wars

---

[1] *Sovietskaya istoricheskaya entsiklopedia (Soviet Encyclopaedia of History)*, Vol. 3, p. 872.

waged by backward classes, wars waged for the purpose of perpetuating class oppression and wars waged for the purpose of eliminating oppression...."[1]

No secrets would have existed if the Second World War had been one of liberation from the beginning. Liberators waging a just war are legitimately proud of their exploit, and have nothing to hide.

A war may be unjust on both sides, if both pursue aims of conquest. A just war is just on one side only. If one side responds to aggression with a just war of liberation, the war of the other side is one of conquest and enslavement, and unjust. People are hardly likely to rally to that sort of war. That is why secrecy and deceit have a field day.

Unjust wars were always garnished with falsehood, deceit and provocation. Foul play necessitates foul means.

Those who pursue imperialist policy, of which war is but a continuation, choose to act in secrecy, especially in the preparatory stage. They dread publicity, knowing that it may boomerang. Those who pursue fair policies have a stake in public knowledge. Lenin said: "We must explain the real situation to the people, show them that war is hatched in the greatest secrecy...."[2]

Secrecy covered the preparations for the First World War, and likewise those for the Second. The direct war architects, the German imperialists, professed to be lovers of peace. Hitler's nazi party, which seized power in Germany in 1933, assured foreign statesmen that it had no concern more urgent than that of safeguarding peace. In the meantime, doing the will of its backers, the monopolies, it prepared frantically for a war for world supremacy.

The Munichites of Britain, France and the United States, eager to channel German aggression eastward, against the Soviet Union, encouraged the German fascists and pretended to accept Hitler's reassurances. They lifted their eyes to heaven and extolled peace, and also, in the same breath, praised the nazi methods against the disobedient. The voices of those cooking up war blended in singing specious paeons to peace.

This mixture of pacific oratory and bellicose intention needed the weapon of secrecy to be effective. In the name

---

[1] V. I. Lenin, *Collected Works*, Vol. 29, p. 343.
[2] *Ibid.*, Vol. 33, p. 447.

of this secrecy the briefcases of German delegates to the disarmament conference were closely guarded, as were the doors of that Munich hall where the fate of Czechoslovakia was sealed, giving the green light to nazi aggression.

The criminal Munich deal struck by Britain and France with Hitler Germany and fascist Italy was paraded as an act of peace, though it was really an act of encouraging aggression and, in that sense, an act of war.

Secrecy was an amenity for those that yearned for war, and for those, too, who were opening up the way for Hitler's conquests. The veils, at least many of them, have been lifted by now, but some still shroud the truth. Take a recent West German volume, *Wahrheit für Deutschland*, whose writer, Udo Walendy, pleads for justice, for a "truth for Germany", denying her war guilt. Page through it and you will smell gunpowder, acrid smoke, and blood; you will see the secrecy that shrouded Hitler's war preparations used in a new way, for new ends.

Walendy quotes prolifically the pacific declarations of the war culprits. He strains to show that none of the German leaders wanted a world war. What they wanted was "merely" to extend German territory. Yet the other powers did not wish to meet Germany halfway. It is their fault the war broke out.

The drum-beaters of the neo-nazi National-Democratic Party of the Federal Republic of Germany, of whom Udo Walendy is one, repeat the Hitler clique's claims in explaining the causes of the Second World War, unmasking the NDP as successor and heir to Hitler's defunct National-Socialist Party.

It may be proper to note that two phases are evident in West German historiography. During the first, from the war's end to approximately 1965, veteran historians (Walter Goerlitz), Hitler generals (Kurt von Tippelskirch, Erich Manstein and Heinz Guderian), and younger writers (Hans-Adolf Jacobsen, Jurgen Rohwer and K. D. Erdmann) alike, endeavoured to exonerate the German General Staff and German imperialism of the war guilt and of the inhumanities of the nazi army. They put all the blame on Hitler. In the second phase, however, embracing the more recent years, with the National-Democratic Party stepping on to the FRG scene, Hitler, too, is being exonerated.

The West German revenge-seekers and militarists now

insist that Germany and her leaders were not to blame for the war. Czechs, Poles, Russians, Ukrainians and Byelorussians were guilty, for instead of acknowledging German territorial claims, instead of bowing to them, they put up a fight. The war was to their intransigence.

And what about the atrocities? The newly-fledged fascists reply there had been none, that no 12 million people had been exterminated in nazi death camps. They declare all documents testifying to atrocities to be false and the material evidence — instruments of torture, gas chambers and the mountains of human ash — to have been fabricated postwar by Germany's enemies. In a collection of articles by NDP ideologists, *Europe in Flames*, atrocities are blandly denied. Referring to Dachau, the neo-fascists say: "Until May 1945 it had no gas chambers. These were built later by German POWs on the orders of the American occupation authorities."[1] Yet it is common knowledge that the American occupation authorities and statesmen, and the British, too, chose to minimise the instances of nazi evil, and were certainly disinclined to exaggerate them. The neo-fascists follow Hitler's explicit advice: The more monstrous the lie, the better.

That literature of this sort has appeared is indicative. One wonders whether men of power are again, for the third time, trying to guide history along the vicious circle: secret war preparations, sudden attack, extermination of millions, total defeat and then again war preparations in secrecy, camouflaged with honeyed words of peace.

Secret diplomacy is the resort of those who pursue unpopular policy and have reason to conceal their intentions. When the October Revolution triumphed in Russia, the Soviet Government at once declared its rejection of secret diplomacy. It said in the historic Decree on Peace, drawn up by Lenin and adopted by the Second All-Russia Congress of Soviets: "The Government abolishes secret diplomacy."[2] Ever since, publicity instead of secrecy has been the basis of Soviet foreign policy. Genuinely democratic policy must be open.

To be sure Soviet measures related to defence were concealed in wartime. But once concealment was no longer necessary, the facts were instantly published. This was true, for example, of the Yalta Conference decision of the Soviet

---

[1] *Europa in Flammen 1939-1945*, Bd. 1, Vlotho-Weser, 1966, S. 421.
[2] V. I. Lenin, *Collected Works*, Vol. 26, p. 250.

Union's joining the war against Japan, kept secret for a year. Publicity is part of honesty. When after the war ended many secrets were revealed, it was discovered that the Soviet Union had done nothing in secret from its wartime allies.

Could the same be said of the other members of the anti-fascist coalition? It could of the Resistance Movement, but not of the governments of the United States and Britain. They represented countries that became combatants by virtue of the inexorable logic of history in a war that developed into a just war of liberation. But even in such a war, they would not disavow their selfish and ultimately anti-popular aspirations. The contradiction between the objective nature of the war and the subjective designs of the US and British rulers kept surfacing at every point. For a long time they sabotaged a second front, concealing the true purpose of the delay. Nor did they forego secret negotiations with nazi chiefs and chieftains. They manufactured their own plans for a post-war world arrangement contrary to the joint decisions of wartime allied conferences. Naturally, these plans were kept secret.

Apart from imperialist secrets related to the preparation and conduct of the war, there were "secrets" of a different kind. These were "secrets", or, more precisely, riddles related to the process of history, for the true sense of many historical developments is concealed from the casual observer. It is the task of the investigator to probe these developments and pinpoint the laws that impelled them.

To limit investigations to the superficial aspects of phenomena is not merely easier, but also, for many, more profitable. Some phases of the Second World War are reminiscent of scenes from old operas, where the actors chant, "We march, we march, we march!", while marking time. In the meantime, others do the marching through raging enemy fire. Yet no sooner the war ended than those who talked big but did little, began declaiming that their shouting had made the enemy bastions collapse. And new secrets appear in place of the old.

Lastly, some "secrets" are ascribable to absence of information. This applies to the "secret", or rather the miracle, of the Soviet resistance and victory, which took many a friend of the Soviet Union, and certainly its enemies, by surprise. Those who knew of the intrinsic strength of the Soviet socialist society saw no miracle in that the Soviet Union withstood the incredible difficulties of a war against a strong enemy, and ascended to victory. In a way, that victory was preordained. But even those who know, will do well to look back again on the wartime attainments of the Soviet people and review the factors that assured the Soviet triumph.

People were the makers of the victory—the people of the Soviet Union, who bore the brunt of the war, the peoples of the United States and Britain, the peoples of France, Yugoslavia, Poland, Czechoslovakia, Belgium, Greece, Italy, and all those countries that were the theatre of the Resistance. Glory to them!

Chapter One

Secrecy—the Watchword

1. World Imperialism Is the Culprit

It took several decades—from the conclusion of the Austro-German Treaty in 1879 to the forming of the Entente in 1904-1907—to prepare secretly for the First World War. Secret preparations for the Second World War began soon after the First ended, and consumed nearly two decades. Two military coalitions confronted each other long before the First World War: the Triple Alliance and the Entente. There was only one coalition before the Second World War: the Berlin-Rome-Tokyo axis. Britain, France and the United States did not gang up against Germany for the simple reason that they refused to lose hope until the day the war broke out (and even after) of coming to terms with the nazis against the Soviet Union.

This difference in the prewar setup reflected deep-going changes in the world arrangement. On the eve of the First World War the globe was totally a capitalist playground, whereas before the Second World War the Soviet Union, the world's first socialist state, was well launched and developing rapidly. That was the new substantive point that distinguished the situation before the Second World War from that before the First. This time, the imperialist states were bent on resolving their contradictions at the expense of the USSR.

The second war, like the first, materialised due to the acute contradictions of the imperialist system—contradictions between the biggest capitalist powers, each of which was out to seize new territories, subjugate peoples and establish its supremacy. That was what led to the First World War, which culminated in a redivision of the world in accordance with the existing balance of power. Defeated Germany was deprived of her colonies and of some of the neighbouring territories seized by German conquerors. Yet the social system in Germany withstood the revolutionary onslaught of the people.

The lessons of that war, of the disastrous defeat, were lost on the German monopolists. On the eve of the first war they clamoured for "a place in the sun", whereas after it they also had a thirst for revenge. Revenge was what rallied all German aspirers of conquest. And by reason of the uneven economic and political development of capitalist countries, Germany soon caught up and then surpassed Britain and France, her European rivals, economically and militarily. This added fuel to the revenge-seeking ambitions of the German rulers.

The process was gradual and in the earlier stages a minimum of effort could have averted the subsequent course of events. But neither Britain nor France (nor the United States for that matter) did anything about it. On the contrary, their rulers displayed a "sense of affinity" with the German militarists. Their policy of abetment was camouflaged with assurances to the world that Germany had changed, become democratic, and would never again be a threat to her neighbours.

The American, British and French monopolies reckoned that German military revival would compensate for the old world's general debility contracted after socialism triumphed in the USSR. German militarism would not have recovered as swiftly as it did if international reaction, mostly the US monopolies, had not given it a helping hand. Monopoly quarters in the US, Britain and France hand-fed hitlerism, assisting the militarists in their new fascist cloak to prepare for the *Drang nach Osten* with the avowed purpose of destroying the Soviet Union.

The myopic anti-Soviet policy of the European and American imperialist bourgeoisie, steeped in hostility for the socialist system and backed by Right Social-Democratic leaders, bordered on outright betrayal of national interests, overstepping that border here and there, in face of the mounting nazi threat. The secret preparations of the Second World War are, in fact, a startling illustration of how the class limitations of the reactionary bourgeoisie and its blind hatred of communism delivered the European countries to disaster and enslavement by German fascist invaders.

In the years preceding the war, the imperialist states converged along the anti-Soviet course. Yet, uniquely, their convergence blended with a further sharpening of the imperialist drives for world rule. That was why the Second World War at first broke out as a collision of two capitalist groups.

World imperialism was thus the sole culprit of the Second World War.

Once again imperialist Germany was its immediate initiator. After its defeat in 1914-1918, German imperialism became more aggressive. Its thirst for world power, an incurable disease, assumed monstrous proportions: it did not hesitate to begin plotting a new war.

The German monopolies sensed that resistance of the patriotic democratic section of the nation could spike their expansionist designs that gravely menaced the Germans themselves. So they delegated power to the Hitler clique, which, they saw, would impose acquiescence on the people by unmitigated terrorism.

The fascist coup took place early in 1933. The nazi seizure of power marked a realignment of strength among the monopoly bourgeoisie. The making of home and foreign policy fell under the total control of the moguls of the heavy and arms industry and the most aggressive and most reactionary segment of German finance capital.

The close alliance between the nazi clique and the German financial oligarchy was cemented by members of the former soon becoming millionaire monopolists. Hermann Goering was the foremost, amassing a fortune by plundering "non-Arian" financiers. His concern had a capital of RM 6,000 million, with a fortune of over $3,500,000 in the United States.[1] Joseph Goebbels became a millionaire by marrying Magda Quandt, a banker's daughter. Adolf Hitler, too, the fascist dictator, was a capitalist of considerable means.

Even before coming to power the nazis were financed by monopolists. Afterwards, this financial support became a regular subsidy. An Adolf Hitler Fund for German Economy was founded on Krupp's initiative in May 1933, compounded from obligatory levies on wages and salaries. The workers

---

[1] G. Rozanov, *Germaniya pod vlastyu fashizma (Germany under Fascist Rule)* IMO Publishers, Moscow, 1961, p. 140.

were made to enrich their most bitter class enemy. The revenue amounted to RM 8,400,000 in the first year, and to RM 20,000,000 in the second.[1]

The nazis dealt ruthlessly with their political opponents long before they came to power, and shed all restraint once the bourgeois machinery of state fell under their control. Prisons and concentration camps densely dotted the country; camp barracks became a graphic architectural symbol of nazism. "The evolution from baroque to barrack was, in a way, a historical process illustrating the development of German culture under Hitler's rule,"[2] wrote Balis Sruoga, a Lithuanian writer and ex-inmate of a nazi death camp.

Nearly a million people[3] languished in prisons and camps, with 200,000 executed or tormented to death. The Communists were exposed to the most brutal treatment of all.

The main nazi aim was to prepare, trigger and prosecute a world war that would place the German monopolies into a position of unlimited power. Home and foreign policy was centred totally on this ultimate aim. Planning the "total" campaign, the hitlerites knew that in common their adversaries possessed superior strength. It, therefore, became their main diplomatic objective to keep them divided. Though reckless to the extreme, this policy paid off.

While the Soviet Union called unceasingly for a united front of peaceful nations to repulse the aggressive nazis, the rulers of the United States, Britain and France opposed this in every way. They were aware of the danger emanating from Germany, but assumed that it was insignificant compared with the advantages they would reap from an eventual war between Germany and the Soviet Union. Their plan was simple: let Germany destroy the Soviet Union and crush the labour movement in Europe, whereupon they would dictate terms to a Reich weakened by its effort in the East. The US rulers concealed their policy of encouraging German aggression in Europe and Japanese aggression in the Pacific behind a cloak of neutrality, and those of Britain and France behind non-interference.

The nazis were aware of the expectations of the US, British and French monopolists. They constructed their

---

[1] G. Rozanov, *op. cit.*, pp. 141-42.
[2] B. Sruoga, *Les bogov (Divine Forest)*, Vilnius, 1958, p. 7.
[3] *Geschichte der deutschen Arbeiterbewegung*, Bd. 5, Berlin, 1966, S. 235.

plans on an anti-communist foundation, Hitler and his lieutenants stressing constantly that their war plans concerned the Soviet Union only, not the rest of Europe, and that their purpose was to protect Europe from the "Bolshevik danger". This, they kept saying, was why the West should help Germany fling off the Versailles constraints and rearm.

Hitler put it in so many words to his closest associates: "I've got to play ball with capitalism and keep the Versailles powers in line by holding aloft the bogey of Bolshevism—make them believe that a nazi Germany is the last bulwark against the Red flood. That's the only way to come through the danger period, to get rid of Versailles and re-arm."[1]

His secret manoeuvres succeeded. The US, British and French governments showed extraordinary zeal in clearing Germany's path. These upholders of Western democracy went so far as to aver that German fascism was a special kind of "democtatic arrangement". And Hjalmar Schacht, the German banker who toured the United States soon after the nazi coup, lecturing before financiers in the biggest cities, did his utmost to back up this specious propaganda. He said, among other things, that the fascist regime was the finest form of democracy.[2] His speaking tour firmed up the friendly feelings of the US monopolies towards Hitler and his regime. They stepped up their action, seeking to reinforce the military-industrial potential and the giant army establishment of nazi Germany. It stands to reason that their endeavours were anything but altruistic. General Motors, for one, cleared at least $30,000,000, and this according to minimised estimates, out of which $20,000,000 were reinvested in industries "owned or controlled by Goering and other nazi officials".[3]

Economic ties of Anglo-US monopolies with Germany and their prominent part in restoring the armed forces of the German militarists, constituted the economic basis of the "neutrality" and "non-interference" officially professed by the United States and Britain, respectively.

No capitalist government bothered to act consistently for peace and security against the imminent fascist aggression. And not for a lack of Soviet warnings, which the capitalist press and bourgeois politicians classified as unfounded

---

[1] K. Ludecke, *I Knew Hitler,* New York, 1938, p. 468.
[2] *New York Evening Post,* May 5, 1933.
[3] *Congressional Record,* Vol. 88, Part 10, p. A3135.

"propaganda", on the grounds that the German Government had publicly declared its allegiance to peace and earned the trust of Western governments by its general activity. Nazi war preparations were indeed camouflaged with professions of peace, but their speciousness was obvious.

The Soviet Union advanced the proposal of a united front of peoples and governments against a new world war. This, in fact, was the purport of the Soviet European collective security plan.

Yet the aggressors and their abettors poured scorn on the Soviet idea. The nazi government made its disapproval clear through official channels, announcing its hostility to all treaties of mutual aid against aggression. This was not surprising. Its repudiation of collective security was motivated by aggressive intents. But Britain and the United States, too, came out against it. Meanwhile Mussolini countered with a plan for a united imperialist front, including Germany. He proposed a "quadripartite pact", and accord by the United Kingdom, France, Germany and Italy to revise peace treaties, recognise Germany's "right" to rearmament and assure co-operation against the Soviet Union.

The four-power agreement of understanding and co-operation was concluded soon after the Hitler coup, on July 15, 1933. But its architects went down in defeat in their respective parliaments, which refused to ratify it in face of the public outcry. This ended the first Anglo-French attempt, backed by the US imperialists, to build an anti-Soviet front and prod the reviving German militarism eastward. However, though unratified, the four-power pact served as a prologue to the Munich deal, a fateful factor of subsequent international developments.

The next encouragement of nazi aggression was Britain's and France's refusal to act effectively against the Hitler government in 1935, when it began its series of gross violations of the Versailles military articles and the building up of vast armed forces.

More, unilateral violations of Versailles treaties were followed by a bilateral violation: in June 1935 the British Government concluded a naval agreement with Germany, allowing her to reconstitute a powerful navy, with British firms promising financial and technical aid.

The US, British and French imperialists thought their cherished goal—a German attack on the USSR—very close.

However, far from relieving the imperialist contradictions, their policy of encouragement only added fuel to the fire. The rapid growth of Germany's military-economic potential, coupled with her war preparations, accentuated the unevenness in the development of the capitalist countries, tilting the balance of strength in Hitler's favour. The split of the capitalist world into hostile groups of powers was imminent, paving the way for an armed conflict between them.

The war matured in the womb of the capitalist world. The eruption drew closer. But the process was veiled by the secrecy that impregnated the policy of the Western powers, which thought of war while chattering of peace. The knife to cut the throat of the peace dove was being whetted by the nazis, while the leaders of the United States, Britain and France turned the grindstone. At first, Hitler had not expected this. The German imperialists had every reason to be grateful, but their gratitude was a mere pretence. Their daggers were drawn against France, Britain and the USA, as well as the Soviet Union.

2. The Secret Nazi Plans

Setting its sights on a world war, German imperialism aspired to much more than mere revenge for the 1918 defeat. It craved for world rule, a world-wide colonial empire in which the German monopolies meant to embrace the developed European countries.

The German imperialists' racial theory advocating extermination or enslavement of all other peoples by the German *Herrenvolk* was the ideological groundwork for Hitler's programme of conquest. Hitler described subjugation of other nations as the historical mission of the Germans, destined to provide the world with "a class of new masters". He said this in so many words:

"We want to make a selection for a class of new masters who will be devoid of moral pity, a class which will realise that because of its better race it has the right to dominate others, a class that will be able to establish and maintain without hesitation its domination over the masses."[1]

---

[1] *International Military Tribunal. Trial of the Major War Criminals*, Vol. 7, Nuremberg 1947, p. 152 (further referred to as *IMT. Trial...*).

Extolling aggression and violence, Hitler propaganda created a military cult, depicting war as the most noble of occupations for the German master race. "The divine essence of man (i.e., German—*Deborin*)," wrote Rosenberg, the nazi theorist, "must be defended with blood."[1]

The nazi ideology also rested on the theory of "insufficient living space". Fanning chauvinism, nazi propaganda maintained that all German troubles (especially painful during the world-wide economic crisis of 1929-1933) stemmed from overpopulation. And the solution for this problem, allegedly created by the advancement of other peoples, was said to be conquest of foreign land.[2]

Oswald Spengler, the German philosopher, said in a book in 1933 that immense colonial areas were available that could provide *Lebensraum* for the German race.[3] Hitler declared publicly: "We are overpopulated and cannot feed ourselves from our own land.... The final solution of the vital questions lies in expanding our living space.... If the Urals with their incalculable material resources, Siberia with its rich forests, and the Ukraine with its incalculable grain areas were part of Germany, the latter would attain abundance under National-Socialist leadership."[4]

The German rulers were plotting conquest of European, even of overseas, countries, and the Soviet Union, which they regarded as an object for colonisation, stood high up in their list. One of the leading nazi journalists wrote: "The Germans consider Russia a future colony.... Russia is entering a new stage in her history: it is becoming a colonial country."[5]

Direct war preparations began immediately on Hitler's assumption of power, gaining in intensity in 1936, when the nazi congress in Nuremberg adopted a four-year plan to build up Germany's war-making potential. In 1933, RM 700 million was invested in the war industry, investments rising to RM 9,000 million in 1936 and 15,500 million in 1938, and passing the 1933 level by as much as 1,1250 per cent in 1939.[6]

---

[1] Alfred Rosenberg, *Der Mythus des 20. Jahrhunderts*, München, 1942, S. 114.
[2] In dozens of countries population is denser than in Germany.
[3] O. Spengler, *Politische Schriften*, München, 1933, S. 124.
[4] *Völkischer Beobachter*, Sept. 13, 1936.
[5] *Zeitschrift für Geopolitik*, Heft I, 1936, S. 10-11.
[6] R. Erbe, *Die Nationalsozialistische Wirtschaftspolitik*, Zürich, 1958, S. 25.

Total cost of economic preparations for war passed the RM 90,000 million mark between 1933 and 1939. Out of this sum, 55,000 million was spent on arms production, 10,000 million on acquiring or producing and building up a stockpile of strategic raw materials, and nearly 25,000 million on state military investments.[1]

War production swallowed up tremendous financial and material resources, and a vast amount of labour. Between 1933 and 1939, for example, employment in the Junkers aircraft concern soared from 3,000 to 53,000 workers.[2]

The armed forces for the contemplated aggressive war grew rapidly, as may be seen from the following table:

The Nazi Military Build-up[3]

	1932	1936	1939
Total divisions incl.:	7	36	103
Panzer	—	3	6
Motorised	—	—	8

The German generals, who willingly acknowledged Hitler's leadership, primed for the war with extraordinary thoroughness. They knew it would be difficult for Germany to overcome the rest of the world. That was why they attached particular importance to the surprise element in attack, a factor yielding a distinct edge over the enemy. General Heinz Guderian wrote in an article in 1935, explaining the advantages of a sudden attack: "One night the gates of the plane hangars and army motor pools will swing open, the motors will break into song and the units will head forward. The first sudden strike will capture or destroy the enemy's important industrial and raw-material areas from the air, switching them out of war production. The enemy's government and military centres will be paralysed, and his

---

[1] *Istoriya Velikoi Otechestvennoi voiny Sovietskogo Soyuza (History of the Great Patriotic War of the Soviet Union)*, Vol. 1, p. 24 (further referred to as *I.V.O.V.S.S.*).

[2] IML, *Dokumenty i materialy Otdela istorii Velikoi Otechestvennoi voiny* (Institute of Marxism-Leninism. *Documents and Materials of the Department of the Great Patriotic War*), folio 19208, sheet 2207.

[3] Burkhart Mueller-Hillebrand, *Das Heer 1933-1945*, Bd. 1, Darmstadt 1954, S. 25, Bd. 2, S. 102.

communications crippled. The first sudden strategic assault will carry the troops more or less far into enemy territory."[1]

The generals' accent on a lightning war completely suited Hitler. He told his closest associates that when his government decided war as propitious, he would not indulge in negotiations. "If ever I attack an adversary," he declared, "I would not do it like Mussolini. I would not negotiate month after month and indulge in protracted preparations. I would act as I have always acted: suddenly, streaking out of the night and hitting lightning-like at my opponent."[2]

It was envisaged, moreover, that numerous German agents planted by the aggressor would help considerably in the sudden seizure of the countries concerned.

The nazis began fanning a war hysteria at home long before the hostilities. Speeches by leaders and generals, martial music over the radio, films and fascist songs combined with grandiose military spectacles consisting of stamping soldiers' boots, a rhythmic swaying of helmets, howls of Heil, were to inject faith that Germany was unconquerable, that her claims to world supremacy were justified.

Hitler's brazen behaviour actually covered up apprehensions and cowardice. Tearing down the restrictions set by the Versailles Treaty, the German Government was careful each time to leave itself avenues for hasty retreat. When they realised that resistance would not be forthcoming, however, they grew immeasurably bolder.

It was with second thoughts, teeth chattering from fear, that Hitler set to remilitarising the Rhine zone in March 1936. It seemed impossible that France would show no sign of outrage over this gross violation of treaty commitments by her dangerous neighbour. Yet the Hitler clique got away with it. "Hitler gazed tensely westward on that day, towards Paris and London. He waited 24 hours, then 48. When no intervention resulted, he breathed a sigh of relief. . . . He had gambled, and he won," wrote Otto Dietrich, Hitler's press chief, in his memoirs.[3]

Hitler Germany was more sure of her ground when she intervened in Spain jointly with Italy, and thereafter began preparing new acts of aggression.

---

[1] Heinz Guderian, "Kraftfahrkampftruppen", *Militärwissenschaftliche Rundschau*, No. 1, 1935, S. 75.

[2] A. Müller, *Hitlers motorisierte Stossarmee*, Paris, 1936, S. 31-32.

[3] O. Dietrich, *12 Jahre mit Hitler*, München, 1955, S. 44-45.

What lay behind the inactivity of many of the states selected as objects of fascist aggression? There were two motives:
firstly, the nazi government had prevailed on many statesmen
that its war preparations were aimed "solely" against the
Soviet Union and no Western powers were imperilled;
secondly, and closely associated with the former, some statesmen thought German aggression advantageous, hoping to
share in the spoils with the German monopolies. Take the
utterances in the House of Lords in February 1937 of
Labourite Sydney Arnold, a figure prominent in the Anglo-
German Friendship Society. "If there is another war on
the continent," he said, "and Great Britain stands aside, we
are not likely to be in danger if Germany were amongst the
victorious Powers or the defeated Powers."[1] Replying on
behalf of the government, Lord Halifax, then Keeper of the
Seal, fell in with this view.[2]

Some years after the Second World War, Lyndon Johnson,
the Senator who later became US President, admitted:
"France could have stopped Hitler when he started into
the Saar. France and England combined could have prevented the occupation of Austria or even later stopped the Nazis
at Czechoslovakia. The United States, England and France
could have prevented the rape of Poland...."[3]

But nothing of the kind was done.

Their earliest acts of aggression, committed with impunity,
so encouraged the German imperialists that they went ahead
with their war preparations. That was in 1937. The General
Staff drew up a secret Directive for Unified Preparation for
War, circulated among the troops on June 24. "Inasmuch as
favourable political opportunities have appeared for Germany," it said, "the most must be made of them, implying
such preparations of the Armed Forces as would enable
them to begin the war suddenly... to catch the adversary
by surprise and inflict a devastating lightning stroke."[4]

Hitler endorsed the main points of the directive at a
conference on November 5, 1937. In his three-hour speech
he gave an exposition of war variants. "The question for

---

[1] *Parliamentary Debates*, House of Lords, Vol. 104, p. 303.
[2] *Ibid.*, pp. 339-54.
[3] *Congressional Record*, Vol. 93, p. 4695.
[4] *Tsentralnyi gosudarstvennyi arkhiv Oktyabrskoi revolyutsii (Central State
Archives of the October Revolution)*, file 7445, case 1729, pp. 22-25 (further
referred to as *CSAOR*).

Germany," he said, "is where the greatest possible conquest can be made at the lowest possible cost"[1] in seizing *Lebensraum* in European territories, in countries adjoining Germany.

The secret came out after the war. The world learned of the German government's military instructions. Certainly, this is embarrassing for the present-day revenge-seekers, who therefore declare these publications, particularly the transcript of Hitler's mouthings of November 5, 1937, entirely false.[2] But that will get them nowhere.

Secret nazi documents leave no doubt whatsoever as to when the war decision was taken. British historian W. N. Medlicott notes that Hitler had made up his mind before the end of 1937.[3]

The secret intentions of the nazis and the shady dealings of the other Western rulers were contrasted by the open and fair Soviet attitude. Many Western statesmen thought at the time that surely something must have been concealed. In his day, Lenin commented on that sort of mentality. "This old world," he said, "has its own diplomacy, which cannot believe that it is possible to speak frankly and forthrightly. The old diplomacy thinks there must be a trap of some sort here."[4] Now everybody knows that the Soviet proposals of the prewar years were no subterfuge. There was no secret behind them. They served one purpose only: to safeguard and reinforce peace.

Although the Soviet collective security plan was shelved due to the resistance of the aggressor and his abettors, some progress was made all the same. Public pressure in France and Czechoslovakia compelled their governments to conclude with the Soviet Union treaties of mutual aid against aggression. The instruments were signed in May 1935 and could have become pillars for all-European collective security. Their fulfilment by the signatories, coupled with support for collective security from other European states, would have blocked German fascist aggression, delivering the peoples of Europe from the ordeal of the Second World War.

But the governments in Paris and Prague, pressured by home reactionaries, Hitler Germany and Anglo-American

[1] *CSAOR*, case 71, p. 113.
[2] *Europa in Flammen 1939-1945*, Bd. 2, S. 318.
[3] Medlicott, *The Economic Blockade*, Vol. 2, London, 1959.
[4] V. I. Lenin, *Collected Works*, Vol. 33, p. 150.

diplomats, had no intention to extend relations with the Soviet Union. The mutual aid treaties were, in effect, stillborn. Czechoslovak President Beneš told Ernst Eisenlohr, German Minister in Czechoslovakia, that the "pact with Russia was the relic of a former epoch, but he could not just throw it into the wastepaper basket".[1] The President heaped scorn on an instrument that could have safeguarded his country's national existence.

Léon Blum, French Prime Minister, too, admitted later that his government's conduct over the treaty with the Soviet Union differed from that of the Soviet side. "The Russians," he wrote, "were very desirous of accords between the General Staffs of the two countries (without which, it may be added, the treaty was indeed ineffective — *Deborin*). But this was not done and Russian insistence was opposed by a generally dilatory response. Russia offered us — and herself solemnly carried out the offer — to communicate full information about her military resources, her industrial resources and the facilities it could place at our disposal in case of a European conflict. In return, it demanded similar information, but this information was withheld."[2]

Paul Reynaud, also at one time Premier of France, revealed that the Soviet Union had offered its aid to France on land, sea and air in the event of a war, both by armed action against the common foe from its own territory and by providing armed forces for joint operations from French territory.[3]

The Italo-German intervention in Spain, like Italy's war against Ethiopia, was the first serious test of the fascist war potential. It encouraged the German and Italian rulers, for no collective action was taken against them. Britain and France assumed their "non-intervention" posture and the United States that of "neutrality", condoning the aggression and blockading Republican Spain. Obviously, they reckoned on the fascist states shedding every restraint after their success in Spain and dragging the world into the abyss, when they would warm their hands beside the flames of war. Their secret designs offered the fascist aggression great possibilities.

---

[1] *Documents on German Foreign Policy 1918-1945*, Series D, Vol. 2, p. 132.
[2] P. Reynaud, *Memoirs*, Vol. 2, Paris, 1963, p. 162.
[3] *Ibid.*

On the other hand, however, the Spanish war showed that in a world engagement invaders are bound to encounter powerful popular resistance. International brigades of anti-fascists from 54 countries[1] fought valiantly in Spain for peace and democracy against fascism. On the sun-scorched Spanish soil a broad international anti-fascist front defended the interests of the Spanish and all the peoples of Europe against the Italo-German troops.

That explains the hesitant German tactics in the early months of the Spanish war. Seeing this uncertainty, the Western governments decided to prod the nazis to new acts of aggression, for which a series of secret talks and conferences was held in November 1937.

Halifax conferred with Hitler in Obersalzberg (Berchtesgaden) on behalf of the British Government and the French cabinet with the same degree of secrecy with Johannes Welczek, the German Ambassador in Paris. Besides meeting Eisenlohr Beneš even stooped to meeting Gestapo representatives. In San Francisco, too, prominent US industrialists and politicians held a secret conference with German diplomatists.

The parleys were part of a Western scheme, a secret effort, to engineer a world war. Spokesmen of the Western "democracies" extolled Hitler for his terrorising Germany's best people and made pompous speeches about Germany's mission as a "fortress against Bolshevism". Hinting transparently at an Eastern campaign, Washington, London and Paris urged Hitler to haste in seizing Austria, Czechoslovakia and Poland.

The US monopolists went the farthest in their secret contacts with the nazis. In San Francisco they agreed that Germany and the United States should co-operate, for the potential markets, China and Russia, cannot be organised without the active collaboration of American capital.[2] That was a step toward a negotiated division of the world. However, the actual situation, highlighted by a sharpening of imperialist contradictions, prevented these plans from materialising.

British Prime Minister Neville Chamberlain publicly encouraged fascist aggression against Austria and Czechoslovakia. "I say," he declared in the House of Commons on

---

[1] *I.V.O.V.S.S.*, Vol. 1, p. 111.
[2] *Congressional Record*, Vol. 88, Part 10, pp. A-3134-35.

February 22, 1938, "we must not try to delude ourselves, and, still more, we must not try to delude small weak nations, into thinking that they will be protected by the League against aggression."[1] For the hitlerites this was tantamount to an assurance that they could go ahead with impunity.

A week later, on March 1, German troops poured into Austria, soon thereafter incorporated in the German Reich. The *Anschluss* was officially recognised by the British and French governments, which thereby betrayed the national interests of all the European peoples. Austria's annexation reinforced Germany's position in Central Europe, enabling it among other things to encircle Czechoslovakia.

The Soviet Government was the only one to denounce the German aggression and warn against its dangerous implications for peace. The Soviet statement said, in part: "...this time the violence has been perpetrated in the centre of Europe and has created an indubitable menace not only for the eleven countries now contiguous with the aggressor, but also for all European states, and not only European ones. So far the menace has been created to the territorial integrity and, in any case, to the political, economic, and cultural independence of the small nations, whose inevitable enslavement will, however, create the premises for pressure, and even for attacks against the large states as well."[2]

The Soviet Government urged a discussion of practical measures either in or outside the League of Nations. It urged all governments, especially the big powers, to work together for the "collective salvation of peace".[3]

The British Foreign Office, fearing that someone would jump ahead of it, sent a reply signed by a minor official, saying that any discussion of collective measures to prevent the spread of aggression was, of all things, unlikely to have a "favourable effect upon the prospects of European peace."[4]

The British refusal coincided with those of the US and France. Heedless of the consequences, the West persisted in its disastrous policy of encouraging Hitler. Now, the fate of Czechoslovakia, one more independent state, hung in the balance.

---

[1] *Parliamentary Debates, House of Commons*, Vol. 332, p. 227.
[2] *Documents and Materials Relating to the Eve of the Second World War*, Vol. 1, Moscow, 1948, pp. 90-91.
[3] *Ibid.*
[4] *Ibid.*, p. 92.

3. The Hidden Meaning of the Munich Deal

Capturing Czechoslovakia was for Hitler Germany a far more difficult job than Austria. Apart from the absence of any valid pretext for crushing the sovereign Czech and Slovak state, the latter's international position was conspicuously stable. Czechoslovakia was an ally of the Soviet Union and France, and any head-on aggression would run into the resistance of Czechoslovak patriots and their allies. The biggest deterrent of all was the Soviet-Czechoslovak Mutual Aid Treaty, for there could be no doubt as to the USSR's living up to its commitments to the letter. The other factor was Czech and Slovak patriotism blending with the patriotic and internationalist sentiment of workers and other progressives in Britain and France, where a strong movement was in motion to protect Czechoslovakia.

These factors were a headache for the British and French rulers, convinced that the German government had made its future moves conditional on the outcome of its claims to Czechoslovak territory. A perfidious plan crystallised, assuming special prominence in the secret war preparations. In substance, it was designed to frighten the peoples with threats of war and, exploiting their peaceful aspirations, meet the German demands, clearing the path for the nazi war machine. The British and French governments wanted merely a guarantee that German guns were trained eastward, away from them.

Blackmail with war as a stake — and this in order to unleash a war — was a novel dodge in the secret book of imperialist diplomacy. The blackmail began in May 1938, when nazi Germany failed to overcome at once the resistance to her plans of taking Czechoslovakia. In that critical hour, British and French diplomacy picked up the cue. They claimed that due to Czechoslovak reluctance to meet Germany half-way a war was likely to break out any day. This was tantamount to shifting the guilt on the victim of aggression. The British and French governments undertook a "peace-making mission".

To begin with, ex-Foreign Minister Lord Runciman was hastily dispatched to Prague as mediator. This amounted to outright incitement, for he was known as a nazi sympathiser. The move was to back up the German intentions, to avert a nazi retreat and portray the predatory fascist demands as legitimate and reasonable, forcing the Czechoslovak Government to bow and reject French and Soviet assistance. The French Government, for its part, cast about frantically for a valid excuse to shirk its obligations. The Soviet Union, meanwhile, declared its determination and readiness to render every possible aid, including armed assistance, denying everything that was alleged to obstruct such aid. The Soviet stand was publicly announced, and also communicated to the governments of Czechoslovakia and France.[1]

The USSR made the most of all opportunities to organise resistance to fascist aggression and render Czechoslovakia armed support, let alone political and moral aid. Regrettably, its efforts were rejected by the Czechoslovak Government under President Beneš.

In the meantime, Chamberlain twice held secret talks with Hitler. His attitude delighted the nazi dictator. The Fuehrer could barely conceal his joy. During their second meeting in Bad Godesberg on September 22, 1938, the two came to terms on the dismemberment of Czechoslovakia. But one point still had to be settled: the resistance of Czechoslovakia and of progressives in Britain and France had to be squashed.

That was when blackmail by suggesting war was used to the fullest. A partial mobilisation was carried into effect in France on September 21. Trenches were dug and anti-aircraft guns stationed in Paris squares and streets. Evacuation of the French capital started. In Britain, the Navy was alerted, sandbags covered shop and office windows in London, and schoolchildren were shipped out of the city. The US Government advised its citizens to leave Europe due to "imminence of war".[2] Pacifist books describing war horrors, heretofore banned in Britain and France, were run off the presses hastily. The Western governments made a show of lamenting that they might have to go to war against a "guiltless" Germany on behalf of "intransigent" Czechoslovakia. Chamberlain said this in so many words over the radio:

"How horrible, fantastic, incredible, it is that we should be digging trenches and trying on gas-masks here because of a quarrel in a far-away country between people of whom we know nothing."[3]

---

[1] *Novyie dokumenty iz istorii Myunkhena (New Documents Concerning the History of Munich)*, Moscow, 1958.
[2] *New York Times*, Sept. 27, 1938.
[3] Winston Churchill, *The Second World War*, Vol. 1, London, 1955, p. 283.

That was how the groundwork was laid for betraying Czechoslovakia and European peace.

In those critical days, the Soviet Union renewed its proposal of a broad international conference to prevent further aggression: it would "search for practical measures to counteract aggression and save the peace by a collective effort".[1] If the Soviet proposal had been accepted, it would have effectively blocked fascist aggression. But that was farthest from the minds of Hitler's abettors.

Western intentions were not to repulse Germany, but to compel Prague to bow to her demands. Giving way to Western pressure, the Czechoslovak Government under President Beneš surrendered unconditionally, accepting Hitler's extortionate demands. This was tantamount to national betrayal.

On September 29-30, 1938, the heads of government of Germany, Britain, France and Italy gathered in Munich. France and Britain burned their bridges: the idea of collective security lay buried. The conference that abandoned Czechoslovakia to the tender mercies of the nazis was the main stepping stone to a second world war. The aggressor, who barely had time to digest Austria, could not believe his eyes. Munich prodded him on to new acts of brigandage. It wrote finis to the idea of a united front against Hitler and his ambitions, paving the way for a united front against the Soviet Union in the interest of German fascism. Eager to direct aggression eastward, the French and British governments sought pledges that no aggression would follow against them. On the second day of the Munich conference, September 30, an Anglo-German non-aggression declaration was signed, with a similar Franco-German declaration signed on December 6, 1938, consummating France's rejection of her mutual aid treaty with the Soviet Union.

Now, 30 years later, the vast majority of historians of different schools, assess the Munich deal in much the same terms as the Soviet Union did in the wake of the event. Herbert Feis, a US historian, writes: "The Munich agreement had allowed Hitler to tear Czechoslovakia apart, leaving Poland and the Soviet Union exposed to German assault."[2] Michael Freund, a West-German historian, chimes in: "With Bohe-

---

[1] *Vneshnyaya politika SSSR (USSR Foreign Policy)*, Vol. 4, Moscow, 1946, pp. 391-92.

[2] Herbert Feis, *Churchill-Roosevelt-Stalin. The War They Waged and the Peace They Sought*, London, 1957, p. 4.

mian soil resounding to the tread of marching Germans, the whole world caved in. The cornerstone had been pulled out of the order erected by the Versailles Treaty. But that was not all. The path to the East had been paved for the German Reich."[1]

The Munichites saw to it that the secrecy shrouding the birth of war should become denser still. The critical war step was described as salvation from war. Chamberlain received a hero's welcome on his return to Britain. Girls in snow-white dresses presented him with flowers. His portraits, framed in laurel wreaths, were displayed in all respectable clubs. His umbrella was described as an emblem of peace. Medallions were on sale, depicting the umbrella crossed by a peace palm. Streets formerly named Peace were renamed Neville Chamberlain. Chamberlain made a triumphant entry into Parliament. His claim that he had secured "peace for our time"[2] evoked an ovation. What Chamberlain did not say was what kind of peace he had secured.

Chamberlain assumed that having given Hitler the green light in the East, he had ruled out war in the West. But the nazi leaders had their own ideas. Ribbentrop, for one, said derisively to Hitler: "That old man has today signed the death warrant of the British Empire and left it to us to fill in the date."[3]

After Munich the war drive was redoubled. At first Germany seized part of Czechoslovakia, then the rest of it. Then it grabbed Memel, now Klaipeda, from Lithuania, and saddled Rumania with an unequal economic treaty, turning her into Germany's economic appendage. In the meantime, Italy overran Albania.

The fascist rash spread over Europe. No longer was there any doubt left in anyone's mind as to the kind of "peace" achieved in Munich. Yet the governments of the United States, Britain and France still acted as neutral observers, letting no opportunity escape, however, to remind Hitler about his promised eastward crusade. If they ever intervened in the course of events, it was unfailingly in Germany's favour. Take Spain: helping the Italo-German intervention-

---

[1] M. Freund, *Deutsche Geschichte*, Gütersloh, 1960, S. 623.
[2] Edgar Holt, *The World at War 1939-1945*, London, 1956, p. 10.
[3] Hugh Dalton, *The Fateful Years. Memoirs 1931-1945*, London, 1957, p. 195.

ists conclude the war, they untied the nazis' hands for new ventures.

The Soviet Union was the only country that pulled no punches in exposing each act of fascist aggression and coming out in defence of the victims. In a note to Germany on March 19, 1939, the Soviet Government refused to acknowledge as lawful and consistent with the principle of self-determination the rape inflicted on Czechoslovakia. It described her occupation as an arbitrary act of violence and aggression.[1]

Far from bettering the international position of Britain and France, the Munich deal had lamentable consequences for those two countries, and for Poland. Before Munich the German leaders and generals wrangled behind the scenes over the direction of fresh armed campaigns. Some suggested the course of least resistance—starting the war for world supremacy by attacking Britain, France and Poland, the latter being the ally of the former two. Others, on the other hand, suggested war against the Soviet Union with Polish aid. The friends and foes of the second alternative equally feared Soviet strength. Diplomat Ernst von Weizsaecker revealed later that the nazis believed the Soviet Union to be more dangerous than any other adversary.[2]

After Munich, the choice was clear: the Western countries would be attacked first, but to avoid a war on two fronts the German generals suggested crushing Poland first of all. Here was how they reasoned: in case of a German attack on Britain and France, their ally Poland would be more likely to come to their aid than if the reverse happened and Poland were attacked first. Hitler spoke with contempt of his Munich collocutors and their policy: "I have witnessed the miserable worms ... in Munich. They will be too cowardly to attack."[3]

Besides, attacking Poland appeared more attractive to the German generals, because it would place their troops along the Soviet border, securing a staging area for a subsequent assault, envisaged after Germany's victory over the Western powers.

Prior to Munich, the General Staff worked on a war plan against Poland merely provisionally. After Munich, it was completed in double quick time. On April 11, 1939, it was

---

[1] *USSR Foreign Policy*, Russ. ed., Vol. 4, p. 411.
[2] Weizsaecker, *Erinnerungen*, München, 1950, S. 230.
[3] *Nazi Conspiracy and Aggression*, Vol. 7, Washington, 1946, p. 753.

endorsed by the government. War hovered over the continent. Yet it was not too late to block the avalanche by extraordinary collective action.

4. Designs of the Abettors of Aggression Exposed

The veil of secrecy that covered the Munich deal did not delude the Soviet Union. The USSR evaluated Munich at once as a gross betrayal. Yet the Soviet leaders would not abandon the idea of uniting the peaceful European countries against nazi aggression.

That is why the USSR agreed to negotiate with Britain and France in 1939. With peace a vital stake in its grandiose plans of construction, the Soviet Union tried sincerely to reach agreement, and hammer out a treaty for effective mutual aid against aggression guaranteeing the security of countries in Central and Eastern Europe. That treaty would provide for the forms and magnitude of mutual aid against any attack. What Moscow did not want was a scrap of paper instead of a treaty. "They were in earnest," Arnold Toynbee, the English historian, wrote of the USSR, "in wishing to conclude a military convention as soon as possible."[1]

But was that what the British and French governments wanted? At times, points of contact appeared between the Soviet and French positions, but none between the Soviet and British.

The British and French governments were in no way motivated by the desire to avert German aggression when consenting to negotiate with the USSR. As a matter of fact, what they wanted was the very reverse. The parleys with the USSR were only meant to allay and deceive home public opinion, which clamoured for an alliance with the USSR to repulse the nazis. But that, too, was secondary. The main objective was to put the choice before the German Government: either we, the British and French, erect a coalition with the Soviet Union against Germany if she imperils the Western powers, or you, Germany, better start your war against the USSR with our, British and French, support.

At the same time, the British and French governments hoped to saddle the Soviet Union with commitments, the

---

[1] *Survey of International Affairs, 1939-1946. The Eve of War, 1936.* Ed. by A. and V. Toynbee, London, 1958, p. 481.

fulfilment of which would inexorably draw the USSR into a war with Germany in the absence of any definite commitments on the part of the British and French. And in the event of Germany's turning westward, the British and French hoped to secure Soviet aid. The consent of the British and French governments to negotiate with the Soviet Union was, thus, merely another move in their double game, a projection in new garb of their Munich policy. They hoped that by going through the motions of coming to terms with the USSR, they would spur Germany into concluding a far-reaching agreement with them, which, while unprejudicial to the British and French monopolies in the world market, would ensure Germany's attacking the Soviet Union.

This view of the Anglo-French stand in the 1939 parleys with the USSR is long known to progressive historians. Now it has been reconfirmed by many new documents, as the memoirs of men involved in those events.

Iain Macleod, Neville Chamberlain's biographer, says: ". . . Chamberlain was reluctant to acquiesce in the opening of negotiations with the Soviet. He did so only under strong pressure from the French Government and from public opinion at home as reflected in the Press, in Parliament and in the anxieties of his Cabinet colleagues."[1] On March 26, 1939, before the parleys began, Chamberlain put down in his diary: "I must confess to the most profound distrust of Russia."[2] Subsequently, Macleod wrote: "He was neither elated when the negotiations seemed to be going well, nor cast down when they seemed to be going badly..."[3] And Lord Halifax, then Britain's Foreign Minister, commented: "It was desirable not to estrange Russia but always to keep her in play."[4] Exactly! That was the official British line.

This policy, then secret, was reflected in Britain's memorandum to France on May 22, 1939. "It would seem desirable," it said, "to conclude some agreement whereby the Soviet Union would come to our assistance if we were attacked in the West, not only in order to ensure that Germany would have to fight a war on two fronts, but also perhaps for the

[1] I. Macleod, *Neville Chamberlain*, London, 1961, p. 273.
[2] Keith Failing, *The Life of Neville Chamberlain*, London, 1946, p. 403.
[3] I. Macleod, *op. cit.*, p. 273.
[4] *Documents on British Foreign Policy 1919-1939*, Third Series, Vol. 5, London, 1952, p. 331.

Ribbentrop greets Chamberlain on his arrival in Germany

Daladier signing the Munich agreement

German troops marching into the Prague Castle

Angry crowds meet the nazi invaders in Prague

The nazi hordes invading Poland

Churchill and his generals hoped that such barricades would stop German tanks

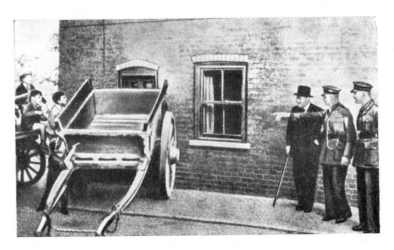

The nazi invaders in Paris

The nazi "new order" in Poland

Nazi troops invading the Soviet Union

Nazi tanks destroyed near Smolensk

German officers and men taken prisoner near Smolensk

reason ... that it was essential, if there must be a war, to try to involve the Soviet Union in it."[1] In other words, the idea was to secure Soviet aid and, if possible, expose the USSR to a German attack, while assuming no commitments to aid the Soviet Union in case it was attacked.

This coloured the behaviour of the British and French governments in their negotiations with the Soviet Union; they were insincere to the extreme. And doubly so, because Anglo-French attempts were simultaneously made to obtain closer contacts with Germany. Secret Anglo-German talks took place in London in June-August 1939 concerning agreements formalising an alliance against the Soviet Union. During these talks, the British spokesman, Minister Robert Hudson, told his German opposite number, Helmuth Wohlthat, that if Britain and Germany were to come to terms, broad opportunities would arise for the two countries in the British Empire, China and Russia. Hudson stressed specially that in Russia "there was a possibility for Germany to take part in vast economic activities".[2] This was as much as saying that Britain was eager to slice up the world between herself and Germany, prodding Germany to engage in economic expansion and also attack the USSR.

Though every minute counted, Britain and France employed dilatory tactics in the talks with the USSR, and to speed them up the Soviet Government suggested parleys by military missions of the three countries in Moscow. The suggestion was accepted, and a French delegation came to London in order to depart for Moscow jointly with the British. This was when Ivan Maisky, Soviet Ambassador to Britain, had a very revealing talk with the head of the British delegation to Moscow. Here is Maisky's record of it:

"*I*: 'Tell me, Admiral, when are you leaving for Moscow?'

"*Reginald E. Drax*: 'That hasn't been settled, but in the next few days.'

"*I*: 'You are flying, of course? Time is precious: the atmosphere in Europe is extremely tense.'

"*Drax*: 'Oh no! We of the two delegations, including the technical personnel, are about 40, and there is the luggage... It would be inconvenient to fly.'

---

[1] *Ibid.*, p. 646.
[2] Herbert von Dirksen, *Moscow–Tokyo–London. Twenty Years of German Foreign Policy*, London, 1951, p. 238.

"*I*: 'If flying is unsuitable, perhaps you will go to the Soviet Union in one of your fast cruisers?... That would be forceful and impressive—military delegations aboard a warship.... Besides, it would not take too long from London to Leningrad.'

"*Drax* (with a sour expression): 'No, a cruiser won't do either. If all of us were to go aboard a cruiser, we should have to evict several dozen of its officers and take their place in their cabins.... Why cause inconveniences? No, no, we shan't go by cruiser.'

"*I*: 'In that case you will perhaps go by one of your speedy liners?... I repeat, time is short and you must get to Moscow as quickly as possible.'

"*Drax* (obviously reluctant to continue): 'I really can't say... Transportation is in the hands of the Ministry of Trade.... Everything is in its hands. I have no idea what will happen.'"[1]

What happened, however, was that the delegations left London as late as August 5, 1939, aboard a combined freighter-passenger doing 13 knots and arriving in Leningrad on August 10.

When the talks began at last, it was discovered that the British delegation was not empowered to work out and conclude any pertinent convention. The secret was out!

The British and French spokesmen had no intention of concluding a mutual aid treaty with the Soviet Union. They referred to the Polish Government's refusal to join the USSR in any concerted measures repulsing German aggression. Yet it was they who had inspired Poland's refusal, just as they had inspired a similar refusal by the Baltic states. It was also discovered that in some cases the British and French negotiators did not even consult the governments concerned when they pleaded their refusal.

To make the negotiations founder was a preconceived Anglo-French plan. On July 10, Britain's Ambassador in Germany told the French Foreign Minister: "... the negotiations with the Soviets had reached a stage when they lacked a sense of realities.... The important thing was to end negotiations one way or another as soon as possible."[2]

---

[1] I. Maisky, *Kto pomogal Gitleru (Who Helped Hitler)*, Moscow, 1962, pp. 152-53.

[2] *Documents on British Foreign Policy 1919-1939*, Third Series, Vol. 6, London, 1953, p. 331.

The Soviet Union realised it could not succeed in reversing the Anglo-French stand by merely negotiating. Other assurances were required. Just when the talks of the military missions in Moscow were stymied by the British and French delegations, on August 20, 1939, the German Government offered to conclude a non-aggression treaty with the USSR. This was a renewal of previous proposals, turned down while hope still existed of a mutual aid agreement with Britain and France.[1] When this hope was dashed, the choice had to be made. The Soviet Union had to foil the German plan of attacking with Japanese involvement and supported by Britain, France and the USA. A meaningful step had been taken at Munich towards a united anti-Soviet front, while Japan, which feared missing the bus, made a try at grabbing a slice of the Mongolian People's Republic, a friend of the USSR.

These factors could not be left out of the reckoning. The situation in the Far East was still simmering, despite the crushing setback suffered by the Japanese at the hands of the Red Army. Japan's rulers were obviously waiting for Germany to attack the USSR.

Yet the nazis were still hesitant, inclining towards immediate war against the Soviet Union one day—which the rulers of the USA, Britain and France encouraged—and shying from the prospect of a war the next.

But this uncertainty, obviously, could not go on for ever. If the Soviet Union rejected the German proposal or dallied with the reply, the balance could tilt against it. And this at a time when German aggression against the USSR had to be averted in order to frustrate the plans of a world "crusade" against the socialist country, to eliminate the threat of the bloc whose creation had been discussed in Munich and to win time and build up defences. In the circumstances, the choice had narrowed. But one thing could be done: the German proposal had to be accepted.

The non-aggression treaty between the Soviet Union and Germany was signed on August 23, 1939, effective for 10 years. On Moscow's part it was a natural reaction to the Western powers' deal with Germany in Munich.

During the Anglo-French-Soviet negotiations, the Polish Government took a highly negative view of co-operating with

---

[1] *I.V.O.V.S.S.*, Vol. I, p. 175.

the USSR in terms of mutual aid against aggression. Out of hand it refused all Soviet aid. So there was no question of Soviet commitments vis-à-vis Poland in the Soviet-German talks. "The only thing that could still be done," *Pravda* reported on September 23, 1939, "was to save the Western Ukraine, Western Byelorussia and the Baltic republics from a German invasion. The Soviet Government received German assurances that the line formed by the rivers Tissa, Narev, Bug and Vistula would not be crossed."[1]

The Soviet-German non-aggression treaty greatly annoyed the Munichites in the USA, Britain and France. They realised that their designs had failed. The same annoyance is displayed in certain official publications seeking to conceal the true story behind the outbreak of the Second World War and keep a secret that had long since ceased to be one.[2] Attacks on the treaty and its misinterpretation are frequent among reactionary writers. West-German historian Kurt Assmann, for one, who endeavours to vindicate the nazi aggression and its abettors, swings out at the treaty and peddles the old lie about an alleged deal partitioning Poland.[3]

Yet writers unafraid of the truth, no matter how distasteful to them, admit that the USSR had acted wisely. Arnold Toynbee holds, for example, that the head of the Soviet Government had not only "saved Russia from war, but he had done so without any sacrifice whatever—or rather, with immense gain. Without firing a shot, he had recovered for Russia much of the territory which she had lost in the days of her weakness, and which every Russian held to be part of the national apanage."[4]

Ernst Niekisch, another bourgeois historian, wrote: "Soviet vital interests required destroying the English-German relations so thoroughly and so conclusively as to end the fear of an Anglo-German conspiracy against Soviet existence. The Soviet-German non-aggression treaty was no doubt a bold, even reckless, undertaking. Yet the situation in the world was so complicated that it spelled the deliverance of Soviet Russia."[5]

---

[1] *I.V.O.V.S.S.*, p. 176.
[2] E. g., *Nazi-Soviet Relations*, Washington, 1948.
[3] Kurt Assmann, *Deutsche Schicksalsjahre*, Wiesbaden, 1951, S. 113-18.
[4] *Survey of International Affairs, 1939-1946. The Eve of War, 1939*, p. 594.
[5] Ernst Niekisch, *Das Reich der niederen Dämonen*, Hamburg, 1953, S. 292.

The Soviet-German non-aggression treaty secured a temporary peace for a considerable portion of Europe, affording the Soviet Union a distinct gain in time. This largely predetermined the favourable outcome of the Second World War. The treaty altered the course of events and paved the way for the future alliance of the USSR, USA and Britain against Hitler Germany, contributing prominently to Germany's defeat in the context of the coalition of freedom-loving peoples.

As a side effect it compelled Japan to check her aggression against the Mongolian People's Republic and the USSR. The Hiranuma Cabinet, which insisted on continuing the aggression, was forced to resign and the Japanese Premier referred ruefully to the treaty as having caused the shift in the policy he had recommended to the Emperor.[1]

* * *

Those were the secrets that the governments of Germany, Italy, Japan, the United States, Britain and France resorted to as cover for engineering the war. Many of them, however, were exposed by Soviet foreign policy and progressives abroad at the time. The situation in which the Second World War was precipitated differed from that directly preceding the First World War.

---

[1] *The Times*, Oct. 4, 1939.

Chapter Two

Governments Surrender, the People Fight On

1. The Polish Tragedy

The German Government began its succession of wars for world rule with the intention of first crushing countries whose governments, prompted by anti-Soviet sentiment, condoned and comforted aggressors. A provocation typical of German militarist methods provided a pretext for attacking Poland.

The story of that provocation was a war secret guarded by the German Government under the code name of Operation Himmler. The "operation" was carried out by the military, which organised an attack by a group of SS-men and criminal elements disguised in Polish army uniforms on the town of Gleiwitz near the Polish border. Before dawn on September 1, 1939, German radio stations interrupted their usual broadcasts to announce a "Polish attack". They switched in Gleiwitz and listeners heard confused noises, revolver shots and Polish speech with strongly German overtones.

Not more than a few hours passed before the flames of war were alight. The battleship *Schleswig-Holstein* opened fire on the town and fort of Westerplatte, but neither artillery, air-raids nor unceasing groundattacks could subdue Polish resistance. The defenders repulsed 13 large-scale enemy attacks, making Westerplatte a symbol of Polish heroism.

The 57 German divisions (2,500 panzers and 2,000 planes) that lunged into Polish territory on September 1 at 04.45 hours consisted of two operational groups striking from north-west and south-west, with a frontal thrust from the west playing a secondary role. The two operational groups converged swiftly on the capital, with orders to surround and destroy the Polish troops west of the Vistula.

Operational Group South under General Karl Rudolf Gerd von Rundstedt was to strike from Silesia in the general direction of Warsaw with General Walter von Reichenau's 10th Army possessing half the available panzer force of 1,000 tanks, breaking through and capturing the capital.

The bulk of Poland's armed forces were east, not west, of Warsaw, massed against the Soviet Union in conformance with the Poles' pro-Western policy. Just 22 army formations were west of the capital, and as many as 30 east of it.[1] Trusting its allies, who had given assurances that Germany would not attack, the Polish Government did not order mobilisation until August 31. As a result, something like one-third of the Polish army had not been properly primed when the Germans attacked. Some divisions were still en route to assigned districts, others rail-borne. With the war at its height, only 33 divisions were deployed against the aggressor.[2] And the plight of the Polish army was made more desperate still by the fact that its Supreme Command, and the government for that matter, did not believe effective resistance possible.

The abyss that lay between the prewar reactionary Polish regime and the people was evident more than ever during the war. While the army and the people fought heroically, the government, stricken by panic, pleaded for British and French aid. The bourgeois-landlord regime proved unable of uniting the country in the hour of trial, while the people, hating the nazi invaders, were ready to fight, their patriotism fettered by the corrupt political system.

Anti-Soviet in foreign policy and anti-people in home policy, the Polish Government was in no condition to fight a just war of liberation. In contrast, the people rallied and fought for their freedom and independence from the beginning until the day the country was cleared of nazis. The war was not a continuation of the unpopular politics of the ruling classes. It was rather a rejection of it and a token of its bankruptcy. The accent was on the traditions of Polish struggle for national liberation, which created a moral uplift.

Hitler Germany, on the other hand, was fighting a distinctly imperialist war of conquest. Bent on gaining world supremacy

---

[1] *Polskie Sily Zbrojne w drugiej wojnie Sviatowej*, Vol. 1, London, 1951, p. 1.
[2] *Ibid.*, p. 267.

and enslaving all peoples of the earth, the German imperialists intended to destroy a large part of the population of overran countries, especially the Slav people. Their war threatened biological existence of entire nations. Polish patriots were aware of this, though official propaganda in Poland, Britain, France and the United States concealed, rather than revealed, Hitler Germany's true aims.

Nazi historians and journalists portrayed the German aggression as "defence against" "Polish provocation", making the most of the propaganda potential created by Operation Himmler, exposed at the Nuremberg trials. Hitler's specious version is still being exploited by some West-German writers. Udo Walendy, for example, asserts the world war did not begin on September 1, 1939; "the German press," he says, "had been ordered to report 'retaliatory fire', not 'war', and everything was done to limit the conflict."[1] The writer's method is a devious one: he vindicates the war of conquest begun by Germany and blames its growth into a world war on Germany's adversaries. But the war was bound to become world-wide, for that was predetermined by Germany's aim: attainment of world rule. It is quite another matter that the German Government would have preferred to destroy one country before tackling the next, in order to avoid the emergence of an anti-fascist coalition.

Some West-German historians describe the German campaign in Poland as an outstanding feat of German arms, a model of precision in carrying through the preconceived plan. But that is not true. Polish resistance wrought havoc with the schedule set by the Wehrmacht command; this is borne out by the heroic defence of Warsaw, which began on September 8 and continued until September 28.

The 4th Panzer Division, 10th Army, which reached the Polish capital on September 8 from the south-east, encountered unexpectedly stiff resistance by the garrison and volunteers. Four tanks of the forward group were put out of action instantly and a 30-panzer drive was repulsed the following day. Some of the tanks fell into traps dug by Warsaw's citizens, and fire was set to many others with gasoline-filled bottles.

The Polish Government abandoned Warsaw on September 6. Soon it crossed the Rumanian border. The defence of

---

[1] U. Walendy, *Wahrheit für Deutschland*, Vlotho-Weser, 1965, S. 432.

Warsaw was organised by city President Stefan Starzynski and Magistrate Janusz Regulski. Polish Communists and Left Socialists, held in prisons and concentration camps until then, were in the front ranks, many having broken out of confinement, picking up whatever arms they could and going into battle.

Left leaders had begun forming workers' battalions on September 5, three days before the Germans came to the walls of the city. In due course these became the main volunteer force fighting the invaders and were reorganised into a Workers' Brigade for the Defence of Warsaw. Command of the Brigade was in the hands of Communists and Left Socialists, specifically, Socialist Marian Kenig. Among its members were Wladyslaw Gomulka and other Polish Communists, as well as Pavel Marishchuk and other comrades of the West Ukrainian Communist Party. Poles, Ukrainians, Byelorussians and others fought shoulder to shoulder. The defence of Warsaw brought together patriots of different parties and classes, uniting the finest sons of the nation in the common fight against aggression.

In the first days of the defence of Warsaw a large part of the German force was drawn off by a large-scale battle west of Warsaw, lasting from September 9 to 18. Between the rivers Vistula and Baura, its tributary, General Kutrzeba, in command of the Polish Poznan Army, counter-attacked the German 8th Army in defiance of Supreme Commander Rydz-Smigly's order to the contrary. Early in the battle the Poles smashed the nazi 17th and 30th infantry divisions, opening the way into the rear of German troops advancing on Warsaw. The success could not be developed, however, due to contradictory High Command instructions and absence of coordination between commanders of the Poznan and Pomorze armies.

All the same, the battle on the Baura detained the nazi strike force for several days, drawing it away from Warsaw. German troops suffered considerable casualties, but after Polish resistance west of the Vistula was crushed, Warsaw became their main objective. The general assault was made by a large force, though day after day the vicious attacks were repulsed with heavy losses for the nazis. Defending the capital became a national mission for its populace.

On September 28 the city fathers signed the surrender instrument, but part of the troops and many of the inhabitants would not accept defeat and continued to resist another two or three days. Not until the morning of October 1 did the German armies enter the half-destroyed city.

Hitler Germany turned Poland into a colony. The western provinces were incorporated into the Third Reich, and the rest converted into a governorship. The nazi governor, Hans Frank, wrote in his diary: "I was assigned to undertake the administration of the conquered areas and given a special order to devastate them mercilessly as a war theatre and a conquered land, reducing the region to a pile of rubble economically, socially, culturally, and politically."[1]

Plunder of the Poles' national heritage began, their culture was destroyed, the population systematically exterminated and the able-bodied driven off to Germany to do forced labour. More than six million Polish lives was the toll of the war and fascist occupation.[2]

The nazis, who thought their hard line would break the nation's resistance, did not reckon with the Polish people. The occupation was not the end, but rather the beginning of a new stage in the popular fight for freedom and independence. That this new stage of resistance was a continuation of the earlier stand is illustrated by the fact that the Workers' Brigade for the Defence of Warsaw survived and conducted guerrilla actions in and outside the city. The resistance movement spread rapidly throughout the nazi-occupied area.

2. The First Nazi Retreat

The German invasion of Poland and the rapid advance eastward showed beyond a doubt that Hitler wanted to take up favourable positions along the Soviet border for a subsequent attack. Nothing could guarantee that, intoxicated by the conquest of Poland and encouraged by the Western powers, he would not attempt an immediate assault on the Soviet Union. Western reactionaries followed the developments with bated breath, hoping their aim was near.

The Soviet Union was not going to be caught unawares. Reserves in six military districts were called up for training, while troops of the Kiev and Byelorussian military districts

---

[1] S. Piotrowski, *Dziennik Hansa Franka*, Warsaw, 1957, p. 96.
[2] *I.V.O.V.S.S.*, Vol. 1, p. 313.

were put on the alert. Special front commands were formed. The situation became most strained in the middle of September. The Germans went beyond the line where they were to have stopped under a Soviet-German understanding. They crossed the Western Bug and San and entered the Western Ukraine and Western Byelorussia, annexed by Poland in 1921.

The Soviet Union was compelled to take action. The German advance had to be halted and the nazi troops prevented from marching to the Soviet frontier. Neither could it be indifferent to the lot of its brothers, the Western Ukrainians and Byelorussians, deprived of equal rights in prewar Poland and then totally abandoned to their fate.

When the Polish state collapsed, Soviet troops were sent to liberate the Western Ukraine and Western Byelorussia. This was an internationalist duty. It was the only possible help they could then render to the neighbouring peoples. Furthermore, the campaign had to be undertaken to prevent Germany from thrusting to the Soviet border, which could be expected in a matter of six to eight days, considering the rate of the nazi advance.

Soviet war historian D. Proektor wrote:

"In the circumstances, marching to halt the victorious aggressor and compel him to withdraw meant salvation in the nearest future for hundreds of thousands of people of nations soon to be drawn into the vortex of a world war; it meant salvation for hundreds of towns; it meant winning hundreds of days of peace, shortening the Second World War thereby, because the decisive event, the Great Patriotic War, began in circumstances far less favourable for Hitler than if the Red Army had not moved to meet his armies at the height of their victories."[1]

The Soviet operation alarmed the nazi command, General Nicolaus von Vormann, a member of Hitler's Headquarters, recalls in his memoirs.[2] The Headquarters debated whether to come to blows with the Red Army or to bide its time and retreat. In the end, it decided on the latter course.

"That," Proektor writes, "was the first order of retreat issued by the Hitler Wehrmacht in the Second World War.

---

[1] D. Proektor, *Voina v Evrope 1939-1941 gg (War in Europe 1939-1941)*, Moscow, 1963, p. 116.

[2] Nicolaus von Vormann, *Der Feldzug 1939 in Polen*, Weissenburg, 1958, S. 153-55.

Significantly, it was issued in connection with a Red Army advance, whose move westward was, kilometre by kilometre, a move towards the future still very distant victory of the anti-Hitler coalition. Who can tell how many people in different countries owe their lives to these kilometres marched west by the Red Army in those autumn days of 1939?"[1]

Few Western politicians saw the Soviet action in the proper focus. Winston Churchill was extremely perspicacious in this respect. Of the Red Army move to the western borders of the Ukrainian and Byelorussian territories, he said: "That the Russian armies should stand on this line was clearly necessary for the safety of Russia against the Nazi menace. At any rate, the line is there, and an Eastern front has been created which Nazi Germany does not dare assail."[2]

The German retreat had a strong bearing on the attitude of many European countries. For one thing, the bourgeois governments of Estonia, Latvia and Lithuania, which had previously rejected Soviet proposals, agreed to conclude treaties of mutual aid against aggression, Estonia signing it on September 28, 1939, Latvia on October 5, and Lithuania on October 10. The signatories undertook to give each other every possible aid, including military, in the event of a direct attack or threat of attack by any European great power.

The treaties prevented seizure of Estonia, Latvia and Lithuania by Hitler Germany, already poised to overrun them. In that part of Europe, too, the full power of the Soviet Union deterred German aggression. The Soviet line of defence moved farther west and Germany was again compelled to desist.

Regrettably, the Soviet efforts to firm up the peace front along its north-western frontier were resisted by Finland's rulers, whose endeavours to turn their country into an anti-Soviet staging area accorded not only with German wishes, but also those of the British, French and US governments, which exerted unprecedented pressure on Finland. They hoped that a Soviet-Finnish conflict would pave the way for a deal with Hitler. That was the mainspring of the Soviet-Finnish war, the blame for which lies not only on certain Finnish groups, but also on their Western abettors. Nor did the

---

[1] D. Proektor, *op. cit.*, p. 117.
[2] Winston Churchill, *The Second World War*, Vol. 1, London, 1948, p. 403.

attitude of these Finnish groups change after Finland's defeat in the resultant war against the Soviet Union and the conclusion of a peace treaty on March 12, 1941, under the terms of which, among other things, the signatories undertook to refrain from any armed attack on each other.

The objective sense of this succession of events is obvious: the Soviet Union blocked the road for the German troops, forcing them to stop. If the Soviet moves had been supported by the governments of the United States, Britain and France, the German road to aggression could have been blocked by collective measures both in East and West even in those opening months of the Second World War. But that went against the plans of those still trying to engineer a world crusade against the USSR.

3. Behind the Scenes in the Phoney War

The German attack on Poland put the British and French governments in difficulties. They were committed to assist their eastern ally in the event of an attack, but had no intention of living up to their obligations, still hoping that the German armies would confine their actions to the East only.

Mussolini, who used Chamberlain's and Daladier's mood, suggested a new conference, similar to that in Munich, on September 2, 1939. The British and French were quick to express consent, though with some reservations. So did the Polish Government. Again, political leaders of these states began speaking of "general appeasement".[1] Addressing the French parliament, Daladier assured the world no Frenchman would ever fight to conquer foreign soil.[2] Hitler understood this to be a reassurance that Poland's allies would leave her in the lurch. Berlin, having regarded Mussolini's initiative as a way of sounding out Britain and France, was now sure of its ground. The nazi government rejected the idea of a new international conference out of hand.

Chamberlain and Daladier, meanwhile, were faced with a public outcry they could not control. Discontent over

---

[1] France. Ministère des affaires étrangères. Documents diplomatiques 1938-1939, Paris, 1939, p. 315 (quoted in Gelbbuch der Französischen Regierung, Basel, 1940, S. 393).
[2] Weltgeschichte der Gegenwart in Dokumenten, Bd. III, München, 1956, S. 411.

their policy of appeasement, tantamount to encouragement of aggression, ran high. The more farsighted Western leaders saw the imminent danger of a nazi assault. Besides, to bow to Germany once more and flout the commitments given to Poland meant relinquishing important international positions and recognising Germany as victor in the imperialist struggle, as hegemon in bourgeois Europe, thus reducing Britain and France to second-class powers.

It was impossible to continue the Munich policy by previous means. New methods were required. Britain and France declared war formally on September 3, 1939, giving as the reason their commitment to Poland, a lofty motive intended to give the Anglo-French war against Germany a just liberative complexion.

But continuing the Munich policy by new means could be neither just nor liberative. It was an imperialist policy of phoney war, its purpose being merely to convince Germany that the British and French governments were determined to maintain their international position and compel her to accept a new deal with the ultimate aim of a world-wide imperialist crusade against the Soviet Union.

This war aim was revealed by top British statesmen. Chamberlain, for one, named Hitler's betrayal of his anti-Soviet promises as the main cause of Britain's entry into the war. Hitler had sworn for years, he said, "that he was the mortal enemy of Bolshevism; he is now its ally".[1] And Halifax, speaking in the Commons on October 4, 1939, said that by signing the non-aggression treaty with the USSR, the rulers of Germany reversed "the most fundamental principles of their policy, which they had for long years most vehemently proclaimed."[2] The same idea was set out at greater length by Lord Lloyd in a brochure published in November 1939 in London with an introduction by Halifax.[3] Chamberlain, too, indicated, that Britain declared war on Germany because Hitler, who had promised war against Bolshevism, had "betrayed ... the whole Western civilisation" by concluding a non-aggression pact with the USSR.[4]

---

[1] *The British War Blue Book. Documents Concerning German-Polish Relations*, London, 1939, p. 195.
[2] *The Times*, Oct. 5, 1939, p. 3.
[3] Lord Lloyd of Dolobran, *The British Case*, London, 1939, pp. 53-60.
[4] *The British War Blue Book*, No. 144, p. 195.

Thus, the British and French rulers were least of all concerned with combating fascism or halting its aggression, but purely with channelling aggression in the direction they desired. This was the reason for their reluctance to aid Poland and the reason why they viewed her tragic plight so dispassionately.

Here is how Zbigniew Zaluski, the Polish war historian, describes Britain's and France's policy in September 1939: "Poland, the victim of Hitler Germany's brazen attack that threatened her biological existence, counted on the help of her allies, while these allies were bent on appeasing Hitler Germany and goading her to fight against the Soviet Union, to fight on Poland's ruins against the only country with a vested interest in defending Poland's independence, the only country that had for a long time endeavoured to safeguard that independence, the only country able to deliver Poland from the nazi yoke."[1]

Regardless of the intents of the British and French governments, their declaration of war on Germany was also undeniable evidence of the sharpness of the imperialist contradictions. These contradictions between the United States, Britain and France, on the one hand, and Germany, Japan and Italy, on the other, obstructed their new deal against the Soviet Union.

The Anglo-French declaration of war was received differently by aggressor and victim. The former was quite sure that the Western powers would take no field action. "That they have declared war on us...," Hitler said, "does not mean they are going to fight."[2] Meanwhile, the Polish Government trusted that it would get help; doubly so on receiving an official reply to its specific operational proposals from the French Foreign Ministry. "Tomorrow, or at the latest in the morning of the day after," it said, "a strong attack by French and British bombers will be made against Germany, which may even be extended to hit the rear formations on the Polish front."[3] But in vain did Poland in her agony wait for help, even if only from the air. The few British and French planes that appeared over Germany confined themselves to dropping leaflets denouncing the policy of the Hitler govern-

---

[1] Zbigniew Zaluski, *Przepustka do historii*, 2nd ed., Warsaw, 1963, p. 53.
[2] Erich Kordt, *Wahn und Wirklichkeit*, Stuttgart, 1948, S. 218.
[3] *Polskie Sily Zbrojne w drugiej wojnie Swiatowej*, Vol. 1, Part II, p. 433.

ment that had flouted the promise of acting jointly with the
Western powers against the USSR.

The Anglo-French betrayal of Poland was no casual act.
It was part of a deliberate and planned policy. The British
Chief of Staff had decided in July 1939, months before the
nazi assault on Poland, that it would be undesirable to relieve
German pressure on Poland at the beginning of the war and
more advisable to wait for the final outcome.[1]

The Anglo-French war against Germany between September 3, 1939, and April-May 1940, was contemptuously christ-
ened a "phoney war". It was war without acts of war. While
nazi troops sowed death and destruction in Poland, the
Anglo-French command entertained its soldiers, passively
installed in the front-line, with football matches.

The balance of strength in the West offered the British and
French abundant opportunities. At the beginning of September, France had 110 divisions, with a British expeditionary
corps of five divisions arriving to reinforce them.[2] Germany
mustered but 23 poorly armed divisions against them, and
after the war Hitler's generals admitted that if the allies had
mounted a strong offensive, the Wehrmacht would have
collapsed, because "the bulk of the combat-ready German
formations had been flung against Poland, while the Western
front was manned mostly by unready divisions incapable of
offensive action".[3]

German weakness in the West derived not only from the
main forces having been deployed against Poland. There
was a political reason. The underlying purpose was to persuade Britain and France that Germany had no intention
of attacking in the West. The Western powers were inclined
to accept this version. For their part, they gave to understand
that they had no unfriendly intentions either, despite the state
of war. This attitude had a corrupting influence on the army
and rear in France, eroding faith in the need for repulsing
the aggressor. Defence preparations were stepped down,
with the "phoney war" and its politico-moral and military
effects preparing the ground for France's defeat.

Progressives, all true patriots in France and Britain denounced the "phoney war". They saw through it. They saw

---

[1] J. R. M. Butler, *Grand Strategy*, Vol. II, September 1939-June 1941.

[2] Gamelin, *Servir*, Vol. 3, Paris, 1947, p. 35.

[3] *Mirovaya voina 1939-1945*. Sbornik statei (*World War 1939-1945*.
Collection of articles), Moscow, 1957, p. 37.

its secret sense—the intention of the British, French and US governments to facilitate a German attack on the Soviet Union, on the one hand, and Germany's intention to secure favourable conditions for smashing her Western friends, now turned foe. Disclosing the secret went against the interests of either side. To conceal it, the French Government, for one, mounted a repressive offensive on the home "front".

The anti-Soviet and anti-democratic campaign in France, Britain and the United States reached its peak during the Soviet-Finnish war. It seemed then that international reaction was close to achieving its aim: the launching of an anti-Soviet crusade. The general staffs in France and Britain were fitting out an expeditionary corps to help Finnish reaction and preparing an attack against the Soviet Union in the South. Neither did they scrap their war planning (against the Soviet Union) after the conclusion of the Soviet-Finnish peace treaty.

The French General Staff had completed a plan for Operation Bakou, envisaging a sudden air assault on the Soviet Union's key economic centres, undermining the country's military-economic potential, to be followed by a ground invasion. The plan was submitted to the government on April 4, 1940, and soon thereafter the final date for the attack was set for the end of June or early July, 1941.[1]

Britain's Chiefs of Staff Committee took part in drawing up the plan. It continued work on it even after France lay crushed, and even when the prospect of a German invasion loomed large for Britain herself. On June 12, 1941, the Committee decided on steps setting the stage for a swift air strike from Mosul against the oil refining plants in Baku.[2]

At the height of the danger to the survival of the peoples of Eastern and Western Europe, instead of repulsing the enemy, the rulers of Britain and France dreamt of an alliance with it and plotted an attack on the Soviet Union—the only country capable of delivering the world from the brown plague of fascism.

4. France Defeated

The phoney war had a most demoralising effect on the army and people in France and Britain. It affected war production, basically no higher than in peacetime, with a

---

[1] D. Proektor, *op. cit.*, pp. 139-40.
[2] J. R. M. Butler, *op. cit.*, pp. 543-44.

considerable quantity of arms, vehicles and equipment routed to Finland.

Germany, meanwhile, lost no time in stepping up arms output, building up her armed forces and charting the plan of a war in the West.

On October 19, 1939, the German High Command completed the first variant of an offensive known under the code name of *Fall Gelb* (Operation Yellow), which by and large reproduced the German plan in the First World War, the Schlieffen Plan. The main blow against France was envisaged across the northern Belgium and southern Holland, hooking round the Maginot Line, and followed by an invasion of northern France.

By the end of December 1939 this variant was scrapped and replaced with a new one: Army Group B would pin down the enemy frontally in northern Belgium, drawing away the main forces, while Army Group A would break through in depth with a large mobile force to the Channel across Luxembourg, the Ardennes and northern France, cutting off the main mass of enemy troops.

Adopting this plan, the German High Command counted on the drooping morale of the British and French troops, and especially the low morale of their commands. The large-scale flanking manoeuvre would expose the German forces to possible encirclement. Success depended on the paralysis spreading swiftly among the British and French military leaders. Hitler's generals counted on it.

There was one more reason that prompted the German command to abandon the original Operation Yellow variant. The monopolies, eager to lay their hands on the Belgian, Dutch and French industries, wished them to escape the destruction that hostilities would be sure to wreak. They wanted them as a supply source for the subsequent phases of the war for world supremacy. A frontal assault in the industrial north would impair its economic potential; a flanking movement left the hope of averting destruction.

Success hinged largely on whether or not the French and British commands would deploy their main forces in Belgian and Dutch territory north-west of the planned Army Group A hooking manoeuvre. To mislead the allies, the nazi command decided to let one of the earlier variants of Operation Yellow, envisaging a frontal attack, fall into enemy hands, disregarding the fact that this would put the Anglo-French leaders wise to nazi preparations of a Western offensive (which the allies were long inclined to consider unlikely). On January 10, 1940, a German aircraft with Helmut Reinberger, a liaison officer carrying blueprints of the early Operation Yellow variant, faked a forced landing near the Belgian town of Michelin. The pretext: it had lost its bearings. Now the French and British were convinced that if Germany were to launch an offensive, she would strike in the north, though it would be more logical to surmise that the Germans would abandon the captured variant.

In the meantime, Berlin decided to conquer Denmark and Norway before launching out on Operation Yellow. The two countries were on the right flank. They were seafaring nations, and, besides, the German monopolists displayed a keen interest in the Scandinavian iron ore; also, the move was prompted by the obvious Anglo-French intention of introducing allied troops into Norway.

The *Weserübung* (Weser Exercise), code name for the invasion of Denmark and Norway, was launched on April 9, 1940. The Danish king and government abandoned every thought of resistance, ordering the Danish forces to lay down their arms. The Norwegians, however, resisted staunchly. Their shore guns sank a nazi heavy cruiser and two light cruisers. Fierce fighting broke out on land. But the nazi agents in the country — traitor Quisling, Norway's War Minister, among them — succeeded in disrupting the resistance. Quisling's name eventually became the synonym of treachery.

The British reacted by landing troops in Northern Norway. But these were soon defeated, Germany gaining complete control of the country. The nazi flank and rear were thus well covered, communications with Norway and Sweden protected, and the German air and naval forces gained new bases against France and Britain.

Having occupied Denmark and Norway, the Germans struck on May 10, 1940, invading Belgium, Holland, Luxembourg and France. That was the end of the phoney war.

By then Operation Yellow had been completely reworked and replaced by the *Sichelschnitt* (Sickle Cut) plan, to which the German command committed 136 divisions against the 142 Allied divisions, 2,580 panzers against 3,000 Allied tanks and 3,500 aircraft against the Allies' mainland-based 2,738 (with another 1,246 stationed on the British Isles).[1] Army Group A, the strike force, had 45 divisions, of which seven panzer and three motorised (all in all, Germany engaged ten panzer divisions against France).[2]

Until May 10 Belgium, Holland and Luxembourg had been neutral countries. For want of a pretext to attack them, the hitlerites again resorted to a provocation. Freiburg, a German university town, was bombed during the night and early morning of May 10. The raiders' demolition bombs hit a girls' boarding school and a hospital. The casualties were appallingly high. Bomb fragments were dug up from the ruins of buildings and promptly placed on the Freiburg burgomaster's desk. He was horrified to see a German trade mark on them. After the war the secret came out: the raid was by the 51st Luftwaffe squadron. It was to create the appearance that the German thrust into the neutral states was in response to the latter hitting Freiburg from the air.

The German invasion of Belgium and Holland spurred the Anglo-French command into action. Troops left their fortifications and marched to meet the foe. One of the weakest French armies, half of it poorly trained reservists (2nd Army of 5 infantry and 3 cavalry divisions), was deployed to cover the frontier with southern Belgium. The French 9th Army (6 infantry, 2 cavalry and 1 motorised divisions), somewhat to the north of it, was no better prepared for combat.[3] In the breakthrough area, the nazi Army Group A held an overwhelming advantage in strength. Its panzer force breached a 90 kilometre frontage between Sedan and Namur and drove north-west to Paris, wreaking havoc in the rear of the French and British troops. The French Government discussed a possible German entry into the capital. But the nazis veered sharply north and headed for the Channel.

The rapidity of their advance exposed them to peril. General Rundstedt's forces cut a narrow corridor between the enemy armies. If the latter converged, the nazi breakthrough force would be between the hammer and the anvil. The matter was debated by the governments and military leaders of France and Britain, but nothing of practical value was

---

[1] *I.V.O.V.S.S.*, Vol. I, p. 219.
[2] D. Proektor, *op. cit.*, p. 224.
[3] *Ibid.*, p. 170.

done, although by then the intentions of the German command were clear.

As soon as the nazi objective of breaking through to the coast ceased to be a secret, the British Admiralty ordered shipowners (on May 14) to prepare their vessels for a possible evacuation of the British expeditionary corps. The co-ordination of French and British troops diminished visibly.

On May 21, Rundstedt reached the coast and on the following day captured Boulogne. By that time Army Group B was approaching Ostend and Zeebrugge from the east. Forty-nine Allied divisions — 22 Belgian (which surrendered on May 25), 9 British and 18 French — were pressed against the shoreline by the giant German horseshoe in the Dunkirk area,[1] facing the prospect of total annihilation.

At a critical hour for the Anglo-French, however, assault was called off. Visiting Rundstedt's headquarters in Charlesville on May 24, Hitler issued the order to desist. He did not explain why, thus creating one more secret of the Second World War.

Today, we have sufficient evidence to unravel the mystery known as the Dunkirk miracle. The "miracle" was the prelude to a nazi scheme: to obtain the surrender of France in a day or two, conclude an armistice with Britain, and then, with her support, attack the Soviet Union. A fairly transparent hint of this is contained in Fieldmarshal Erich von Manstein's memoirs.[2] Hitler's speeches of the last few months of the Third Reich contain a revealing statement to the same effect. "Churchill," the Fuehrer rued, "was quite unable to appreciate the sporting spirit of which I had given proof by refraining from creating an irreparable breach between the British and ourselves. We did, indeed, refrain from annihilating them at Dunkirk."[3]

The Dunkirk evacuation (Operation Dynamo) from May 26 to June 4, 1940, was carried out under the protective cover of the British Navy and the French ground army. Tens of thousands of British civilians — fishermen, sportsmen and merchant sailors — helped save the British expeditionary troops, shipping 338,000 men who had abandoned all their

[1] G. A. Deborin, *The Second World War*, Progress Publishers, Moscow, p. 80.

[2] E. Manstein, *Verlorene Sieg*, Bonn, 1955, S. 122.

[3] *The Testament of Adolf Hitler. The Hitler-Bormann Documents (February-April 1945)*, 1962, p. 108.

heavy arms, across the Channel. The bulk of the French soldiers, however, were abandoned to their fate.

On June 5, the German offensive was resumed. By then the French had but 60 divisions left. Defeat and occupation was imminent. The evil flower of treason bloomed. Treason, in fact, had been implicit in the policy of the French government since the push-off of the German offensive as an outcome of its entire preceding policy. Men who favoured surrender were quickly inducted into the cabinet. The final step was taken on May 18, when Marshal Petain was made Vice-Premier. Already on May 15, the French cabled London: "We have lost the battle... The road to Paris is open."[1] On June 10, General Maxime Weygand, French Commander-in-Chief, said he saw hardly any way of preventing the enemy from overrunning all of France. He, Petain and Reynaud (who assumed the Premiership) rejected Churchill's advice of adopting guerrilla warfare rather than lay down arms.[2]

On June 10, fascist Italy joined the war against France and Britain. Her rulers wanted a share in the spoils. Count Ciano, Italy's Foreign Minister, said later that Mussolini, too, wanted to pillage.[3]

In Canget, a castle near Tours, during a cabinet sitting on May 13, Weygand argued in favour of immediately abandoning Paris and of total surrender. He referred to the danger of "anarchy" and "social disorders", resorting to the favourite "argument" of all traitors—the bogey of communism. "Maurice Thorez," he said, "has installed himself in the Elysee Palace." The Communists had begun seizing control of Paris.[4] His lie was instantly repudiated. Home Minister Georges Mandel telephoned the Paris Prefect, Langeron, who replied: "Paris is calm."[5] But the traitors in the government could not care less for the truth: they decided not to defend the capital. Surrender thus became a foregone conclusion.

William Bullitt, US Ambassador to France, undertook to mediate the surrender of Paris. On June 14, 1940, German troops entered the French capital unresisted. And on June 22 France signed an act of surrender. Displaying a sense for

[1] P. Reynaud, *La France a sauvé l'Europe*, Vol. 2, Paris, 1947, p. 94.
[2] D. Proektor, *op. cit.*, p. 361.
[3] Pietro Badoglio, *L'Italie dans la guerre mondiale*, Paris, 1946, pp. 47-48.
[4] P. Reynaud, *op. cit.*, p. 323.
[5] R. Langeron, *Paris. Juin 1940*, Paris, 1946, pp. 36-37.

the dramatic, the nazis staged the signing ceremony in the same railway carriage near Rethondes in Compiègne in which the French accepted the German surrender on November 11, 1918.

The national tragedy of France was a natural sequel to the preceding events. Not the Germans became the tool of the imperialist policy of the USA, Britain and France; it was the last-named that fell victim to the Germans, and it began to look like Britain would soon be next, and then the United States. Having isolated the USSR, the British and French governments destroyed every chance of unity against aggression and were then themselves isolated in face of the fascist German aggression. True, German military superiority and employment of new effective offensive tactics did play a certain part in the French defeat, but military superiority alone, without the political factors, was never decisive. But British and French military strategy was an offshoot of the Munich policy. The Munich "appeasers", preoccupied with hatching war against the Soviet Union, exposed their countries to nazi aggression, covering themselves with shame as traitors and gravediggers of their own peoples.

The betrayal of the French ruling group extended to long after the armistice. The invaders divided the country into two zones: the east, north and west of France, with the bulk of the nation's industry, was occupied by the nazis, while the south and part of the central territory comprised the unoccupied zone. The Petain government of this zone, installed in Vichy, consisted of traitors and collaborators. The Vichy dictatorship centred its efforts on breaking the resistance of the people and furnishing the German fascists with every facility in the unoccupied part of the country. Petain and his ministers opposed the popular resistance and helped the nazis combat the patriots.

But neither the disgrace of surrender nor the Vichy regime could destroy the fighting spirit of the French. What had happened in Poland, Denmark, Norway, Belgium and Holland, held true again: the government surrendered, the people fought on.

5. What Was "The Battle for Britain"

In many histories that appeared postwar in Britain, France, and the United States, the war is broken down into "battles". There is the Battle for Poland, the Battle for

France and then the Battle for Britain. Yet luckily for her people, there was no ground fighting in British territory. Then, is the term, Battle for Britain, legitimate? To answer the question, turn to the facts.

The German High Command had been preparing to invade the British Isles since September 1939, having begun planning the operation soon after Poland's defeat. Its operational plan bore the code name Sea Lion. On July 16, 1940, the Wehrmacht received Directive 16 on preparing landing operations against Britain. The directive read: "This operation is dictated by the necessity of eliminating Great Britain ... and if necessary the island will be occupied."[1]

On September 9, 1940, the OKW (High Command Armed Forces of Germany) drew up the Orders Concerning the Organisation and Functioning of Military Government in England, which left no doubt as to the fate the nazis prepared for the population of the British Isles. They intended to wipe out all known progressives, all political leaders and intellectuals. Able-bodied men were to be shipped out of Britain.[2] Sentence of death was to be passed for every form of resistance. The German monopolists, meanwhile, had a detailed plan ready of how they would strip and plunder England's economy. Those were the aims for which the Military Government was to be set up.

Walther Darré, Hitler's "expert on racial problems", declared: "As soon as we beat England we shall make an end of Englishmen once and for all. Able-bodied men will be exported as slaves to the continent. The old and weak will be exterminated."[3]

The hour after France's surrender was a critical one for Britain. She now stood face to face with Germany, without an ally and, certainly, was unable to go it alone, especially after most of her armaments had been lost in Dunkirk. Churchill was quite explicit on this score after the war: "Our armies at home were known to be almost unarmed."[4]

Britain's plight was the result of her prewar policy, but also of the phoney war. Harold L. Ickes, the US statesman, commented: "Britain kept hoping against hope that she could

[1] Peter Fleming, *Invasion 1940*, London, 1957, p. 15.
[2] *Ibid.*, p. 261.
[3] Comer Clarke, *England Under Hitler*, New York, 1961, p. 51.
[4] Winston Churchill, *The Second World War*, Vol. II, London, 1955, p. 226.

embroil Russia and Germany with each other and thus escape scot-free herself. She got caught in her own toils and in so doing has lost the respect and the sympathy of the world generally."[1] The Germans were brazenly obvious with their preparations to invade the British Isles. A month after France's defeat 168 transports, 1,910 barges, 419 lighters and 1,600 motorboats were concentrated along Europe's northern shores—the southern shore of the Channel; it seemed the invasion would begin any day.[2]

But, in fact, the nazi government and generals had no intention of putting the invasion scheme into practice. They hoped to conquer Britain, to occupy her, without large-scale armed action. That was the upshot of the German "peace" proposals, made in quick succession after Hitler's speech in the Reichstag on June 19, 1940 on the occasion of the victory over France. Elucidating the proposals, Admiral Erich Raeder told his staff that Hitler "is firmly convinced that England's defeat will be achieved even without the landing."[3]

However, the German "peace" offers were in vain. London did not bite at the bait, although on the British Isles too, there were men of Petain's ilk. De Gaulle says in his memoirs that in Britain in those days "the initiated bandied the names of politicians, bishops, writers and businessmen, who if opportunity presented, would come to terms with the Germans in order to assume government under their control."[4]

But the dominant sentiment was to reject German hegemony, tantamount to suicide for Britain as a great power. Despite pro-fascist tendencies, Britain's ruling class was opposed to surrender, and inclined to defy the nazi claim to world supremacy. The scales were tilted by the determination of the people to fight fascism and defend independence. In the existing political situation going against their will was for the rulers a risky proposition. They might have lost their class ascendancy.

Besides, they had everything to gain from the people's hatred of fascism, from open battle under the banner of British democracy against their bitterest imperialist rival.

[1] Harold L. Ickes, *The Secret Diary*, Vol. 2, New York, 1954, p. 705.
[2] Kurt von Tippelskirch, *Geschichte des zweiten Weltkriegs*, Bonn, 1951, S. 117.
[3] Peter Fleming, *op. cit.*, p. 116.
[4] Charles de Gaulle, "Mémoires de Guerre", *L'Appel*, Paris, 1954, p. 87.

Expecting Britain to surrender without an invasion, Berlin gave priority to an entirely different course, finalised when the German success in France became a foregone conclusion: to strike next against the Soviet Union, the main barrier on the way to German supremacy. The German imperialists were afraid that the Soviet Union would grow stronger with the passage of time. Not only were they impatient to attack in the East. They had made up their minds to conserve the maximum possible strength for war against the Soviet state. That is why, with vessels concentrating along the Channel coast to scare Britain with the prospect of invasion, German ground forces were being rail-borne in the opposite direction.

The Soviet Union saved England from invasion by just existing and strengthening its forces. Long before the Great Patriotic War, the USSR sluiced off considerable nazi strength from the West, delivering European peoples from fresh Wehrmacht incursions and facilitating the genesis of Resistance.

Abandoning the idea of invading the British Isles, the German chiefs decided on terrorist measures to bring the English to their knees. They rained bombs on British cities and blockaded Britain from the sea. In Directive No. 17, dated August 1, 1940, Hitler described this as the overture to Britain's collapse.

The regular air-raids began early in August. At first, they came day and night, and in force. In the first raid on the British capital, the London docks were the main target, their huge warehouses filled with food and depots with materiel. Incendiary bombs caused a colossal fire. Eyewitnesses relate that flames leaped sky-high as artillery shells and cases of TNT exploded. Fire in a warehouse where pepper was stored filled the air with pungent particles. Flowing rum formed a flaming stream, merging with the "lava" of burning sugar. Flames of all colours leaped about the docks, while burning rubber emitted clouds of choking black smoke. Tea burned brightly, producing a peculiar sweetish, nauseating smell. Smoke from the burning grain overcast the skies. From September 7, 1940, London lived through 65 nights of unintermittent bombing. On November 14, five hundred nazi bombers demolished Coventry, the heart of Britain's aviation industry.[1]

---

[1] *I.V.O.V.S.S.*, Vol. 1, p. 290.

In the aggregate, however, the air assault yielded but a meagre success. British anti-aircraft defences stiffened. In the tensest months of the air war, from August to October 1940, the Luftwaffe lost nearly twice as many planes as the RAF.[1] Though exposed to air attacks, the British aviation industry stepped up production.

The sea-blockade, consisting of piratic air, submarine and surface attacks on merchant vessels carrying freight to Britain, was a peril that had to be eliminated at all costs, for Britain's sea losses were near disastrous, exceeding the maximum capacity of her shipyards at least threefold. Marine communications were largely disrupted. And it was not until after July 1941 that Britain's plight was visibly relieved thanks to stubborn Soviet resistance.

In sum, the main armed forces of Germany and Britain did not come to grips at all. Seen from that angle, no Battle for Britain ever occurred. That battle was fought in an entirely different area--chiefly the moral-political. The ordeal to which the British nation was subjected in those months was terrible. The war was visited on the Englishman's home in the full sense. People in the towns fought the fires and quickly repaired the havoc wrought by the air raids. The Home Guard was on the alert, ready to fight in the event of an enemy landing. Workers did not leave their benches even when enemy planes roared overhead. The merchant seamen took their ships out to the sea fearlessly, defying nazi submarines and learning the art of concealment from lurking periscopes.

Far from breaking their will, the trials of those days steeled the British nation. Their determination to fight on to the end was never stronger. For the British Government no policy was conceivable other than to survive, to win time. The phoney war and the political hide-and-seek with German fascism, on which Hitler had banked, were buried beneath the hail of German bombs.

6. The Unvanquished

The nazi "new order" rested on the assumption that hyperbolised terror and the physical extermination of millions of people would bend the survivors to its will. And the slavish

---

[1] *Voyenno-istorichesky zhurnal*, No. 2, 1967, p. 33.

servility of the Quislings and Petains seemed to bear this out. But the events soon dispelled the illusion.

Powerful popular movements, later named the Resistance, began in all nazi-occupied countries. And the nazi dream of a vanquished Europe went up in the flames lit by the Resistance.

From the first days Czechoslovakia was occupied, before the outbreak of the world war, the people resisted the arrogant invader. In 1940 a wave of strikes swept Slovakia. And from the beginning of September a resistance movement gradually gained momentum in Poland.

The French surrender sparked a broad movement of national resistance. One trend in the movement consisted of sections of the bourgeoisie and "middle" classes who had had no part in treason and the cowardly capitulation. They responded to General de Gaulle, who issued his first appeal for resistance from London on June 18, 1940. The other trend was that of the working people, born of their patriotic determination to save the nation from extinction. Political and economic resistance combined with a gradually mounting armed struggle.

Historians of the French Resistance tell of its beginnings. In the back room of a small café in Dechy (Nord department) a dozen people gathered at the beginning of August 1940 to swear vengeance. Heading this group was a 20-year-old Italian, Eusebio Ferrari, and Félicien Joly, a Frenchman, also aged 20, was made his deputy. A red cloth streamer inscribed "Courage and Faith", the slogan of the first French Resistance groups, appeared the following day on the pilon of a power transmission line. The Ferrari group began by attacking nazi soldiers and organising sabotage in war factories. In December 1940 they derailed a German military train and blew up a power station.

Pierre Georges, a legendary Resistance fighter subsequently known as Fabien, organised young people in Lyons, then Marseilles, then Corsica. Jean Mérot did the same in Toulon. One of the most battle-steeled fighters, Charles Debarge, began with a handful of followers. His small band blew up a catering establishment filled with Germans, following up with raids on German posts and with a few larger acts of diversion. On May 15, 1941, he and a few other Resistance fighters led the strike of 100,000 miners in Nord Department. The following episode, described by Charles Tillon, shows the kind of strike it was. "In Bruay, on June 8, a nazi emissary asked the miners:

'You have enough bread, enough meat and soap; what more do you want?' A worker shouted: 'We want rifles!' '[1]

The Resistance movement in France originated on French soil, in the thick of the people. It was the beginning of a full-scale war of liberation by civilians against invaders. Similar developments were seen in Belgium, Norway and other nazi-occupied European countries.

On April 6, 1941, Hitler made his sneak attack on Yugoslavia and Greece. What had happened in the West somewhat earlier, was repeated: Yugoslavia surrendered on April 18 and Greece on April 27. The surrenders were signed by delegates of the governments and military commands, and were not accepted by the people.

The Yugoslav workers and peasants began collecting arms and the first partisan groups formed in the mountains and forests, especially in Bosnia and Herzegovina. Early in May 1941 Communist Party leaders conferred in Zagreb at a secret meeting-place of the Central Committee, adopting the decision to prepare for an armed rising.

The people in Greece rose to the occasion, with detachments of insurrectionists forming in the country and committing the first acts of diversion. Manolis Glezos, a man of courage beyond compare, performed his deathless feat: on May 31, 1941, risking his life, he tore down the nazi flag from the Acropolis, replacing it with the Greek national flag. It was a bold call to arms.

A distinctly new factor came into evidence. The general crisis of capitalism, which had prompted the national betrayal of the big bourgeoisie and landowners in the nazi-attacked countries, saw the masses rising against the aggressors. The war gradually became a people's war, a just war of liberation.

The liberative aims of the Resistance movement and its identity with the national interest and international duty attracted more and more people, exerting a powerful influence on the nature of the war. The Communists played a prominent part in this, being always to the fore of the Resistance in all countries.

The nature of the war changed completely after the Soviet Union, attacked by the nazis, was drawn into it.

This was the main factor, making it a just war of liberation.

---

[1] Charles Tillon, *Les F.T.P. Témoignage pour servir à l'Histoire de la Résistance,* Paris, 1962, p. 89.

Chapter Three

Collapse of the Barbarossa Plan

1. Secret Intents of the German Monopolists

In their drive for world supremacy the German imperialists attached the prime importance to conquering the Soviet Union, destroying the Soviet system and enslaving the Soviet people. Naturally, they kept these intentions secret for a long time. In the meanwhile, nazi leaders issued assurance upon assurance that they were only thinking of "protecting" Western civilisation and culture from Bolshevism. Yet if world civilisation and culture needed protection, it was from the nazi vandals.

The leaders of fascist Germany did not intend to give up their plans, despite signing a non-aggression treaty with the Soviet Union. Adolf Hitler, fascist dictator and supreme commander of the Wehrmacht, said so plainly on November 23, 1939. "I was not sure for a long time whether I should first strike in the East and then in the West.... It so happened, of necessity, that the East was left out for a time.... Moreover, we have the treaty with Russia. But treaties are observed only for as long as they are useful."[1]

Initially, he planned to attack the USSR in the autumn of 1940. Strategic deployment of troops from France to Poland began soon after the former's defeat. The drafting of the war plan was speeded up.

Hitler's intention of attacking the Soviet Union was revealed by him to a conference of German generals on July 31, 1940. "Once Russia is beaten," he said, "England's last

---

[1] Max Domarus, *Hitler. Reden und Proklamationen 1932–1945*, Bd. II, Erster Halbband, München, 1963, S. 1423.

hope will vanish. Germany will then be master of Europe and the Balkans. The conclusion: for this reason Russia must be done away with."[1] The dictator did not, however, set out all the war aims. He held that the generals and admirals knew them: the ultimate objective was to conquer the world for the German monopolies.

The conference examined the first variants of the operation plan and put off attack day to the spring of 1941. The war plan against the USSR (Directive No. 21, Plan Barbarossa) was approved on December 18, 1940. Its operational guideline was formulated as follows:

"The German Armed Forces must be prepared, even before the conclusion of the war against England, to crush Soviet Russia in a rapid campaign."[2] On April 30, 1941, the date of the attack was tentatively set for June 22, and the final order to jump off on that day was issued on June 17.

The nazis meant to destroy the Soviet state and enslave its people. "The war is to be one of extermination," said Hitler on March 30, 1941. "Unless we look at it that way, we may defeat the enemy, but the Communist danger will reappear 30 years hence. We do not make war to preserve an adversary.... In the East firmness is a boon for the future."[3]

So the German imperialists would destroy not only the Soviet state, which they hated, but also the bulk of its population. "The war against Russia," Hitler told his generals, "will be such that it cannot be conducted in a knightly fashion. This struggle is one of ideologies and racial differences and will have to be conducted with unprecedented unmerciful and unrelenting harshness.... German soldiers guilty of breaking international law ... will be excused."[4] And OKW, the Wehrmacht command, accepted Hitler's admonition as mandatory.

The crimes against the Soviet people were planned in advance. Through their generals, the German monopolies ordered the total extermination of all protagonists of the Soviet system, all who came under the head of "Bolshevist commissars and communist intellectuals".[5]

---

[1] *Ibid.*, S. 1565.
[2] *Hitler's War Directives 1939-45*, London, 1964, p. 49.
[3] M. Domarus, *op. cit.*, Zweiter Halbband, S. 1682.
[4] William L. Shirer, *The Rise and Fall of the Third Reich*, New York, 1960, p. 830.
[5] *Voyenno-istorichesky zhurnal*, No. 2, 1959, p. 82.

On May 13, 1941, the German Government issued a decree concerning the exercise of military jurisdiction in the Barbarossa area and concerning special measures of the troops. The decree required "complete lack of mercy to the civilian population" and execution of all partisans and citizens rendering the least resistance or suspected of contact with partisans. "Suspects" were to be shot at once, without a trial. German soldiers and officers were relieved of responsibility for crimes committed against prisoners of war and peaceful citizens. The decree envisaged punitive operations against the population, introduced the criminal hostages system, wholesale repressions and unbridled violence.[1]

No less disgraceful a document was the OKW directive to exterminate captured Red Army political officers and employees of Soviet government institutions, issued on May 12, 1941. It classified all political officers and employees of government, municipal and economic offices as especially dangerous to the plan of colonising the Soviet Union. Political officers were not to be treated as prisoners of war and were to be killed on the spot. It was considered needless to bring them to any rear area. Some government employees were to be allowed to live for a time, for they could be useful in implementing orders of the occupation authorities. Subsequently, they would also be destroyed.[2]

A brutal routine was devised for POWs whose life would at first be spared. It was a routine that doomed them to a slow death. Hermann Reinecke, a Lt.-General and Chief of the POW Affairs Department of the High Command, was the man who worked it out on orders of the German authorities. Briefing his subordinates in a secret conference in Berlin in March 1941, he said camps for Russian POWs would best be situated in the open. On August 6, 1941, the High Command issued a directive that had been drawn up in advance, "Food Ration of Soviet Prisoners of War", which read: "We are not obliged to supply Soviet prisoners of war with food."[3]

Not prisoners only, but the entire Soviet people, were to be deprived of food. Speaking behind closed doors on June 20, 1941, A. Rosenberg gave the following instructions:

---

[1] *CSAOR*, file 7445, registration No. 2, case 166, sheets 65-70.
[2] *Ibid.*, file 7021, registration No. 148, case 156, sheets 4-5.
[3] *IMT. Trial*, Vol. VII, p. 350.

"The southern territories and the Northern Caucasus will
have to serve... for the feeding of the German people. We
see absolutely no reason for any obligation on our part to
feed also the Russian people with the products of these
territories."[1]

Rosenberg was put in charge of a bureau to solve the
question of *Ostraum* (eastern space). The bureau, founded
in early April 1941, worked in two main directions: a) it
plotted the partitioning and colonisation with Germans of
the Soviet territory and b) planned the extermination of the
Soviet civilian population. On July 17, 1941, the bureau
was converted into a Ministry for the Eastern Occupied
Areas.

Rosenberg's initial plan was to set up a number of German-
controlled puppet states, which Berlin rejected as too liberal.
A new plan was drawn up and adopted, lacking even this
fictitious appearance of statehood. Under it the entire territory
of the Soviet Union would be Germany's colonial "Eastern
space". Elucidating it, Rosenberg declared: "The Soviet
Union will no longer be the *subject* of European politics; it will
become the object of German *Weltpolitik*."[2]

For administrative convenience the Soviet Union would be
carved into four Reichskomissariats: "Moskau", "Ostland",
"Ukraine" and "Kaukasus". A fifth, "Turkestan", was also
contemplated.[3] Anticipating events, Berlin appointed the
Reichscommissars (Siegfried Kasche for Moscow) and 1,050
junior commissars for the regions.

By special order, Gestapo chief Himmler drew up a general
Plan Ost (East Plan) for the subjugation by fire and sword of
all peoples in Eastern Europe. The plan was ready long
before the attack on the Soviet Union and envisaged the
total extermination of Poles, Ukrainians and other Slav
nations. All education, save for primary and "special"
schools, was to be wiped out in order to eradicate national
cultures. In the "special" schools pupils would be taught
counting (at most up to 500), signing their name, and the
divine commandment to obey the Germans, to be honest,
diligent and obedient. Learning to read was considered
superfluous.

---

[1] *CSAOR*, file 7445, registration No. 1, case 1666, sheet 197.
[2] *IMT. Trial...*, Vol. XXVI, p. 613.
[3] A. Dallin, *Deutsche Herrschaft in Russland. 1941-1945*, Düsseldorf, 1962.

Commands and requisite equipment were created in advance for the wholesale extermination of the civilian population. "We," Hitler declared, "are obliged to depopulate as part of our mission of preserving the German population. We shall have to develop a technique of depopulation.... If I can send the flower of the German nation into the hell of war without the smallest pity for the spilling of precious German blood, then surely I have the right to remove millions of an inferior race that breeds like vermin."[1]

Another nazi programme outlined the procedure of plundering the Soviet Union. Goering was appointed to control the seizure of the Soviet economy. A detailed programme was drawn up, named Directive for the Operation of the Economy in the Newly-Occupied Eastern Territories.

To attain these secret aims Hitler planned a piratic attack. In the meantime, the plans and preparations were thoroughly camouflaged.

The German imperialists inveigled their allies—Hungary, Rumania, Italy, Finland, Croatia and Slovakia—into taking part in the war, and came to terms with their friends in Bulgaria and Spain, and in the unoccupied part of France. To obtain the support, or at least the neutrality, of Britain, Rudolf Hess, a top-ranking nazi leader, went on a special mission to contact the British Government.

The German economy was on a war footing long before the war. The German imperialists and generals had a ramified war economy, which experienced only slight strain in the early period of the war. The territorial seizures, the occupation of country after country and the enlistment of other countries as satellites, added to the economic potential of the nazi war machine, with the shortage of manpower compensated by the use of foreign labour forcibly shipped to Germany. By December 1940 as many as 1,300,000 foreigners were put to work in German factories.[2]

Military production in 1940 was 76 per cent up on 1939 and as much as 22 times up on 1933.[3] Production of tanks, tractors, warplanes and naval vessels increased spectacularly. The armed forces had huge dumps of arms and materiel. The stockpiles were so great that some months after the

---

[1] *IMT. Trial...*, Vol. XIX, p. 498.
[2] *I.V.O.V.S.S.*, Vol. I, p. 375.
[3] *Ibid.*

attack on the Soviet Union production of shells and cartridges was even deliberately somewhat reduced. These days West German researchers blame Hitler for not expanding war production before attacking the USSR. But, in fact, war production soared and the drop in the output of shells and cartridges only speaks of the vastness of the stocks.

Mobilisation and deployment of forces for the war against the USSR was largely completed before June 1, 1941. Germany had more than twice as many troops and warplanes as at the beginning of the Second World War, as shown in the following table.

Germany's Armed Forces[1]

	Sept. 1, 1939	May 1, 1940	June 1, 1941
Divisions, total	103	156	214
Panzer	6	10	21
Motorised	8	8	14
Panzers (in service)	3,200	3,387	5,640
Warplanes (in service)	4,405	5,900	10,000

By June 21, 1941, as many as 190 divisions were poised along the Soviet border, of which 153 German, including 17 panzer and 13 motorised, and two brigades and support units (24 divisions, the General Headquarters reserve, were en route), and 29 allied divisions and 16 allied brigades. All in all, troops deployed against the Soviet Union totalled five million men and officers. Warplanes added up to 4,940 and tanks to 3,410. Eighty-five warships, 109 special-purpose vessels and 86 submarines were massed for action in the Northern seas.[2]

The German army, mobilised and armed to the teeth, had nearly two years of combat experience and consisted of superbly trained men and officers conditioned in the fascist spirit.

The troop masses deployed along the Soviet border were prepared to strike in key strategic directions, where the German generals had built up a considerable numerical ad-

---

[1] *Ibid.*, p. 382.
[2] *Ibid.*, p. 384.

vantage and superiority of arms. Never in history were such colossal masses of men and equipment concentrated before the war to discharge strategic assignments. The generals thought they would thus make short work of the Soviet Union. In a conversation with his army commanders on December 5, 1940, Hitler said: "... It is likely that the Russian army, once hit, would face a still more disastrous collapse than France."[1]

The self-confident German command drew up on June 11, 1941 Directive 32 on what was to follow the conquest of the Soviet Union, envisaging the invasion of Britain, seizure of Gibraltar and all British support points in the Mediterranean and Middle East, the invasion of Iraq, Syria and Iran, and the conquest of Egypt. This was estimated to take a matter of weeks, after which Germany's war effort would extend to other parts of the globe.[2]

German imperialism envisaged a drive across Afghanistan into India as a stage in its battle for world supremacy. The decision to draw up a plan of this operation was taken by Hitler on February 17, 1941.[3] Capture of India, coupled with operations in the Middle East and the Mediterranean, was expected to sluice off Britain's armed forces, sap resistance and cause her collapse.[4]

The nazis expected Britain to surrender without an invasion. But they would strike if necessary, and continued preparations. The Luftwaffe was cast in the main role for the destruction of Britain and, eventually, of the USA. This was spelled out in the so-called Goering Programme, which envisaged a spectacular increase in planes production.[5] A steep expansion was also envisaged of the navy and, chiefly, of the submarine force. On March 30, 1941, Hitler said that following the Operation Barbarossa "it is necessary to start sweeping construction of naval vessels".[6]

Air raids on US cities were to begin in the autumn of 1941. Hitler mentioned this on May 22, 1941.[7] On July 25 he told

---

[1] Helmuth Greiner, *Die Oberste Wehrmachtführung 1939-1943*, Wiesbaden, 1951, S. 326.

[2] *Wehrwissenschaftliche Rundschau*, Heft 3, März 1956, S. 134-35.

[3] *Kriegstagebuch des Oberkommandos der Wehrmacht*, Bd. 1, S. 328.

[4] *Wehrwissenschaftliche Rundschau*, Heft 3, März 1956, S. 134.

[5] *Kriegstagebuch...*, *op. cit.*, S. 1016.

[6] Andreas Hillgruber, *Hitlers Strategie, Politik und Kriegsführung 1940-1941*, Frankfurt am Main, 1965, S. 381.

[7] *Ibid.*, S. 380.

his generals that he "intended to take vigorous action against the United States".[1]

Brutal treatment of the population of the British Isles was outlined in a plan drawn up by the summer of 1940, and a similar plan was envisaged for the people of the United States.

The vast store of documents left behind by the Hitler government and German military Command reveal a sinister secret: the German monopolies' plans for winning world supremacy and the way they were going to go about it. We now see how the German industrialists and their generals, driven by a thirst for more wealth, arranged the sequence of military actions that would win them the world. Concentration and death camps scattered all over Europe, were also to be set up across the ocean. Prison barracks would be the main type of architecture in all countries, with the smoke from the cremation furnaces to hang over the globe.

The peril that menaced the Soviet Union was a peril also for all states and nations. For all of them the German fascists planned the same fate—a colonial regime, slave labour, the overseer's gun and asphyxiation in gas chambers. The only way to thwart this monstrous scheme was to destroy the gigantic nazi war machine that had already overrun 15 countries. Could the Soviet Union do it? Could it deliver mankind, its culture and civilisation from the 20th-century barbarians armed not with arrows and spears, but with tanks, planes and automatic firearms? This was the question—a question of life and death—for all the people on earth.

2. Perfidy and Surprise

The nazis knew it would not be easy to defeat the Soviet Union. They intended to make the most of perfidy and surprise, the long-time tools of aggression.

The attack was to be carried out without a warning, without preliminary demands, talks or pretexts. And to the public Hitler intended to portray the sneak attack as a preventive war: the Soviet Union, he would say, had to be attacked to avert an imminent Soviet attack. The facts upset this legend.

[1] *Ibid.*, S. 380.

To assure surprise, the nazis employed a set of deceptions. Some were enumerated in the Directive on Concealing Preparations for Operation Barbarossa, which said, among other things: "Reports of new means of attack and transport are to create the impression that preparations to attack the Soviet Union are meant to camouflage the landing (in Britain—*Ed.*) ... Deployment of troops for 'Barbarossa' is to be portrayed as the greatest deceptive action in the history of wars, aimed at covering up final preparations for the invasion of Britain."

With the same motive, the Germans sold the Soviet Union samples of their panzers and planes and let Soviet representatives visit industrial installations, including war factories, confident that in the brief time before the assault on the USSR Soviet designers, fliers and tankers would learn nothing useful from them. This also revealed their basic recklessness and disdain for the imminent adversary.

The nazi talks with the Soviet Commissar of Foreign Affairs in November 1940 were also part of the camouflage. Ribbentrop suggested that the Soviet Union should join the Germany-Italy-Japan military bloc, though actually it was erected against the USSR. Naturally, the Soviet delegation turned the offer down.

Despite these manoeuvres to conceal Hitler's nefarious intentions, the secret was cracked by Soviet intelligence officers. One of these, Richard Sorge, informed Moscow not only of the date of the attack, but of the invaders' initial attack strength, the operational and strategic targets of the nazi Command and direction of the main blows. In two successive radiograms, on June 15, 1941, he wired: "The war will begin June 22", and "Attacking on a wide front at dawn June 22."[1]

The Soviet Government was then fortifying the country's frontiers, though its efforts were impeded by the international set-up. It had no knowledge of how the British and US governments would react to a German attack on the USSR. Not improbable was it to think that they would offer some kind of support to the Germans. Every Soviet act of fortifying the western frontiers was, if journalists discovered it, presented falsely in the British and American press. Provocative reports to that effect had to be denied. One TASS denial said:

---

[1] *Voyenno-istorichesky zhurnal*, No. 12, 1966, p. 101.

"According to a United Press correspondent's cable from Vichy, the Soviet Union is massing large forces along its western frontiers. Diplomatic circles in Moscow, UP alleges, are referring to large-scale concentrations along the western frontiers…. TASS is authorised to declare that the suspiciously strident report … is a figment of the author's imagination."[1]

The British Government's treatment of Hess was perturbing. True, Hess's proposals of peace and an alliance against the Soviet Union were obviously unacceptable to Britain after the preceding months of the war. But neither did the British Government reject the offer publicly, encouraging Hitler to attack eastward. Soviet historian V. Trukhanovsky draws the conclusion that "Hitler was sure the attack on the USSR would not lead to war on two fronts and that if Britain did not help Germany against the Soviet Union she would at any rate place no obstacles to the war against the socialist state. There was one more aspect to this question. The British Government ardently desired that Germany should commit error in this issue, for this error would mean Britain's salvation. … In May-June the British Government's reaction to the Hess mission was such as to fortify Hitler in his view that an arrangement could be reached if development were given a 'push' by an attack on the USSR."[2]

The US and British governments were active in other areas, too, prodding Germany to come sooner to grips with the Soviet Union. In the spring of 1941 British Intelligence in New York, working jointly with the Federal Bureau of Investigation, planted the following false report in the German Embassy in Washington: "From highly reliable source it is learned USSR intends further military aggression instant Germany is embroiled in major operations."[3]

With everything to win from stretching out the peace, the Soviet Union had to reckon with the fact that certain groups in Britain and the United States wished to hasten the nazi attack. In the circumstances, it was important to observe meticulously all the non-aggression treaty stipulations. German Ambassador Werner von Schulenburg wrote from Moscow that the Soviet Government was "due to the present

---

[1] *Izvestia*, May 9, 1941.

[2] V. Trukhanovsky, *British Foreign Policy During World War II*, Moscow, 1970, p. 154.

[3] H. Montgomery Hyde, *Room 3603, The Story of the British Intelligence Centre in New York During World War II*, New York, 1963, p. 58.

international situation, which it views as grave, trying to avert a conflict with Germany".[1]

Hitler Germany held strong, though temporary, triumphs: her economy was militarised and the country on a war footing; the preparations for war of conquest had been long and thorough and her army had acquired combat experience in the West; her arms and troops deployed in the border areas were superior. Besides, Germany had at her command the economic and manpower resources of nearly all Western Europe. In countries overrun by the nazis, the arsenals, vast stores of metal and strategic raw materials, and the steel and war factories were operating for the conqueror. The Soviet Union, its troops lacking experience in large-scale operations, was faced by a powerful military machine.

Those were the factors that contributed to the Soviet Army setbacks at the beginning of the war.

At dawn on June 22 the fascist armies jumped off, delivering a sudden and perfidious blow of immense power without so much as a declaration of war. The Wehrmacht and its allies—190 divisions in all, comprising 5,500,000 men—crossed the border while air armadas showered bombs on Soviet cities and thousands of guns and tanks opened fire.

Hitler's war against the Soviet Union was reactionary, imperialist, aggressive and unjust. So were its aims. German imperialism set out to destroy the Soviet Union and clear the way to world supremacy. It set out to destroy the Soviet system, to capture the land and wealth of the country, to instal German landlords and capitalists in the conquered land, abolishing the statehood of the Soviet people and wiping out Soviet culture.

The nazi treacherous attack exposed the USSR to great peril. The Soviet people were assaulted by a perfidious and brutal enemy who had an immense military potential and would shrink at nothing.

3. The "Secret" of Soviet Resistance

Their hatred for the Soviet Union, for socialism, blinded the German monopolists and their generals. They were totally unaware of the changes in the life of the Soviet Union. The

---

[1] *Die Beziehungen zwischen Deutschland und der Sowjetunion 1939-1941,* Tübingen, 1949, S. 389.

country had been converted by heroic efforts inspired by the Communist Party from an agrarian into a highly industrialised power. In 1940, Soviet heavy industry was producing 12 times as much as prewar Russia, and the machine-building industry 50 times as much as in 1913.[1] The redeployment of industry, its move to the East, begun before the war, helped the nation to survive the initial onslaught. Against 1913 the share of the eastern regions in the economy had by 1940 increased in power output twice over, coal output nearly threefold, oil 350 per cent and steel 50 per cent.[2]

Yet the Soviet economic potential was still far lower than that of Hitler Germany and the nazi-occupied countries.

However, the Soviet heavy industry provided the resources for the technical rearmament of the Red Army, the Navy and the Air Force. This against a setting of general scientific progress. Soviet researchers, designers and inventors applied their genius to the new technical problems facing the nation's defence.

Shortly before the German attack highly sophisticated arms had been designed and prepared for mass production, among them the heavy KV and the medium T-34 tanks. Put into the field, they proved superior to anything produced before in the line of armour. New planes were designed—the armoured attack aircraft IL-2, and the fighter planes YAK-1, LAGG-3 and MIG-2. Dive-bomber P-2 was in use for daylight raids until the end of the war. Another outstanding innovation was the lorry-mounted jet mortar, fondly known by soldiers as Katyusha.

Arms production had increased, though until the outbreak of the war it was substantially less than that of nazi Germany. From 1929 to 1941 light, medium and heavy artillery increased seven times over in number and anti-tank and tank artillery 17 times over. The armoured force grew 150 per cent between 1934 and 1939, and for each plane available in 1930 there were 6.5 in 1939.[3]

When the Second World War began, the Soviet Government took steps to expand arms production. Decisions were passed to modernise existing plane factories and to build

---

[1] *Narodnoye Khozyaistvo SSSR*, Statistichesky Sbornik (*Soviet Economy. Statistical Yearbook*), Moscow, 1956, p. 45.

[2] E. Lokshin, *Promyshlennost SSSR 1940-1963 gg.* (*Soviet Economy 1940-1963*), Moscow, 1964, p. 32.

[3] *Voyenno-istorichesky zhurnal*, No. 3, 1967, p. 55.

new ones. Ammunition production was to be boosted —factories were expanded and new ones built to produce gun powder, shells, and other ammunition. In addition to the Kirov Works in Leningrad and the Kharkov Plant, the tractor factories in Stalingrad and Chelyabinsk began converting to tank production.

Mass production of new plane and tank models commenced in 1940. That year and the first six months of 1941, Soviet industry produced 3,719 planes and 2,083 tanks of new designs,[1] not nearly enough for the Armed Forces. Meanwhile, the Soviet Navy was equipped in 1941 with some 500 new vessels.

With reports of German attack preparations reaching Moscow from various quarters and army intelligence reporting vast troop concentrations along the frontier, measures were taken to enhance combat readiness in the first half of 1941.

Divisions were moved closer to the western border throughout April, May and June from the interior and the Far East, while the border zone divisions were deployed still closer to the frontier. When Germany attacked there were 170 divisions and 2 brigades, totalling 2,900,000 men, in the western zones, but the enemy surpassed Soviet strength 1.8 : 1, with a 1.5 : 1 edge in medium and heavy tanks, a 3.2 : 1 edge in warplanes of the latest design and a 1.25 : 1 edge in guns and mortars.[2]

What served the country well in face of the nazi assault was the deployment of armies of the High Command reserve along the Western Dvina and the Dnieper.

On June 12-15, 1941, the command of the border military districts in the west received order to deploy divisions stationed in depth closer to the frontier and to areas designated in the defence plans. On June 19, orders came for the commands of the North-Western, Western and South-Western fronts to move into field posts, followed up on June 21 with a directive forming a new front, the Southern.[3]

However, many of the measures were uncompleted when the war broke out. "Particularly deplorable were the con-

---

[1] *Kommunist*, No. 12, 1968, p. 65.
[2] *50 let Vooruzhonnykh Sil SSSR (Soviet Armed Forces in 50 Years)*, Moscow, 1968, p. 252.
[3] *Kommunist*, No. 12, 1968, p. 68.

sequences of the delay in putting on a combat footing those troops in the border military districts and fortified areas that were to engage the enemy the moment he struck. This was due largely to the error of judgement as to the probable time of fascist Germany's attack".[1]

A Defence Commissariat telegram warning that "a sudden German attack is possible in the course of June 22-23" was transmitted at 23.45 hours on June 21.[2]

Having built up considerably superior strength in the main directions, the enemy mounted a sudden attack against unalerted Soviet troops in the border area. This frustrated the troop movements to the frontier that had already begun. In the first days of the war the Soviet Union suffered considerable losses in men and materiel, the strength ratio tilting still more drastically in favour of the invader. The Soviet air force, too, was hit hard. Sudden air strikes at airfields, coupled with the Red Army shortage of planes of latest design, enabled the Luftwaffe to gain command of the air.

The enemy seized the strategic initiative along the entire front and drove on steadily. Assault groups consisting chiefly of panzer and motorised divisions thrust forward, suppressing Soviet resistance. Fighting bitterly, the Red Army retreated. The mobile nazi formations hooked round the Soviet defence flanks and cut deep into the rear. The Soviet troops tried but failed to disengage themselves from the persistent foe, were often encircled, and fought in extremely unfavourable conditions.

The Soviet troops abandoned towns and villages with a heavy heart. Their setbacks perturbed the nation. The blockade tightened round Leningrad, the cradle of the October Revolution. Heroic efforts were demanded of those in the rear, most of whom were women whose husbands had gone to the battle-lines, and adolescents. People near the combat areas came out in the hundreds of thousands to build fortifications. In the cities, they stood guard over the nation's property during air raids, and hunted for saboteurs and spies.

No other country in the same predicament could have survived. But the heroic Soviet people, led by the Communist

---

[1] *Soviet Armed Forces in 50 Years*, Russ. ed., p. 251.
[2] *Kommunist*, No. 12, 1968, p. 69.

Party, the people that had built socialism despite the hostile capitalist encirclement, arose as one to stem the nazi tide.

The scale of the fighting increased. There were no prolonged lulls. Each day the Soviet-German front became more and more the main and decisive theatre of the Second World War.

The Communist Party called on the nation to rally and drive out the enemy: to preserve the socialist system, the honour and independence of their country, to smash the invader, liberate the enslaved nations of Europe, the German included, and to afford them the freedom of choosing their political and socio-economic order. The war became the Great Patriotic War of the Soviet Union. Resisting the treacherous nazi attack, the Soviet people affirmed the just, anti-fascist, liberative character of the war.

Acting on Lenin's precepts relating to the defence of the socialist homeland, the CPSU Central Committee and Soviet Government drew up measures to assure the mobilisation of all resources. A summary of what had to be done was contained in the Central Committee and Council of People's Commissars directive of June 29, 1941, which was the basis for Joseph Stalin's radio address to the nation on July 3.

The Presidium of the Supreme Soviet announced a general mobilisation on the first day of the war. All groups (born between 1905 and 1918) in all military districts save the Central Asian, Transbaikal and Far Eastern, were called up. Martial law was proclaimed in some republics and regions. The Headquarters of the Supreme Command was formed on June 23, consisting of the People's Commissar of Defence Marshal S. K. Timoshenko (chairman), Chief of General Staff General G. K. Zhukov, J. V. Stalin, V. M. Molotov, Marshals K. Y. Voroshilov and S. M. Budyonny, and People's Commissar of the Navy Admiral N. G. Kuznetsov. On June 30 the Presidium of the Supreme Soviet, the Party Central Committee, and the Council of People's Commissars also formed the State Defence Committee, appointing Joseph Stalin its chairman. The decision said: "The full power of government shall be concentrated in the hands of the State Defence Committee",[1] which immediately launched a mammoth national effort, mobilising men and resources.

---

[1] *KPSS o Vooruzhonnykh Silakh Sovietskogo Soyuza (The CPSU on the Armed Forces of the USSR)*, Moscow, 1958, p. 357.

The nazis encountered stubborn resistance the moment they crossed the border. Having lost some 300,000 men and officers in the conquest of Poland, France, Norway, Denmark, Belgium, Holland, Yugoslavia, Greece and Luxembourg, Germany's ground forces lost as many as 389,924 in just the first 53 days of the war against the USSR (from June 22 to August 1, 1941).[1]

Soviet resistance in the frontier battles astounded the nazi command. The German generals had expected a walkover. Now they had to face up to the fact that the Barbarossa schedule had been based on fallacious assumptions. On June 24, 1941, General Franz Halder, Chief of the OKH General Staff, wrote in his diary: "The enemy in the frontier area put up a resistance almost everywhere.... No sign of the enemy's operational withdrawal so far."[2] And Hermann Hoth, Commander of the Third Panzer Group, admitted years later: "In the vicinity of the frontier ... the enemy was flung back, it is true, but recovered quickly from the surprise and mounted counter-attacks with reserves and tank groups rushed up from the rear, stemming the German advance again and again."[3]

Despite the surprise element and the fact that for the first time in history an aggressor committed so vast a force in the opening battle, the Soviet troops kept their head, retained faith in ultimate victory and rendered determined resistance. Their courage in face of overwhelming odds gradually sapped the nazi power.

The now legendary resistance of the Brest Fortress, the garrison of which fought for over a month against a vastly superior enemy, was a feat among many similar ones. On its ruins are left the inscriptions of its defenders. One of these, made by a mortally wounded soldier, reads: "I shall die, but never surrender! Farewell, my country. July 24, 1941."[4]

The 13th border post of the 90th Frontier Detachment, commanded by A. V. Lopatin, fought for 11 days in a ring of enemies, while men of the 9th post, 92nd Detachment, under N. S. Slyusarev, flung back the invader in a hand-to-hand clash. Nor did they flinch when 10 panzers were sent out against them.

---

[1] *Voyenno-istorichesky zhurnal*, No. 12, 1967, p. 81.
[2] *Ibid*., No. 7, 1959, p. 88.
[3] Hermann Hoth, *Panzer-Operationen*, Heidelberg, 1956, S. 68.
[4] *I.V.O.V.S.S.*, Vol. 2, p. 19.

The feats of valour performed in the early days of the war were an inspiration for the Soviet nation and all champions of freedom and independence in the rest of the world. They became the hallmark of the Patriotic War to be emulated by other heroes. On the first day of the war, airman D. V. Kokorev, discovering that he had run out of ammunition, continued his pursuit of an enemy Messerschmitt-110 and slashed off its tail with his propeller. On July 26, Captain N. F. Gastello directed his plane, which had caught fire, at a concentration of German lorries and gasoline carriers. The explosion was costly for the enemy, who paid a high price for the lives of the Gastello crew.

The population in the frontier zones and beleaguered towns helped fortify the defences. A partisan movement began on the first day of the war, soon growing into a force that struck terror into the nazis.

Foreign observers wondered about the secret of the Soviet resistance. But few could answer the question correctly. To do so they had to know the nature of the Soviet system, its material potential, and the makeup of the Soviet man.

Two diametrically opposite social systems—fascist imperialism and socialism—had come to grips, and the question was: Which was the more viable?

The main source of Soviet power lay in the socialist system, triumphant in the country by virtue of the immense reconstruction accomplished by the people led by the Party. The reconstruction involved a radical change in society's class structure, giving birth to a state without exploiting classes and class antagonisms, a homogeneous society of working people. The socialist state was the bearer and champion of their interests.

All grounds for differences between government and people, differences that usually surface in a war, no longer existed. All sections of the Soviet people regarded the policy of their government as their own, backing it and determined to uphold it. Trust in the government was boundless. In a society resting on antagonistic class interests, war rouses the masses against the government's policy. In Soviet society, based on the identity of the class interest of workers and peasants, the war fused the masses with the Communist Party and the Soviet Government.

The moral and political unity of the people had been forged long before the war. It was an entirely new factor in the relationship of people among themselves, and vis-à-vis the state. The unity was of great potency, producing a society fused into a mighty whole; the wishes, aspirations and actions of millions blended into one.

Workers, peasants and the intelligentsia were firmly resolved to defend the socialist state, defying difficulties, defying death, defying hardship. This determination spelled doom for all enemies.

The Leninist solution of the nationalities question in the multinational Soviet Union had a strong bearing on the strength of the Soviet socialist society. The USSR had become a community of equal socialist peoples. The friendship of the peoples of the USSR was a prominent factor in the country's power of resistance. Loyalty to socialism became a feature of the national character.

Soviet patriotism combined with genuine proletarian internationalism. The people fought in a patriotic war that was at once internationalist in the loftiest sense of the word. They performed their mission of liberation with unexampled bravery, helping the nations of Europe fling off the fascist yoke. Men and women alike were consumed with bitter hatred of the nazi killers, while conscious of their internationalist bonds with the working people of Germany. It was farthest from their thoughts to impinge on the sovereignty and continued existence of the German nation; instead, they offered the Germans a hand of friendship, helping them emerge from the shame with which nazism had covered them.

The Great Patriotic War revealed the spiritual mould of the Soviet man—his faith in victory, hatred of the enemy, love of country and deep loyalty to the Communist Party and the socialist cause.

Naturally, the outbreak of the war terminated all socialist construction in the country. The Party and the government advanced a new slogan, "All for the Front, All for Victory!". It was converted into constructive acts, into a material force the impact of which the nazi invaders soon experienced in full measure.

4. Moscow, the Hero City

In the beginning of the Great Patriotic War the tide went against the Soviet Armed Forces. In the first three weeks of the war the Red Army abandoned Latvia, Lithuania,

Byelorussia, a large slice of the Ukraine and Moldavia. The nazis thought the war was all but won. On July 11, 1941, General Halder wrote in his diary that the Soviet front, "behind which reserves existed no longer, cannot be held".[1]

The German Command was confident that their road to Moscow would lie open once they captured Smolensk. On July 10, 1941, began the German offensive against Smolensk; the city was captured on July 16 despite stout Soviet resistance. But when the nazis moved on east from Smolensk, they ran into fresh resistance. More, in a fierce counter-attack the Red Army temporarily captured the northern part of the city, stalling the German advance for several weeks.

Early in September Soviet troops east of Smolensk, near the towns of Yelnya and Yartsevo, mounted an offensive of their own. They liberated Yelnya and in so doing smashed a large nazi force.

The Red Army displayed heroism and tenacity, and a burning wish to turn the tables in the Smolensk Battle. The German blitzkrieg was beginning to fold. The nazis saw that their intention of entering Moscow on the march was a pipe-dream—doubly so since the flanks of Army Group Centre, driving towards the capital, were exposed both north and south. To play safe, Hitler decided to wheel part of his troops northeast and another lot southeast.

In the northeast, the nazis laid siege to Leningrad. However, their effort to take the city proved in vain. Blockaded Leningrad, its population suffering terrible hardships, drew off the bulk of Army Group North, of which only six divisions could be spared to help in the Moscow offensive.

The courage of Leningrad's defenders and civilian population was unexampled. When the fascist ring closed round the city at the end of August, a population of 2,500,000 was almost totally cut off from the rest of the world.[2] The food stores in the Badayev warehouses were destroyed in a fire caused by nazi shells and bombs. The power supply failed. Electricity was available only for the Smolny,[3] the bakeries and Army Headquarters. The water supply was cut off. The daily bread ration dropped to 125 grams for children and

---

[1] Franz Halder, *Kriegstagebuch*, Bd. 3, Stuttgart, 1964, S. 64.
[2] *Izvestia*, February 10, 1968.
[3] *Smolny*—architectural monument of historic significance, headquarters of the armed uprising in November 1917. At present, seat of the Leningrad Regional Committee of the C. P. S. U.

disabled people and to 250 grams for those who worked. People died in the streets from hunger and exposure. To stay alive, people ate carpenter's glue and leather belts. And the torments of hunger were aggravated by the winter's cold.

But nothing could break the spirit and the discipline of the Leningraders. In a research institute the staff preserved a valuable collection of grain samples. When enemy shells crashed into vans carrying bread passers-by helped reload the bread on some other vehicle, never taking a loaf themselves.

Poets, writers, musicians, artists, scientists and designers worked on. The Leningrad factories produced war supplies in the immediate proximity of the battle-line. This courage and dedication surpassed anything known heretofore.

In the southeast, the German Command headed for Kiev. In the fighting for the Ukrainian capital, the Soviet troops were compeled to withdraw. But their heroic stand had a bearing on subsequent developments at the approaches to Moscow, helping frustrate the nazi aim of a blitz victory.

After a few successful flanking operations to the South and North of its Army Group Centre, the Germans were poised for a general offensive against Moscow. Hitler and his generals knew that Moscow's industries figured prominently in the Soviet economy. Besides, Moscow was a crucial communication centre, and a seat of culture. More, it was of the utmost significance as the capital, from which the Communist Party and the Government guided all peacetime activity and were then organising the nation's war effort. Moscow, in short, was the standard-bearer in the fight for liberation, the pride and hope of the peoples, a wartime centre coordinating the efforts of all the freedom-loving forces risen or rising to combat German fascism.

The German imperialists were sure that once Moscow was conquered the Soviet people would surrender.

Following the pattern set in their assaults on the Western countries, the German Command kept up the air offensive against the Soviet capital begun on July 22. But it collapsed: an ingenious system of anti-aircraft defences and the courage of the defenders saved Moscow from large-scale destruction. Only 120 out of the 4,212 nazi planes which took part in the 36 raids from July 22 to October 1, managed to reach the limits of the city.[1]

---

[1] *I.V.O.V.S.S.*, Vol. 2, p. 232.

As a precaution, part of Moscow's population spent the nights in the tunnels of the Moscow underground, where all essential services, including the medical, were made available. There, deep below the surface, 217 infants came into the world in the summer and autumn of 1941.[1]

General Headquarters and the General Staff had their offices in Metro Station "Kirovskaya". On the platform, fenced off from the tracks with a light plywood partition, the strategists performed their operational work. The signals centre was at one end of the station, and Joseph Stalin's study at the other. True, not once did Stalin go to the underground shelter.[2]

The men assigned to guard Moscow's military establishments displayed great courage. Private A. V. Teterin, called up in the spring of 1941, was on guard duty outside the Defence Commissariat when a nazi incendiary bomb hit the building in the night of September 21. His attempts to extinguish the bomb failed. So he covered it with his body and put out the fire, but paid for this with his life, dying from severe burns.[3]

Having made up their mind to launch a general offensive on Moscow, the German Command prepared Operation Typhoon. For the assault it massed 75 divisions, including 14 panzer and 8 motorised—a force vastly superior in men and arms to the Soviet troops defending the city.

The OKW order to prepare Operation Typhoon was signed on September 16, 1941, accompanied by two "instructions" concerning secrecy, the manner of seizing Moscow and the treatment of its population. The city was to be cut off from all communication lines; fire was to be opened on anyone trying to leave city limits and pass through the nazi lines; no German lives were to be risked in attempts to save Russian cities from fires; and their population was not to be fed at Germany's expense.[4]

The nazi offensive started on September 30 and began gathering momentum on October 2. That day in a public statement Hitler said: "At last, the stage has been set for the last powerful blow that will crush our foe before winter. All prep-

---

[1] *Literaturnaya Gazeta,* Dec. 3, 1966.

[2] S. M. Shtemenko, *The Soviet General Staff at War (1941-1945),* Moscow, 1970, pp. 39, 45.

[3] *Ibid.,* p. 42.

[4] *Voyenno-istorichesky zhurnal,* No. 10, 1961, p. 87.

arations have been completed to the extent that is humanly possible. This time, each step has been planned out to put the enemy in a position in which we can deliver the mortal blow. Today is the beginning of the last great and decisive battle of the year."[1]

Bitter fighting erupted. The Soviet troops held their ground, inflicting considerable losses on the enemy. Although the German armies advanced inch by inch and made considerable tactical and operational gains, they did not attain their set objectives.

The defenders of Moscow were backed up by the entire nation. The people of the hero city participated in its defence. More than half a million Muscovites built fortifications. Eleven divisions and 87 destroyer battalions were formed of civilian volunteers.[2] In the meantime, some 40 partisan detachments launched operations behind the enemy lines. As many as 3,600 self-defence groups totalling 81,600 men were formed on the residential principle, in addition to 12,736 volunteer fire-fighting crews comprising 205,000 men.[3] The mobilisation of all available manpower was directed by the Moscow Committee of the Communist Party.

At this hour of peril, scorched by fires from the approaching battle-line, turned into a military camp and arsenal, pitted with anti-tank ditches and "dragon's teeth", Moscow did not waver. It stood its ground firmly.

The traditional military parade took place as usual in Red Square on November 7, 1941 in open defiance of the nazis, still advancing on the capital and reckoning to hold their own parade in Moscow that day. The parade was a symbol of faith in victory, of courage and tenacity. As the snow whirled loudspeakers in the Red Square boomed out a message that was heard throughout the land and along the front-line. The troops marched from the parade past the Lenin Mausoleum directly to the battle-lines.

On that day ended the first phase of the German fascist "general offensive" against Moscow, brought virtually to a halt by the tenacity and stamina of the Soviet troops and people. Whipped on by the approach of winter, the German generals could not wait to start the second phase. Not only

[1] *Völkischer Beobachter*, October 10, 1941.
[2] G. Deborin, *The Second World War*, Moscow, 1964, p. 201.
[3] *Voyenno-istorichesky zhurnal*, No. 11, 1966, p. 100.

did they draw up an operational plan, but also a plan for the destruction of Moscow and its inhabitants. Speaking to the Staff of Army Group Centre, Hitler said: "The city must be blockaded so as to allow no Russian soldier, no inhabitant, whether man, woman or child, to escape. Every attempt to break out is to be countered with force. The necessary preparations have been made to flood Moscow and its environs.... Where Moscow stands today there will be a large sea which will forever conceal from the civilised world the capital of the Russian nation."[1]

The second phase of the "general offensive" began on November 15-16. But the nazis soon discovered that Soviet resistance had become still more tenacious. The Soviet stand at Moscow was a compound of many feats. One of these was by 28 men of General I. V. Panfilov's 316th Infantry Division, who repulsed 50 panzers, destroying 18. "Russia is huge," said their political office, V. G. Klochkov, "but there is nowhere we can retreat, for behind us is Moscow." This became the motto of all the defenders of the Soviet capital.

During the fighting for Kryukovo, a Moscow suburb on the Moscow-Leningrad railway, three panzers broke through the Soviet lines and headed at top speed for Moscow. A battery of anti-aircraft guns on the highway finished them off. Three giant replicas of anti-tank "hedgehogs" now stand on the spot in tribute to the city's defenders.

Early in December the attack capability of the nazi army petered out. The "general offensive" was over. The blitzkrieg strategy, so successful in the rest of Europe, proved a total flop when used against the Soviet Union. With all the odds weighing heavily against it, the Red Army frustrated the nazi war plan and stemmed the tide. The resistance, the acme of human courage, beyond compare in history, provided the time and opportunity for a gradual shift of the strategic initiative to the Soviet side, coupled, of course, with the political and economic requisites provided by the nation as a whole.

To give the enemy no time to recover, the Red Army mounted a large-scale offensive from Moscow on December 5-6, committing the forces of three fronts—Kalinin (General I. S. Konev), Western (General G. K. Zhukov) and South-

---

[1] Fabian von Schlabrendoff, *Offiziere gegen Hitler*, Zürich, 1946, S. 48.

Western (Marshal S. K. Timoshenko). The thrust developed with good results into a general Soviet offensive in the central theatre. The troops displayed extraordinary enthusiasm. Sergeant V. V. Vasilkovsky covered an enemy embrasure with his body to silence a nazi machine-gun in the clash for Ryabinka village, and a few days later the feat was performed by Private Y. N. Paderin.

The 612th Infantry Regiment was ordered to hook around the enemy lines, wedge itself into the nazi rear, straddle the Minsk Highway and block the approach of German reserves. It withstood the onslaught of a large force of infantry, panzers and the Luftwaffe, cutting the highway at the 141st kilometre sign. How the men fought is described in a death note by one of the soldiers:

"We were twelve, ordered to block the enemy, especially tanks. And we held them. Now there are just three — Kolya, Volodya and I, Alexander. But the enemy keeps coming. We've lost Volodya, of Moscow. The enemy still keeps coming. Nineteen enemy tanks are aflame. But there are just the two of us. We shall stand firm to our dying breath, unless reinforcements come to relieve us.... Now I am alone, wounded in head and arm. The burning tanks are twenty-three. Maybe I'll die. Maybe someone will find this note and remember us. I am Russian, from the town of Frunze. An orphan. Good-bye, friends. Yours, Alexander Vinogradov. 22.2. 1942."[1]

Twelve men armed with hand-grenades, incendiary bottles, anti-tank guns, rifles and submachine-guns destroyed 23 panzers in an unequal engagement, winning unfading glory.

In the counter-offensive at Moscow in December 1941 and in early 1942, the Soviet forces defeated 38 nazi divisions and panzer units. The Red Army drove the enemy out of over 11,000 towns and villages to a distance of 100 to 250 kilometres from Moscow. This was how the tide began turning. Meanwhile, south-east of Leningrad another Soviet offensive in the Tikhvin area added to the success of Soviet arms.

West-German war historian Paul Carell wrote: "...Whatever victories were yet to come, the divisions of Army Group Centre never recovered from the blows they suffered before Moscow. They were never again brought up to full strength,

---

[1] *Komsomolskaya Pravda*, February 22, 1968.

they never recovered their full effectiveness as a fighting force. At Moscow the strength of the German Army was broken."[1] Only in one thing Carell erred: no victories were "yet to come" for Army Group Centre.

Hitler could do nothing to block the inevitable consequences of his defeat. When Berlin received the news of the outcome of the Battle for Moscow "unrest grew among the people. The pessimists remembered Napoleon's war with Russia, and all the literature about La Grande Armée suddenly had a marked revival. The fortune-tellers busied themselves with Napoleon's fate, and there was a boom in astrology."[2]

The German Government blamed the defeat on the generals, many of whom were dismissed, including Fieldmarshal Walther von Brauchitsch, Army Commander-in-Chief, alf commanders of the army groups and many commanders ol panzer and field armies.

The German defeat at Moscow sharpened the antagonisms in the Hitler bloc, above all between Japan and Germany, and Italy and Germany. When the Red Army was still engaged in heavy defensive actions, Japan officially informed Berlin that she had put off the attack on the USSR until 1942. The Red Army victory added to the Soviet Union's international standing and influence. For the peoples it meant that a realistic prospect of at last defeating Hitler Germany had appeared.

Patriots in countries overrun by the nazis took heart. A new stage began in the Resistance movement throughout Europe. Well-organised partisan forces appeared, operating under a considered plan.

Nazi Germany had suffered her first major military defeat in the Second World War. Nineteen forty-one went down in history not only as an arduous, but also a heroic year, a year of the bitterest trials, but also a year of revived hope. The all but superhuman effort of the Soviet people made it a year marked by the beginning of the end for Hitler and his Wehrmacht. No longer was the latter thought invincible and its blitzkrieg strategies went bankrupt.

But the Soviet Union failed to consolidate the turning of the tide, and for a number of reasons, among which the most

---

[1] Paul Carell, *Hitler's War in Russia*, London, 1964, p. 191.
[2] Arvid Fredborg, *Behind the Steel Wall*, London, 1944, pp. 60-61.

salient was the absence of a second front that would sluice off at least part of the German strength from the East.

To sum up, the nazi advance eastward was stemmed, resulting in a temporary strategic equibalance. More, the scene was set for tilting the scales gradually in favour of the Soviet Union.

5. The Pearl Harbor Secret

In December 1941 the US Navy suffered a defeat unique in the history of wars.

It was night, clear and cloudless, on December 7, 1941. The large naval base of Pearl Harbor, Hawaii, slept serenely. US planes were on the ground. In the harbour, behind a coral reef, not barred off from the sea, 93 US warships were packed tightly, the vastness of the 8 battleships rising above them.

In a hut on a mountain, having come off duty two soldiers and a sergeant played idly with a radio locator. At dawn they noticed numerous spots on the screen, which could possibly be water-borne vessels. They informed the officer on duty, but were dressed down for their pains. Neither Japan nor anyone else, the officer said, would ever think of attacking the United States. Yet within 30 minutes the Japanese attack became a stark fact.

At 7.55 a.m. Pearl Harbor was turned into a blazing hell. Several hundred planes rose wave after wave from Japanese aircraft-carriers, raining bombs on US vessels and shore installations. In the first run they encountered no resistance and dropped their bombs unhindered, hitting the targets. Meanwhile, Japanese submarines attacked the anchored warships in the harbour.

In 110 minutes five of the proud eight US battleships were sunk and the remainder badly damaged. The entire crew of more than 2,000 men went down with the battleship *Arizona*. And a few days later a British naval group was sunk in the open sea.

This originated the secret of Pearl Harbor, one of the secrets of the Second World War. It is a mystery how, with a world war ablaze, the US Armed Forces could be in a state of total unpreparedness, taking no precautions against a surprise attack. The shroud of mystery grows denser still when one learns that US intelligence had cracked the Japanese diplomatic code, and had monitored and deciphered communications from Tokyo to Japanese diplomats abroad, including those in the United States. The communications were sufficiently revealing, containing but slightly veiled references to the imminent Japanese attack on Pearl Harbor.

In time the secret was discovered. Japan and the United States had for some time negotiated a settlement. Japan wanted a deal to secure its rear in the event of a war against the Soviet Union. And the US Government tried assiduously to convince the Japanese that they had nothing to fear if they attacked the USSR. Washington was willing to make concessions it would have never otherwise made.

On May 12, 1941, Japan couched her predatory claims in the form of a proposal for elaborating a "joint policy of combating communism". On June 21, 1941, on the eve of Hitler Germany's assault on the USSR, Washington informed Japan of its concessions to the latter and its readiness to continue discussing this joint policy.

The anti-communism reigning in Washington lulled the vigilance of the US rulers. They ignored the indications that Red Army resistance to the nazis had compelled the Japanese militarists to revise the order of their aggression. Though earlier Tokyo had thought of first joining the war against the Soviet Union and turning later against the United States and Britain, they reversed the order in the autumn of 1941.

From then on Japanese diplomacy was busy dulling the vigilance of the US Government and its generals by faking negotiations. And the success was complete. On October 16, 1941, the US War and Naval departments informed the Pacific Ocean Command that "hostilities between Japan and Russia are a strong possibility. Since the United States and Britain are held responsible by Japan for her present desperate situation, there is also a possibility that Japan may attack these two powers".[1] The local commanders, however, gave credence to but the first half of the communication, and totally overlooked the second. They lifted all precautions against a sudden Japanese attack.

Making most of the naval advantage they had gained, the

---

[1] George Morgenstern, *Pearl Harbor. The Story of the Secret War,* New York, 1947, p. 224.

Japanese militarists overran Malaya, Burma, Indonesia, the Philippines and many other islands in the Pacific in a matter of five or six months. The British, US and Dutch armies stationed in those territories were not strong enough to stem the Japanese offensive, largely due to their unpopularity among the indigenous population.

Some time later a popular movement, a desperate fight for national independence, began in the Japanese-occupied Southeast Asian countries and the Pacific islands. Directed at the time against the Japanese, the movement was also against the imperialist colonial system. It was a harbinger, the beginning, of the powerful national liberation surge of the colonial and dependent peoples that later tore down the colonial system.

By the end of March 1942 a mass organisation, the Hukbalahap, was formed in the Philippines that led the struggle against the Japanese. An anti-Japanese people's army was formed in Malaya, and an anti-Japanese national liberation league in Burma. Guerrillas were fighting the Japanese in Indonesia, Indochina and Korea. And in this guerrilla fighting, the Communists, its initiators, stood in the van. The peoples of India were seething. In China, a powerful people's struggle was under way.

The rulers of the United States and Britain were deeply perturbed about mass participation in the anti-Japanese action. They were hostile to the national liberation movement. When the Filipino patriots proposed joint action against the Japanese invaders, Washington turned down the offer.

When making their fatal decision to wage a war against the United States and Britain, the Japanese imperialists left many factors out of the reckoning. To begin with, they did not reckon with the fact that the heroic Soviet resistance to the nazis would enable the United States and Britain to transfer substantial forces to the Pacific. Secondly, they overlooked the fact that popular resistance in occupied territories would pin down considerable Japanese forces. These factors made it possible for the United States and Britain to turn the tide in a war that had begun so unfavourably for them.

There was a big naval engagement in the Coral Sea, near Australia, in May 1942 between Japan and the USA. The adversaries used their air power, while the guns of their warships were silent. The losses were approximately equal. But the Japanese fleet admitted defeat and made off. In

another battle, near Midway, Japan suffered her first major
setback, losing four aircraft-carriers, a cruiser and many
planes. The balance of strength had changed. The Japanese
offensive stalled, and a long pause ensued in the hostilities.

In the meanwhile, the battles on the Soviet-German Front
increased in scale. There were no protracted pauses there.
The decisive Second World War theatre, this Front gained
continuously in importance.

6. The Great Coalition

The embattled peoples of the USSR were not alone. The
world's progressives were on their side. In their own national
and international interests, people all over the world unfolded
an anti-fascist liberation movement. Their determination
and the efforts of the governments of the belligerent countries
to dispel the nazi danger and remain in the saddle, created
a community of aims, leading up to the emergence of an
anti-fascist coalition.

This coalition rested on the just, liberative nature of the
anti-Hitler war—a quality it acquired in full measure with
the Soviet entry into the war. The Soviet war aims were in
full harmony with the nature of the war and the Soviet
Union rightly became the moral and political vanguard
in that great struggle for freedom.

The liberation movement in Yugoslavia flared up with
renewed force after Germany attacked the USSR. On July 7,
1941, in the village of Belaya Tserkov, the partisan group of
Žikica Jovanović clashed with gendarmes in the service of
the occupation authorities. The battle grew into an armed
uprising, spreading throughout Serbia, then to Montenegro,
Slovenia, Croatia, Bosnia and Herzegovina. By the autumn
of 1941 a partisan war engulfed all Yugoslavia.

In Czechoslovakia, due to local conditions, the resistance
assumed other forms—at first those of strikes and sabotage and
of publishing underground anti-fascist literature. The underground *Rudé Právo*, organ of the Communist Party, had a large
circulation. In November 1941 the paper wrote: Czecho-
slovaks "were unbroken by centuries of Hapsburg rule, by
the disgraceful Munich betrayal, or even by the bloody
terror loosened by Reinhard Heydrich, the nazi hangman,
and nothing will break them, whatever trials may lie ahead….

The people will live on, after Hitler, Goebbels, Neurath, Heydrich ... and other carrion is flung on the dustheap of history."[1]

The *Rudé Právo* and other Communist Party publications were directed by Julius Fučík, a gifted journalist. Tracked down and apprehended by the nazis, he went to his death singing the *Internationale*. While in prison, he wrote his well-known book, *A Report with the Noose Round My Neck*, an outstanding work in the humanistic tradition of truly revolutionary literature.

In France and Belgium patriots responded to the nazi attack on the Soviet Union with increasingly powerful acts of sabotage and outright resistance. And on July 14, 1941, the French national holiday, large anti-German demonstrations took place in nazi-occupied Paris.

The peoples in the overrun countries became loyal members of the anti-fascist coalition that began to form round the Soviet Union soon after the German attack on the USSR. Capitalist governments, including those of Britain and the United States, joined that coalition, too, under pressure of their people's anti-fascist struggle and by reason of imperialist contradictions between them.

A historic change occurred in the relations between the Soviet Union and Great Britain. Nor was it a fortuitous one. Long before the war broke out, the USSR had advocated collective action against the aggressor. And in the course of the war Britain realised that her hopes of victory lay in an alliance with the USSR.

Not knowing the Soviet people, Churchill was uneasy: perhaps, he thought, the Soviet Union would surrender? Information from Moscow dispelled his doubts. The British sensed an important change. Churchill said: "We are no longer alone."[2] In a radio speech on June 22, 1941, the Prime Minister stressed that, though still an irreconcilable foe of Bolshevism, he was for an alliance with the USSR because "the Russian danger is ... our danger, and the danger of the United States, just as the cause of any Russian fighting for his hearth and home is the cause of free men and free peoples in every quarter of the globe."[3]

---

[1] *Antifashistskoye dvizheniye Soprotivleniya (Anti-Fascist Resistance Movement)*, Moscow, 1962, pp. 114-15.

[2] W. Thompson, *Assignment: Churchill*, New York, 1961, p. 215.

[3] Winston Churchill, *Great War Speeches*, London, 1957, p. 140.

Franklin D. Roosevelt, the US President, declared his support of the USSR on June 24. That same day, however, Senator Harry Truman gave an interview that sounded like a challenge from the most sinister forces of US imperialism. "If we see that Germany is winning," he said, "we ought to help Russia and if Russia is winning, we ought to help Germany and that way let them kill as many as possible."[1]

But neither Truman nor Moore-Brabazon, British Minister of Aviation, and their followers, could now arrest the emergence of an anti-fascist coalition, the way for which had been paved by years of Soviet efforts to establish a collective security system against aggression.

Among capitalist statesmen, Churchill and Roosevelt probably had the clearest conception of their countries' rockbottom interests. But their stand should not be exaggerated. Any other approach would have spelled defeat for Britain and, later, for the United States. Besides, Churchill's radio speech contained overtones indicating his aversion of the social system in the USSR. The speech was a contradictory one. It favoured an alliance with the USSR, on the one hand, while being frankly hostile to the social system there, on the other. This contradiction explains many of the British and American wartime secrets.

At the beginning of July 1941, the Soviet Government approached Britain, proposing an alliance. The offer was accepted. A joint action agreement was concluded by the Soviet and British governments on July 12 in Moscow, raising the curtain on what would soon become a formal anti-Hitler coalition.

Soon after being drawn into the war, the Soviet Union established diplomatic relations with the émigré governments of some of the nazi-occupied countries—Czechoslovakia, Poland, Belgium and Norway—and concluded formal alliances with Czechoslovakia on July 18 and with Poland on July 30. This was evidence of the Soviet wish that the conquered countries should regain their liberty and statehood.

With the outcome of the war depending on developments on the Soviet-German Front, where Germany kept its main forces, the legitimate question arose of how Britain could help the Soviet Union, preoccupied then in repelling the enemy assault. British sentiment on this score was reflected

---

[1] *New York Times,* June 24, 1941.

in a *Tribune* article: "There is only one question for us in these swift days: what can we do to help ourselves by coming to the aid of the Soviet armies?"[1] The clearest possible reply was contained in the Soviet proposal that Britain should open a second front in Western Europe.

The Churchill Government baulked. It took the risk of withholding aid in an hour when it was most desperately needed. No one could be sure then what turn the events would take. The British PM, for one, thought it possible the Soviet Union would collapse. And for Britain this would be disaster. Yet he put in jeopardy his country's vital interests, compelling the Soviet Union to go alone, deliberately letting his ally exhaust his strength.

In the early months of the Soviet-German war, the British Government, and then also the United States, not yet embroiled in the hostilities, confined themselves to shipping limited quantities of raw materials, war materiel, arms and goods. Anglo-American deliveries to the Soviet Union and Soviet counter-deliveries were examined at the three-power Moscow Conference in September-October 1941, which ultimately adopted a concrete programme.

However, Anglo-American deliveries were a trickle. General John R. Deane, head of the US Military Mission in Moscow, admitted this.[2] Compared with the colossal Soviet effort, US historians admit, they made "but a slight contribution to Soviet defence or to ultimate victory on the Eastern Front".[3] What little arrived, however, was important, for at that time the Soviet Union was straining its energies to the utmost in holding off the Germans.

The anti-fascist coalition continued to expand, joined by General de Gaulle's French National Liberation Committee and the governments of other nazi-occupied countries.

The Soviet attitude to co-members of the coalition was friendly. In the case of de Gaulle, the French bourgeois leader, the Soviet Union was even more considerate than the United States and Britain, which long refused to recognise his Committee. Therefore, early in June 1942 de Gaulle

---

[1] Michael Foot, *Aneurin Bevan. A Biography,* Vol. 1, London, 1962, p. 336.
[2] John R. Deane, *The Strange Alliance. The Story of Our Efforts at Wartime Cooperation with Russia,* New York, 1950, p. 89.
[3] W. L. Lanter and S. E. Gleason, *The Undeclared War 1940-41,* New York, 1953, p. 560.

asked whether "the Soviet Government would receive him and his troops in its territory".[1] True, when the British Government promised a few days later to reconsider his status, he withdrew the question. While friendly to the Free French Movement, the Soviet people were aware that de Gaulle and his Committee represented but a segment of the French freedom fighters, who responded not so much to the General's appeals from London, but primarily to the heroic efforts of the French Communist Party.

After Japan attacked Pearl Harbor the United States, China, Australia and many of the Latin American countries lined up with the coalition.

Its construction was completed in the first six months of 1942. By that time, stimulated by the Soviet victory at Moscow, the Resistance Movement spread like wildfire. On January 1, 1942, a 26-nation declaration of alliance was signed in Washington, its signatories henceforth to be known as the United Nations. A treaty of alliance against Germany and her accomplices in Europe was signed by the Soviet Union and Britain in London on May 26, 1942, also stipulating cooperation and postwar mutual aid. On June 11 in Washington Soviet-American agreement was concluded on mutual deliveries of supplies. A Soviet-American communiqué was published that day, stating that "full understanding was reached between the two parties with regard to the urgent task of creating a second front in Europe in 1942".[2]

The wartime coalition had an immense impact. It was the first try in world history of states with different social systems at uniting for common action—a try that justified its makers, for it provided favourable international conditions for victory over the fascist foe.

The anti-Hitler coalition frustrated imperialist Germany's basic strategy of cutting down its adversaries one by one, preventing co-operation among them and securing for each an international political isolation. The tables were turned: Germany and her allies were increasingly isolated, with the forces of the Axis powers steadily losing strength, and those of the Allies gaining strength.

---

[1] *Sovietsko-frantsuzskiye otnosheniya vo vremya Velikoi Otechestvennoi voiny, 1941–1945 gg. (Soviet-French Relations During the Great Patriotic War 1941-1945)*, Moscow, 1959, p. 82.
[2] *The Times*, June 12, 1942.

Chapter Four

From the Volga to Berlin

1. The Stalingrad Exploit

In early 1942, the Soviet High Command held that the turning of the tide in the Moscow Battle could be consolidated and developed. What was needed was a second front by the United States and Britain. But the governments of those two countries were disinclined to fulfil their commitment. And the nazi intelligence soon found out that no preparations were undertaken.

The absence of a second front enabled Germany to manoeuvre freely with the considerable forces it still had. A new offensive was planned against the Soviet Union along new operational principles necessitated by the breakdown of the Barbarossa Plan.

The new plan was aimed at crushing the main forces of the Red Army, depriving the USSR of its economic potential in the South and then building up for a renewed operation against Moscow.

No longer could the nazis mount an offensive simultaneously in all strategic directions. There were to be successive offensive operations, the first of them on the southern wing.

Hitler's plans for 1942 summer offensive provided graphic evidence of Germany's predatory war aims, outlined forthrightly by Goebbels: "This war is not a war for a throne or an altar, this is a war for grain and bread, a war for a well-laden breakfast, dinner, and supper table... a war for raw materials, for rubber, iron and ore."[1]

---

[1] Joseph Goebbels, *Das eherne Herz*, München, 1943, S. 334-36.

That was not entirely true. The war may have been all that Goebbels said, but it was also waged for nazi world supremacy.

For the southern offensive the nazis massed 90 divisions and 4 brigades out of the total of 229 divisions and 16 brigades that they had on the Soviet-German front at the end of June 1942.[1] These jumped off on June 28, driving for Voronezh. In a month of heavy fighting they advanced 150 to 400 km, but failed to encircle the Soviet troops, which continued to resist courageously, holding new defence lines.

After the initial success, the Germans decided to develop the offensive with two army groups—Group "B" heading for the Volga and Group "A" for the Caucasus. In the meanwhile, Soviet counter-attacks from the North against the flank of the advancing enemy had halted the latter at Voronezh, the main theatre shifting south, in the Stalingrad direction.

The great Stalingrad Battle began with a nazi offensive from the Chir River on July 17. Within the very first weeks the Soviet fighting forces added outstanding exploits of courage and tenacity to their glorious record. At the end of July, near Kletskaya, four anti-armour soldiers of the 33rd Guards Division (P. Boloto, I. Aleinikov, F. Belikov and Samoilov) barred the way to 30 panzers. In three days of fierce fighting they destroyed 15, not letting the enemy pass. Somewhat later, in another sector, 16 men of the 40th Guards Division repulsed five attacks and destroyed six out of the 12 attacking panzers. Feats of this kind were a daily occurrence.

However, vastly superior in numbers and arms, the enemy pressed forward. From July 17 to August 17 the nazis came another 60-80 km closer to Stalingrad. On August 23, they thrust powerfully towards the city proper, breaching the front and pouring into a gap with the Luftwaffe striking massively from the air. Marshal A. I. Yeremenko, who was in command of the Stalingrad Front as a Colonel-General, describes the scene in the afternoon of August 23:

"Stalingrad was enveloped in flame, smoke and soot. Fires broke out all over the city; it was ablaze; the log buildings burned like torches; vast billows of smoke and tongues of flame shot up over the factories; the piers were alight; the oil tanks were like active volcanoes, spitting

---

[1] *I.V.O.V.S.S.*, Vol. 2, p. 418.

lava…. All Stalingrad seemed to be dug up and blackened. A hurricane appeared to have hit the city, raising it into the air and letting the fragments of buildings fall on squares and streets. The air had become acrid and bitter, and difficult to breathe."[1]

Yet the nazis faltered and—much to their surprise—failed to capture the city. The Soviet resistance and counter-attacks stemmed their advance. However, the German offensive potential was still considerable. Daily, fresh masses of men and arms were committed to the battle. And on September 13 came the general assault.

Soviet resistance, directed by now experienced generals, grew firmer by the hour. The splendid Soviet soldier, unshakeably convinced in his cause and coming victory, rose to full stature in the Volga battle. His development was the result of educational work by the Communist Party. The Communists brought out the finest qualities in the Soviet soldiers, who covered themselves with undying glory.

There were many men among the Stalingrad defenders like sniper V. Zaitsev, who destroyed 225 Germans. Zaitsev it was who spoke the phrase that became the motto of Stalingrad: "For us no land exists across the Volga!" Mortally wounded, signaler V. Titayev clamped his teeth on the end of a torn telephone cable, restoring the connection. A handful of Soviet soldiers defended a strategically important four-storey house at which German guns fired up to 120 shells daily, and retained possession until the end of the battle. The building is known by the name of the sergeant in command as Pavlov's House. The squad consisted of Russians (Pavlov, Alexandrov, Afanasyev), Ukrainians (Sabgaida and Glushchenko), Georgians (Mosiashvili and Stepanoshvili), the Uzbek Turganov, the Kazakh Murzayev, the Abkhazian Sukba, the Tajik Turdyiev and the Tatar Romazanov.

At a high price in men and arms, the nazis reached the Volga on October 15, cutting the Red Army front in two. At one time the depth of the Soviet Stalingrad defences, with the Volga behind them, was no more than 700 metres. Yet the Red Army stood its ground. Here, it began its long trek back to the West. On the bank of the Volga was sealed the fate of Berlin. In 1967, Knapton and Derry, two British

[1] A. I. Yeremenko, *Stalingrad*, Moscow, 1961, pp. 134-35.

authors, wrote: "The Russians had sacrificed more men to save one ruined city than the Americans were to lose in combat during all the campaigns of the war. In so doing they had made the defense of Stalingrad a turning point in the history of Europe, if not the world."[1]

The Soviet Command took stock of the opportunities for a counter-offensive that a stout defence, pinning down a huge enemy force at Stalingrad, would create. While defending the city, it maintained positions on the flanks of the German battering ram at Stalingrad, and began concentrating forces north-west and south of the city well in advance.

While the nazi Army Group B unleashed its fury against Stalingrad, part of Army Group A mounted Operation Edelweiss to capture the Caucasus. From Rostov the nazi armies set out south-east.

In defensive battles between the Don and the northern foothills of the Main Caucasian Range, the Soviet troops, fighting in extremely difficult circumstances, displayed incredible tenacity. Repulsing ferocious enemy attacks, counter-attacking strongly, the Red Army backed away to the northern foothills, there to stem the German move in November 1942. All enemy attempts to blast the way through to the Transcaucasus were repelled at a high price for the nazis.

Then came the hour of the big turn in the Great Patriotic and Second World War. In the morning of November 19, 1942, the roar of thousands of Soviet guns and mortars gave notice of the Red Army's offensive at Stalingrad.

The German Command still had a considerable force of 50 divisions massed in the area. True, the enemy no longer had the advantage of superior numbers. Strength was approximately equal. If anything, the Red Army had a slight edge. The ratio in men and officers was 1 : 1, it was 1.3 : 1 in tanks, 1.3 : 1 in guns and mortars, but 1 : 1.1 in planes.[2] The Soviet offensive was made possible thanks to the skill of the Command. While the enemy force had bogged in Stalingrad, the Soviet generals built a decisive superiority in men and arms in the direction of the main blows and delivered two converging ones: one from the north-west against the township Sovietsky, and the other simultaneously from the south.

---

[1] F. Knapton, T. Derry, *Europe and the World since 1914*, London, 1967, p. 270.
[2] *I.V.O.V.S.S.*, Vol. 3, p. 26.

The two Soviet fronts (the Southwestern under General N. F. Vatutin and the Don under General K. K. Rokossovsky) effected a junction and encircled the entire enemy Stalingrad group in less than five days. The Stalingrad Front (under General A. I. Yeremenko) took part in the operation, too. The ring round the Germans shrank to half its original area in the following six days. Twenty-two nazi divisions with a vast amount of weapons and vehicles were compressed into an area of 1,500 sq km, vulnerable from all directions to long-range artillery. Meanwhile, another 12 divisions were wiped out.

The Soviet forces repulsed the attempts to relieve the beleaguered force made by Army Group Don under General Fieldmarshal Fritz Erich von Manstein.

On January 8, 1943, a Soviet offer of surrender was turned down by the encircled German troops. Two days later, the Don Front began a mopping-up operation, slicing the encircled force into parts, isolating each part, and eliminating them one by one. General Fieldmarshal Friedrich von Paulus and his staff were taken prisoner on January 31, and by the evening of February 2 the entire nazi Stalingrad group was either destroyed or captured. By then the prisoners' total climbed to 91,000, including 24 generals.

Hitler Germany proclaimed a day of mourning—a day that for all progressive mankind was a day of hope. The Soviet victory on the Volga put paid to Hitler's plans of world conquest. The official US war history says: "The heroic stand of... Soviet peoples saved the United States a war on her own soil."[1]

While Hitler mourned, the radiant sun of victory rose over the Soviet Union and its Armed Forces. It was still a long way to the West—from the Volga to the Elbe and Spree. But the start had been made, the war reversing its direction from Mamayev Kurgan, the strategic height at Stalingrad, towards Berlin.

Western historians, if in the least objective, admit the crucial significance of the Stalingrad victory, though some falsifiers have still not given up running it down. But the facts are against them. Walter Goerlitz, a West German

---

[1] *The War Reports of General of the Army George C. Marshall, General of the Army H. H. Arnold, Fleet Admiral Ernest J. King,* Philadelphia and New York, 1947, p. 149.

historian, for one, pointed out that "Stalingrad was the turning point in the Second World War".[1] British historian Ronald Seth wrote: "If you are honest, whatever you may think about Communism, you cannot withhold admiration for the Russians and their military leaders, for the courage, endurance and skill in holding the Germans at Stalingrad in 1942, and with Stalingrad as their springboard, eventually turning the tide of war in their own favour, and, incidentally, to the advantage of the Western Allies."[2]

The counter-offensive at Stalingrad grew into a general Soviet offensive all down the line from Leningrad to the Caucasian foothills. In January 1943, the blockade of Leningrad was lifted and the "lifeline" across the ice of Lake Ladoga replaced by railway communications along the lake's southern shore.

New exploits were inscribed in the chronicle of the Soviet war effort. In January 1943, north of Velikiye Luki, a Guards regiment of infantry, 56th Division, attacked an enemy stronghold in Chernushki village. Its advance was stemmed by a machine-gun nest, which kept the soldiers on the ground. Six submachine-gunners dispatched to destroy the machine-gun were cut down before they reached it. A private, Alexander Matrosov, crept towards the machine-gun and, coming to within a few yards from the embrasure, opened fire against it. The fire was well aimed; however, though a mine near the machine-gun was caused to explode, the enemy continued firing. Matrosov leaped and covered the embrasure with his body, thus enabling his mates to rush forward. The battle was won at the price of Matrosov's life, the memory of whom is now revered. He was posthumously awarded the title of Hero of the Soviet Union, and the 254th Guards Infantry Regiment, in which he served, has been given his name.

In the fierce cold of winter, the Red Army advanced west ome 600-700 km, crushing 113 enemy divisions in 4 months and 20 days. It cleared important economic and strategic areas and totally eliminated the threat to the Volga and the Caucasus.

The outcome of the Stalingrad Battle was impressive evidence of the power and viability of the socialist state. The

---

[1] *Entscheidungsschlachten des zweiten Weltkrieges*, Frankfurt am Main, 1960, S. 311.

[2] Ronald Seth, *Stalingrad—Point of Return*, London, 1959, p. IX.

Stalingrad victory had strong international and historic repercussions.

It turned the tide in favour of the Allies in all theatres, including the African and Pacific.

Victory over fascism was dawning. A new phase began for the Resistance movement. The peoples were eager to contribute to the victory and relieve some of the burden borne by the Soviet Union due to the absence of a second front. In this new phase, the nazi invaders were in most occupied countries opposed not by mere partisan detachments, but by well-knit liberation armies.

In Germany proper, too, the Communist Party became more active underground. The number of anti-fascist groups multiplied. The judgement passed down by the nazi judiciary in the case of the biggest and most massive anti-fascist organisation headed by veteran Communists Anton Sefkov, Franz Jakob and Bernhardt Bestlein, said that members of the group "had come to the conclusion that after Stalingrad Germany can no longer win the war, and decided to do everything they could to speed up the defeat of the Third Reich and reestablish peace".[1]

The entire fascist bloc, not Germany alone, was hurled into a crisis by the Soviet victory at Stalingrad. It was a heavy blow for Germany's European allies, who began toying with the idea of quitting the war. The Japanese Government, which had once already postponed the date of its attack against the Soviet Union from 1941 to 1942, postponed it once more until the following year. Meanwhile, Germany's relations with some of the neutral countries, which provided it with extensive aid before Stalingrad, deteriorated.

Joachim Wieder, a West German historian, observes: "The consequences of the German defeat came into evidence everywhere: the neutral powers, Turkey, Spain, Sweden and Portugal began to show restraint; the fighting spirit of Germany's allies sank to nil. The partisan movement in the occupied areas became stronger, the military rebels in the Wehrmacht became stronger too, and so did the opposition throughout the country."[2]

---

[1] Otto Winzer, *Zwölf Jahre Kampf gegen Faschismus und Krieg*, Berlin, 1955, S. 212.

[2] Joachim Wieder, *Stalingrad und die Verantwortung des Soldaten*, München, 1962, S. 289.

The Stalingrad victory firmed up the anti-Hitler coalition. It won admiration everywhere. Only the extreme reactionary element in the United States and Britain was perturbed and irritated. Its hopes of seeing the Soviet Union exhausted and subjugated had collapsed.

Yet grateful mankind gave due credit to the unexampled exploit of the Soviet people at Stalingrad. The word "Stalingrad" heartened all anti-fascists, all champions of national and social freedom. It inspired writers and poets, musicians and painters. "Born I was to sing the immortality of Stalingrad," wrote Pablo Neruda, a Chilean poet in his poem, "A New Song of Love to Stalingrad".[1] Rockwell Kent, the US artist, when making a gift to the USSR of his paintings and books, said in November 1960: "All of us are indebted to the Soviet people for Stalingrad. This gift that I make is an act of gratitude."[2]

Stalingrad is for all a symbol of tenacity and courage of freedom, and of the grandeur and invincibility of social progress, of socialism.

2. Anglo-American Military
and Diplomatic Strategy Secrets

An Anglo-American-Soviet agreement was concluded in May and published in June 1942 envisaging a second front in Europe that year in order to bring closer the victorious end of the Second World War. All the requisites for a second front were at hand: the German troops were deeply involved on the Soviet Front, the United States and Britain had built up strong, well-equipped armies, and the Resistance Movement in Western Europe was powerful enough to support an allied assault against Germany.

Yet the second front was not opened in 1942, and not even in 1943. A veil of secrecy has been cast over British and US wartime strategy, but the reason why the second front was not opened when most needed, cannot be concealed. The British and American rulers were determined to save their strength until the war's end in order to promote their imperialist policy. More, they wanted to see the Soviet Union, their

[1] Pablo Neruda, *Nuevo Canto de Amor a Stalingrado*, Mexico, 1943.
[2] *Pravda*, November 17, 1960.

ally, weakened and exhausted by the single combat. Of course, the truth was kept from the public, while a variety of spurious excuses was tendered. The nazi claim of an Atlantic Wall against a possible Allied landing on the mainland, was exploited to the utmost for this purpose, giving succour to Hitler, who grew more and more convinced that Germany had nothing to fear in the West.

Just eight days after the Anglo-Soviet-American second front announcement, Churchill pleaded with Washington for a postponement, and had no difficulty in convincing the US rulers. Churchill, they decided, would go to Moscow to mollify the ruffled feelings this postponement would create there.

Churchill was anything but enthusiastic about his mission, but his hatred of the Soviet Union was of long standing, and he was pleased with the decision to delay the second front. He described his feeling during the flight to Moscow in his memoirs: "I pondered on my mission to this sullen, sinister Bolshevik State I had once tried so hard to strangle on its birth, and which, until Hitler appeared, I had regarded as the mortal foe of civilised freedom. What was it my duty to say to them now? General Wavell... summed it all up in a poem. There were several verses, and the last line of each was, 'No second front in nineteen forty-two'."[1]

The Soviet Government was informed of this during the tensest days of the Stalingrad Battle (in August 1942). Churchill promised the front the following year. His perfidy strained the system of inter-allied relations. In contrast, the Soviet Government observed all its commitments to Britain and the USA and briefed Churchill on the situation on the Soviet-German Front and the Red Army preparations for the counter-offensive at Stalingrad. As we shall see, the British Premier took this into account in his planning.

While in Moscow, Churchill offered British aid in defending the Transcaucasus. British troops, he said, could be sent in from Iran. His true intentions, of course, had nothing in common with any desire to help. At that same time the US Government offered "aid" to defend the Soviet Far East and Siberia from the Japanese by setting up American air bases there. The Soviet Government declined both offers, designed to take advantage of Soviet difficulties to carry forward

---

[1] W. Churchill, *The Second World War*, Vol. IV, London, 1951, p. 428.

imperialist policy, and this by typically imperialist methods.

The official British and US war histories argue that the second front delay was compensated amply by the flow of supplies to the Soviet Union. Fuller writes: ... "In the autumn of 1942 the economic position of Russia was a desperate one, and had it not been for the steady stream of Anglo-American supplies then pouring into Archangel, it is doubtful whether the Russians would have been able to turn to their advantage the fantastic situation in which Hitler had placed his armies."[1]

That is contrary to the facts. Far from being poured in, supplies were being withheld just at that time.

One of the excuses given for delaying the opening of the second front were the heavy losses sustained by what were really modest-sized British commandoes raiding the shores of Western Europe, e.g., the Canadian divisions at Dieppe. And one of the excuses given for the break in the flow of supplies were the heavy losses sustained by one of the convoys en route to Archangel.

The convoy, consisting of 34 merchant vessels, most of them American, left Iceland on June 27, 1942, accompanied by 28 British and US warships under command of British Rear-Admiral Louis Hamilton. A strong cover force of battleships and aircraft-carriers cruised somewhat to the west. When this convoy, PQ-17, was 200 km east of Medvezhy Island, the Admiralty ordered Hamilton to leave the merchant vessels to their fate and retreat west, because there were "grounds to assume" a German attack. The merchant vessels were told to "disperse and head for Russian ports". The result of this was indeed appalling: German planes and submarines sank 23 ships. As for the German fleet in the fear of which the British cruisers and destroyers had fled, it never even appeared in the vicinity. Yet the whole thing gave the British Government the wanted excuse to stop the flow of supplies to the USSR.

The British and American seamen who delivered the supplies displayed a high degree of courage, scorning danger, seeking honestly to help the Soviet people in their dedicated fight.

Two convoys were sent to the Soviet Union in September and December 1942, but regular communications were not resumed until the beginning of 1943. ... "Until the late

[1] J. Fuller, *The Second World War 1939-1945*, London, p. 186.

spring of 1943," notes US historian Ivar Spector, "the Red Army had to rely entirely upon Soviet resources."[1]

When Italy entered the war in the summer of 1940, engagements were fought in Northern Africa with alternating success. At first, the Italians managed to push back the British colonial army, then the latter mounted a counter-offensive. But when General Rommel and his troops landed in Africa, the British were again flung back to the approaches to the Suez Canal. A threat arose to the Middle East. But the intensity of the fighting on the Soviet front prevented reinforcements from being sent to Rommel. Panzers painted yellow-grey, the "colour of the desert", went to the area between the Don and Volga instead of Africa.

While delaying the second front, the US and British governments, acting on their colonial interests, co-ordinated their operations in Northern Africa: the British would hit the Italo-German divisions at El Alamein, whereupon considerable Anglo-American forces under General Eisenhower would land in the enemy rear.

Taking note of the information he received in Moscow about the projected Soviet Stalingrad offensive, Churchill timed the British push at El Alamein shortly before it. He intended to produce the false impression that the British victory in the African desert, really quite secondary in importance, was the turning point in the war. When word of the victory in Africa reached Britain, churchbells rang for the first time since the war began, while the British Prime Minister declared: "It marked in fact the turning of 'the Hinge of Fate'."[2]

When the El Alamein battle began, Rommel had 96,000 men and 500-600 tanks, whereas the British had 150,000 men and 1,114 tanks.[3] Moreover, two-thirds of Rommel's force consisted of Italian divisions, the men and officers of which had little stomach for the fight.

The British offensive went off to a start on October 23, 1942. At once, the Italo-German forces retreated. Advancing on the heels of the enemy, the British troops covered 850 km in 14 days. By that time, November 8, three Allied

---

[1] Ivar Spector, *An Introduction to Russian History and Culture*, Toronto, New York, London, 1950, p. 350.

[2] W. Churchill, *op. cit.*, Vol. IV, p. 541.

[3] J. Fuller, *op. cit.*, p. 234.

groups of armies landed far in Rommel's rear. One group, from the United States, went ashore in French Morocco, while the other two, consisting of British and US troops from the British Isles, landed at Oran and near Algiers. Ignoring Vichy orders, the French troops stationed in Northern Africa refused to resist the Anglo-American landing.

Yet the Italo-German forces retreated slowly. Caught between the hammer and anvil, they withdrew to northern Tunisia and were finally crowded into the Bona Peninsula, the north-eastern tip of the country, where they surrendered en masse on May 12, 1943. That was the concluding act in Northern Africa.

What the United States and Britain would now do had been decided back in January 1943, at the summit meeting in Casablanca, where Churchill and Roosevelt decided to postpone the invasion of the European mainland until the summer of 1944. Strategically tenable and prepared by Anglo-US workers, soldiers and sailors, the invasion was replaced by exercises. Nor did the British and American commands make a secret of it.

The Soviet Union was informed of the postponement at the beginning of June 1943. The head of the Soviet Government replied that it would create great difficulties for the Soviet Union, which was having to "do the job alone, almost singlehanded, against an enemy that is still very strong and formidable".[1] In the next letter to the British Prime Minister, Stalin said: "I must tell you that the point here is not just the disappointment of the Soviet Government, but the preservation of its confidence in its Allies, a confidence which is being subjected to severe stress. One should not forget that it is a question of saving millions of lives in the occupied areas of Western Europe and Russia and of reducing the enormous sacrifices of the Soviet armies, compared with which the sacrifices of the Anglo-American armies are insignificant."[2]

The perfidy of the US and British governments was not confined to the postponement of the second front. Behind the back of the Soviet Union their representatives conducted secret negotiations with spokesmen of Hitler Germany along

---

[1] *Correspondence Between the Chairman of the Council of Ministers of the USSR and the Presidents of the USA and the Prime Ministers of Great Britain During the Great Patriotic War of 1941-1945*, Vol. 1, Moscow, 1957, p. 132 (further referred to as *Correspondence...*).

[2] *Ibid.*, p. 138.

several channels—through Spain, Sweden, Portugal, Switzerland and the Vatican. In many cases, middlemen were employed.

The focal point in these negotiations was the meeting of Allen Dulles, US Intelligence chief in Europe, with Count Moritz Hohenlohe, Hitler's emissary, in Switzerland. The main theme of their discussion was how to save the nazi regime in Germany and use it to establish US hegemony in postwar Europe—a gross violation of America's and Britain's commitments as allies of the Soviet Union.

The Soviet policy was entirely different. The USSR did its utmost to invigorate the anti-fascist coalition, to support all peoples fighting the nazis. It did its utmost to promote the cohesion of the patriotic forces in the occupied countries and to pave the way for the restoration of independent national states.

The Soviet people showed a warm affection for those Britons and Americans who wanted the war to end as quickly as possible. Public opinion in the United States and Great Britain clamoured for the second front. So did the army ranks and part of the officers. Pressure increased and became an important element in home affairs.

The Soviet Government met the wishes of French patriots eager to contribute to the war effort. A French air squadron, the Normandie, was formed as part of the Soviet Air Force and saw action on the Soviet-German Front. The courage of the French airmen was acclaimed by the Soviet people. The Normandie's splendid fighting record cemented the Soviet-French friendship and contributed to the solidity of the anti-fascist coalition.

The Soviet attitude to France was reflected in the fact that the USSR recognised the French National Liberation Committee before any of the other powers as "the representative of all French patriots fighting against Hitler tyranny".[1]

The Soviet Union aided the Polish and Czechoslovak peoples. The Polish Thaddeus Kosciuszko Infantry Division was formed in the Soviet Union in the summer of 1943. Fighting shoulder to shoulder with the Soviet troops, it acquired combat experience and later became the nucleus of the Army of People's Poland. By the end of 1942 the 1st Cze-

---

[1] *Soviet-French Relations During the Great Patriotic War, 1941-1945*, Moscow, 1959, p. 195.

choslovak Battalion was formed in the USSR, and a 20-year Soviet-Czechoslovak Treaty of Friendship, Mutual Assistance and Postwar Co-operation was concluded in Moscow on December 11, 1943.

The Soviet policy of combining the efforts of all freedom-loving peoples, and its accent on honest fulfilment of allied obligations helped consolidate the anti-fascist coalition, adding to its strength and offering the peoples the prospect of liberation from the fascist yoke, deliverance from enslavement, and revival of national independence and sovereignty trampled by the German invaders.

3. German "Tigers" Smashed

After the Stalingrad defeat Hitler Germany still had great strength and considerable resources, and doubly so because, taking advantage of the absence of the second front, it could deploy troops eastward from the West. The German generals were bent on avenging Stalingrad, regaining the lost strategic initiative and, ultimately, turning the tide of the war in their favour.

Hopes were pinned on new weapons. German industry was working round the clock to produce Panther and Tiger panzers with heavy armour and considerable firing power. It was also building Focke-Wulf-190A planes which flew at over 600 kmph and had four cannon and six machine-guns. "Total mobilisation" enabled Germany to field 42 divisions more on the Soviet-German Front than at the beginning of the war.

Nazi planners drew up Operation Citadel, envisaging a south-eastward drive from south of Orel and a north-eastward from north of Kharkov. German thrusts were to converge near Kursk, cutting off the Kursk Bulge, and encircling and destroying the Soviet forces in that salient. In general outline, the plan followed the lines of the brilliant Red Army operation at Stalingrad. After the initial success the German offensive would develop deeper into Soviet territory, either east to the Volga or north-east to Moscow.

Fifty divisions, with another 20 on their flanks, were massed for Citadel. Almost a quarter of these troops were panzer and motorised units. Never since the war broke out was the deployment of forces so massive on a relatively small frontage, never the deployment of panzers and self-propelled guns so concentrated. More than 2,000 planes—three quarters of the Luftwaffe's strength on the Soviet-German front—would render air support.

On the night before the jump-off, the German troops heard Hitler's message. It said in part: "You will participate in large-scale offensive battles, the outcome of which may settle the war. More than ever before, your victory will convince the whole world that all resistance to the German army is, in the end, futile."[1] What an object lesson of how the German imperialists had digested their Stalingrad experience! They were still dreaming of conquering the world!

The preparations for the German blow were about over. The nazis would strike any minute. Churchill, however, for reasons of his own, kept assuring the Soviet Government that no German offensive would ensue. On June 19, 1943, he wrote that he had reason to believe that Hitler was vacillating and intending "to delay his plans for a large-scale offensive against Russia this summer".[2] On June 27, he wrote that "it may even prove that you will not be heavily attacked this summer".[3] If the Soviet Union had given credence to this information, the German offensive may have spelled disaster.

However, the nazi intention of mounting a large-scale offensive at Kursk did not escape the notice of the Soviet Command, then engaged in planning a fresh offensive of its own. The question to decide was, who would jump first. The Soviet Supreme Command decided to let the enemy do so, in order to mince up his forces in defensive fighting and then go over to the attack. This was the most realistic plan in those circumstances.

The German plan, on the other hand, was stamped with the usual brand of reckless adventurism. The Operation Citadel order issued by OKW on April 15, 1943, expressed confidence that it would culminate in a "rapid and decisive success" and would be a torch that would set the world alight.[4] But the Soviet Armed Forces, with the victories at

[1] *I.V.O.V.S.S.*, Vol. 3, p. 245.
[2] *Correspondence...*, Vol. 1, p. 134.
[3] *Ibid.*, p. 141.
[4] *Kriegstagebuch des Oberkommandos der Wehrmacht*, Bd. III, Halbband 2, S. 1425.

Moscow and at Stalingrad, stood firmly in the way of the German aggressors.

The Soviet Command anticipated the direction of the nazi main blows. A strong defence in depth was built and strategic reserves were activated and made ready for battle. The depth of the defences of the Central and Voronezh fronts, standing directly in the way of the nazi assault, added up to 150 to 190 km. And behind them was stationed the Steppe Front, the Supreme Command's strategic reserve with its own defence lines and fortifications, behind which ran the strategic Don River. All in all, eight defensive zones and lines 250 to 300 km deep were ready by the time the enemy moved into action.

Soviet reconnaissance obtained exact information about the direction of the nazi main blows, and, what was more, about the zero hour. Ten minutes before the enemy began his artillery build-up, at 02.20 hours on July 5, the Soviet guns opened up with a counter-barrage. The nazis suffered considerable casualties and spent something like two hours restoring order in their lines and then began their artillery bombardment. The Soviet side replied with another artillery shoot.

Heavy fighting ensued. The nazi offensive developed slowly, the Germans suffering heavy losses. The Soviet troops engaged in an active type of defence, manoeuvring the reserves and mounting swift counter-blows against enemy wedges. It was the first time the Red Army committed its tank armies and large anti-tank artillery units.

The courage of the Soviet soldiers and officers was boundless. In one air battle A. K. Gorovets, flying a LA-5 built on money donated by the collective farmers of Gorky Region, shot down nine nazi bombers, becoming the world's only flyer to make nine consecutive hits.

The German troops edged forward very slowly. Their last hope was to try to breach the front at Prokhorovka in a narrow sector (8-10 km) and then proceed to Kursk. The nazi command built up a tremendous armour density—something like 100 tanks and self-propelled guns per kilometre of frontage.

The Prokhorovka battle, involving 1,200 tanks[1] and a large number of planes on both sides, opened on July 12.

[1] *Soviet Armed Forces in 50 Years*, Russ. ed., p. 336.

In a week of fighting the Germans advanced some 6-8 km in the Orel-Kursk direction and some 30-35 km in the Belgorod-Kursk direction, and this at an extremely high price: Hitler's finest panzer divisions had ceased to exist. Here is how Goerlitz describes the outcome: "The last of the units capable of attacking burnt to cinders; the neck of the panzer weapon was twisted."[1] The time had come for a giant Soviet counter-offensive, which jumped off duly without the slightest hitch — a model of warcraft. A powerful blow was struck on July 12, 1943. Soviet troops attacked from north-east (Western Front under General V. D. Sokolovsky and Bryansk Front under General M. M. Popov) and south-east (Steppe Front under General I. S. Konev and Voronezh Front under General N. F. Vatutin), with troops of the Central Front (General K. K. Rokossovsky) participating.

The Kursk Battle, in which the German Command reckoned on regaining the strategic initiative, revealed the complete failure of the offensive strategy employed by Hitler and his generals. From then on the strategic initiative never again passed out of Soviet and Allied hands.

The post-Kursk Soviet offensive inflicted heavy losses on the nazis, proving that their defensive strategy, too, was a failure. It became increasingly obvious that Hitler Germany was doomed.

Orel and Belgorod were cleared of the enemy on August 5, and by mid-August the entire nazi group in the Orel area was smashed. Kharkov was liberated on August 23.

Meanwhile, the Soviet offensive gained in scale. Huge tracts of Soviet territory were being cleared. The nazi exodus assumed massive proportions. Gradually, the Kursk counter-offensive developed into a strategic general offensive along the frontage running from Velikiye Luki to the Black Sea.

The Ukraine east of the Dnieper was liberated in August-September 1943. The Soviet troops reached the river simultaneously along a 600-km line. The Dnieper, wide and deep, was a formidable obstacle, on which the nazis pinned their hopes. They fortified the western bank mightily and prepared for a long siege. But the Soviet troops force-crossed the river and captured 23 bridgeheads.

This forced-crossing on the march after the bitter and

---

[1] Walter Goerlitz, *Der Zweite Weltkrieg, 1939-1945*, Bd. II, Stuttgart, 1952, S. 208.

sustained offensive fighting, calling no rest, using everything that floated without a preliminary build-up, without
waiting for special river-crossing equipment, has nothing to
equal it in the history of wars. It was an exploit not of individual heroes, but of large units of attackers. This is reflected
in the fact that 2,000 of those who participated in the crossing
were awarded the title of Hero of the Soviet Union. The first
step had been made in the liberation of the Ukraine west of
the Dnieper.

During the swift Soviet drive to the Dnieper, battles broke
out in the southern sector of the front for the possession of the
Donets Basin. It took less than a month to crush the strong
enemy force there, and liberate the basin.

The Red Army used one of the bridgeheads on the western
Dnieper bank, near the town of Lyutezh, to mount the attack
against the distant approaches to Kiev on November 3, 1943.
And by 04.00 hours on November 6, the day before the 26th
anniversary of the October Revolution, the capital of the
Soviet Ukraine had regained its freedom.

North of Kursk the Red Army performed the Smolensk
Operation, crowned by the recapture of the area between the
rivers Dnieper and Western Dvina, crossed by the main
communication lines from the centre of the country to
Byelorussia. Subsequent offensive operations liberated the
eastern part of Byelorussia.

In the summer and autumn of 1943 the Red Army advanced
300-600 km westward, liberating more than 40,000 localities,
including 162 towns. The time had come for the final banish-
ment of the enemy from Soviet territory. The hour of retribution was drawing closer, too, for Germany proper.

Marshal of the Soviet Union A. M. Vasilevsky summed up
the purport of the 1941-1943 fighting as follows: "We must
stress again and again the organic link between the battle
for Moscow, the battle on the Volga and the Kursk Battle.
Those were the three biggest politico-military events of the
first two years of the Patriotic War, signifying three stages in
the Red Army struggle for the possession of the strategic
initiative, with the Stalingrad Battle turning out to be decisive
in securing a radical change in the course of the Second World
War. The battles on the Kursk Bulge consolidated once and
for all the strategic initiative of the Red Army."[1]

---

[1] *Kommunist*, No. 1, 1968, p. 57.

4. The Teheran Conference

The Red Army victories and public opinion compelled the governments of the United States and Britain, which until then had preferred to discuss military strategy and the postwar arrangement in the absence of Soviet representatives, to agree to joint discussions. The latter half of 1943 saw conferences of the Big Three foreign ministers and heads of government, proving that international co-operation of states of the different social systems was possible and necessary.

At the Big Three (USSR, USA, Britain) Foreign Ministers' Conference, held in Moscow on October 19-30, 1943, the Soviet delegation called on the Allies to step up action and bring closer the victorious end of the war. As the initial item on the agenda, the Soviet spokesmen suggested examining "measures reducing the duration of the war against Germany and her allies in Europe". British General Hastings Lionel Ismay, speaking on behalf of the US and British delegations, declared, however, that the second front could not be opened until 1944, and that only provided a number of especially favourable conditions were at hand.

On the initiative of the Soviet Union the discussion was wound up with a communiqué stating that its participants regarded as their "prime aim hastening the end of the war".[1] The Soviet delegation did not obtain explicit US and British second front commitments for 1944. All the same, the decision adopted on the need for closer military co-operation by the three Powers to hasten the end of the war offered new scope for international co-operation and made so much easier the Soviet efforts to speed the opening of a second front in Europe.

The Conference recognised the need for postwar international co-operation. Its communiqué said: "... it was essential in their (three Powers'—Ed.) own national interests and in the interests of all peace-loving nations to continue the present close collaboration and co-operation in the conduct of the war into the period following the end of hostilities, and ... only in this way could peace be maintained and the political, economic and social welfare of their peoples fully promoted."[2]

The delegations exchanged opinions on the German ques-

[1] *Vneshnyaya politika Sovietskogo Soyuza v period Otechestvennoi Voiny (Soviet Foreign Policy During the Great Patriotic War)*, Vol. 1, p. 412.
[2] *The New York Times*, November 2, 1943.

tion. The Soviet Government held that the legitimate rights and interests of the German nation should be taken into account, with the solution of the question ensuring the complete elimination of fascism and prevention of its revival, and appropriate controls to secure lasting peace in Europe. The US spokesman, State Secretary Cordell Hull, put forward a plan for partitioning Germany. The same idea was projected by British Foreign Minister Anthony Eden, who said use of force should not be discounted in achieving this aim.[1]

The US and British representatives urged the USSR to resume diplomatic relations with the Polish emigré government, broken off a few months previously due to the latter's strongly anti-Soviet policy. Replying to the insistent Anglo-American representations the Soviet spokesman said: "We stand for an independent Poland and are ready to help her. But Poland must have a government with friendly feelings towards the USSR. That is lacking now."[2]

In contrast to plans concerning Austria advanced by certain groups in the United States and Britain without the least consideration for the opinion of the Austrian people, the Soviet delegation declared that the Austrians had the right to an independent national existence and to self-determination. It was the Soviet Union that initiated the issue of the Declaration on Austria by the Conference, saying that the three governments wished to see a free and independent Austria and would enable the Austrian people, like those of the neighbouring countries faced by similar problems, to find the political and economic security that is the only possible basis of a lasting peace. The Declaration also emphasised that Austria "has a responsibility which she cannot evade for participation in the war on the side of Hitlerite Germany".[3]

The Conference discussed Italy. Defeats on the Soviet-German Front, where Italian troops shared the fate of the German, coupled with Italy's loss of all her colonies and the powerful popular movement at home, had precipitated a crisis in the spring of 1943. The Italian monopolists were frightened by the incipient revolution. On July 25, Mussolini was removed

[1] *I.V.O.V.S.S.*, Vol. 3, p. 508.
[2] *Ibid.*
[3] *United Nations Documents 1941-1945*, London-New York, 1947, p. 15.

from power by the King's order, arrested and shipped off to the island of Ponca. The idea was to save the fascist dictatorship by sacrificing the bankrupt fascist dictator. But the people had their own ideas. They demanded peace, freedom and total elimination of the fascist regime. In the circumstances, the Italian Government started secret negotiations with the Anglo-American Command.

On September 3, Italian representatives and officers of Eisenhower's staff, acting on behalf of the United Nations, signed an armistice. It formalised the end of hostilities in Italy, with no mention of her democratic development and elimination of the fascist legacy.

British and US troops began landing in the South. The slow pace enabled the nazi armies to lunge into Italy and capture her northern, central and a large section of southern territories. There the nazis formed a puppet government, of which Mussolini, released from arrest by German paratroopers under Otto Skorzeny, a veteran SS trouble-shooter, was made the head.

As a result, an Italian front appeared, with British and US troops coming to grips with the Germans. New nazi defeats on the Soviet-German front and a spectacular partisan movement in Northern Italy paved the way for what could have been a rapid and crushing defeat of Hitler's armies in Italy. But the US and British commands acted with deliberate slowness, waiting until the nazis should wipe out the Resistance movement in the country. That was why the Allied Command rejected the partisan offer of concerted action, which would obviously have brought Italy's liberation closer.

In the southern part of Italy, the Americans and British established a military administration which retained the fascist legislation and extensively employed the services of Italian fascists. It impinged on the national rights and interests of the Italian people, prejudicing the interests of the anti-fascist coalition and acting contrary to the war aims of that coalition.

At the Moscow Foreign Ministers' Conference, the Soviet delegation spoke sharply against the US and British separatist and anti-democratic policy in Italy. And it won its point with the adoption of the Declaration on Italy, an important victory for the democratic forces. The Declaration championed the legitimate rights of the Italian nation and laid down the principle of democratising the country.

To prevent further separate action by any Allied Power, the Moscow Conference decided to form a European Advisory Commission (consisting of the USSR, USA and Britain) to work out joint three-Power decisions relating to the approaching end of the war, including the armistice or surrender terms for the hostile states. A special resolution was framed concerning behaviour in relation to peace-feelers from the enemy countries; it was aimed at averting new cases of separate secret negotiations. Under its terms, the Allied Powers undertook to inform each other forthwith and conduct mutual consultations "in order to agree their actions" in the event of any proposals from any of the countries of the Hitler bloc.[1]

A Declaration on German Atrocities, adopted on Soviet initiative, provided for the punishment of war criminals by nations against which their specific crimes had been committed, while the main war criminals would be tried and punished jointly by the Allied Powers. The Declaration warned that the war criminals would not escape just retribution, because "the three Allied Powers will pursue them to the uttermost ends of the earth and will deliver them to the accusers in order that justice may be done".[2] The Declaration was a stern warning for the German war criminals, and disappointed those who had wished to protect them.

The Conference discussed ways of assuring universal postwar security and the idea of an international peace-keeping organisation. A Declaration on General Security was adopted, which the Chinese Government also signed, referring to the establishment of "a general international organisation, based on the principle of the sovereign equality of all peace-loving States... for the maintenance of international peace and security".[3]

The Declaration was historic in that it initiated the United Nations Organisation and first formulated its purpose, defining its basic principles as a body for the international co-operation of sovereign states in maintaining peace and security. This destroyed the plans of turning the organisation into a kind of "supra-national government", as certain Western quarters wished. The Declaration envisaged agree-

---

[1] *I.V.O.V.S.S.*, Vol. 3, p. 509.
[2] *United Nations Documents 1941-1945*, p. 16.
[3] *Ibid.*, p. 13.

ment by its signatories on how to regulate armaments and stipulated that after the war's end none would "employ their military forces within the territories of other states except for the purposes envisaged in this Declaration and after joint consultation".[1]

The Conference went down in history of the anti-fascist coalition as a practical proof that international co-operation was possible and fruitful. Its decisions assisted the efforts of progressives to assure a democratic postwar arrangement in the world. More immediately, they helped to invigorate the wartime Anglo-American-Soviet coalition and, moreover, prepared the ground for the first meeting of the USSR, USA and British heads of government.

The Teheran Conference, at which Joseph Stalin, Franklin Delano Roosevelt and Winston Churchill first sat down round the same table, opened on November 28 and closed on December 1, 1943.

Teheran was chosen as the venue after prolonged negotiations. Some city in the Soviet Union would have been preferable, considering that the Soviet leaders directing operations on the decisive war front, could not afford to break off direct communications with the troops. However, considerable pressure was exerted on the US President by those who had wanted to complicate co-operation and pleaded considerations of prestige.

The Allies had to take into account the existence in Iran of a considerable secret German intelligence network. The Soviet Government, for one, learnt that an attack was being planned against the heads of the three Powers. Nikolai Kuznetsov, legendary Soviet intelligence officer posing as Paul Siebert, a nazi oberleutnant, succeeded in winning the friendship of SS Sturmbahnfuehrer von Ortel in the German-occupied town of Rovno. Von Ortel revealed to him the plan of an attack envisaging the landing near Teheran of several groups of paratroopers specially trained in a Copenhagen school to capture and kill the leaders of the Allied Powers. Kuznetsov's information was speedily relayed to Moscow.

Protective measures were taken. The Conference took place in the Soviet Embassy building, where premises were also provided for the US President's residence. The Soviet delegation was lodged in the two-storeyed villa of the Soviet

---

[1] *Ibid.*

Ambassador near the main Embassy building. The British delegation stayed on the grounds of its own embassy, located close to the Soviet.

A military group from the staff of the Soviet Supreme Command and the General Staff was also put up on the Soviet Embassy grounds. Contact was continuously maintained with the troops and war operations were directed along the entire Soviet-German Front.

Just as at the preceding Foreign Ministers' Conference, the main topic in Teheran concerned the second front. Speaking first, President Roosevelt named May-June 1944 as the approximate time for the landing of troops in Europe. "We should very much like to help the Soviet Union and to draw off a part of the German forces from the Soviet front."[1] But, of course, a second front in the summer of 1944 could not be half as useful as a year or two earlier. The 1944 landing was spurred essentially by the interests of the US ruling element.

Stalin stressed in his speech that the invasion of Europe by Allied forces would yield the best results "by a blow at the enemy in Northern or Northwestern France".[2] Churchill, however, suggested stepping up operations in Italy and the Eastern Mediterranean before landing Allied forces in north-west Europe, though, he said, this "could cause some delay in the operation across the Channel".[3] In reply, the Soviet head of government suggested that the Allies should consider Operation Overlord, already prepared, as their main 1944 undertaking—that is, invading north-west Europe with a supporting action in southern France, adding that the invasion should take place not later than May 1944.

In the next two days Churchill continued to insist on his proposal. On November 30 he told Stalin that "a choice has to be made between the date of Operation Overlord and the operations in the Mediterranean",[4] obviously giving precedence to the latter. Seeking to overcome Churchill's objections, Stalin said the Soviet Union would aid Operation Overlord by timing a major offensive in May in order to "pin down the German divisions on the Eastern Front and to prevent the Germans from creating any difficulties for

---

[1] *The Tehran, Yalta and Potsdam Conferences*. Documents, Progress Publishers, Moscow, 1969, p. 9.

[2] *Ibid.*, p. 11.

[3] *Ibid.*, p. 12.

[4] *International Affairs*, No. 8, 1961, p. 115.

Overlord".[1] Thereupon, the Conference agreed scheduling Operation Overlord for May 1944.

Just as at the Foreign Ministers' Conference, the US and British delegates in Teheran raised the question of Soviet relations with the Polish emigré government. The head of the Soviet delegation set out the Soviet attitude: "Russia, no less than the other Powers, is interested in good relations with Poland, because Poland is Russia's neighbour. We stand for the restoration and strengthening of Poland. But we draw a line between Poland and the emigré Polish Government in London. We broke off relations with that Government not out of any whim on our part, but because the Polish Government joined Hitler in slandering the Soviet Union."[2] The discussion of the Polish question yielded no results, because the US and British governments tied the matter in with the policy of the emigré government in London.

At Roosevelt's suggestion, Germany was discussed at some length. Stalin said: "What are the proposals on this matter?" Roosevelt's reply was curt: "The partition of Germany." Churchill was of the same opinion: "I am for partitioning Germany." Stalin's view differed: "there are no steps that could exclude the possibility of Germany's unification.... I don't know that there is need to set up four, five or six independent German states."[3]

At the end of the October 1 sitting, acting on what he had discussed in private with the head of the Soviet delegation, Churchill submitted the following proposal concerning Poland's postwar frontiers: "The hearth of the Polish state and people must be situated between the so-called Curzon Line and the line of the Oder River, including Eastern Prussia and the Oppeln Province as part of Poland."[4] In principle, Stalin expressed his accord.

Eyewitnesses recall that Roosevelt had told Stalin the United States could help the Soviet Union rehabilitate the war-ravaged economy by granting credits of several billion dollars. His country, Stalin replied, would welcome aid from so rich a country as the United States, provided the terms were acceptable.[5]

---

[1] *The Tehran, Yalta and Potsdam Conferences*, p. 38.
[2] *Ibid.*, p. 47.
[3] *Ibid.*, pp. 48, 49-50.
[4] *Ibid.*, p. 50.
[5] *New Times*, No. 49, 1967, p. 28.

Two Teheran documents were made public: the Declaration of the Three Powers on joint action in the war against fascist Germany and on postwar co-operation, and the Declaration of the Three Powers Regarding Iran. The former said the three powers had concerted their plans for the destruction of the German forces and reached complete agreement as to the scope and dates of operations to be launched from east, west and south.[1]

The latter said that the three powers are "at one with the Government of Iran in their desire for the maintenance of the independence, sovereignty and territorial integrity of Iran".[2]

Churchill handed Stalin a sword, a gift from the King of Great Britain to the citizens of Stalingrad in commemoration of the victory. According to an eye-witness account Churchill suggested that the ruins of that hero city should be kept intact, with a new city built nearby, so that the ruins of Stalingrad would remain as a tribute to human endurance. Stalin said that the ruins of only one block or several buildings would be preserved. The whole city would be built anew, rising out of the ashes like Phoenix, he said, and this would be a fitting monument.[3]

The Moscow and Teheran conferences were successful first and foremost thanks to the Soviet Union, whose government was striving to finish the war as quickly as possible, to liberate the enslaved peoples, to organise the postwar world along democratic lines and prevent new imperialist aggression in Europe. The conferences played a positive role, demonstrating that separate meetings by US and British statesmen were ineffective, while joint decisions on the major issues of war and peace were enormously important.

[1] *Soviet Foreign Policy During the Great Patriotic War*, Russ. ed., Vol. 1, p. 425.

[2] *The Tehran, Yalta and Potsdam Conferences*, p. 53.

[3] *New Times*, No. 49, 1967, p. 28.

Chapter Five

The Economic Miracle

1. Heroism in Battle and in Labour

An army has to be fed, clothed, shoed, transported and armed. In this respect, the demands of the Second World War were much greater than of any other war before it. The armies were of many millions, using a great variety of arms and vast numbers of vehicles. To defeat Hitler Germany and her allies militarily, they had first to be defeated economically.

And it was economically that the Great Patriotic War began most unfavourably for the Soviet Union. Having continuously primed for war through nine years and conquered a number of European countries, nazi Germany possessed considerably greater military-economic resources. This may be seen from the following table.

**Output of Key Strategic Materials
in Fascist Germany and the USSR in 1940
(million tons)[1]**

Item	Germany proper (1937 frontiers)	Germany, her satellites and occupied countries	Soviet Union
Coal	251.9	391.2	153.7
Steel	19.1	30.9	18.3
Oil	1.1	7.7	31.1

Although Germany was far behind in oil, it had a well-geared synthetic fuels industry and possessed considerable

[1] *I.V.O.V.S.S.*, Vol. 6, p. 43.

stocks of oil and oil products seized in occupied countries. The German production of arms, meanwhile, was far greater than that of the Soviet Union at the time of the attack.

Furthermore, when the war broke out, with the enemy overrunning important industrial areas, the Soviet situation deteriorated seriously. Against June 1941, the December production of pig iron dropped to less than a quarter, steel and rolled stock to less than a third, rolled non-ferrous metals to a tiny fraction of prewar, and of ball-bearings to less than one-twentieth.[1] Soviet industrial output shrank to under half between June and November 1941.[2] War production, too, declined: war planes to less than a third from September to November, while 303 munitions factories went out of operation totally between August and November.[3]

Suffering losses of this magnitude, no economy in the capitalist world could have revived in war conditions.

True, the Soviet Union had certain industrial resources in its eastern regions, built up under the prewar five-year plans. But these were insufficient to defeat the enemy economically. Eastern production had to be expanded, and considerably so. That is why at the very outbreak of war the Central Committee of the Communist Party and the Soviet Government stressed that the plan of extending war production depended "on the rapid unfolding of a production base in the trans-Volga area, the Urals, Western Siberia, Kazakhstan and Central Asia".[4] Industrial plant from the country's western regions was to be transferred there as quickly as possible.

A mammoth migration began from the country's war-threatened West to the East. Nothing of like proportions has ever been witnessed in history. Hundreds of factories, including war plants, were put on wheels, including equipment usually thought untransportable—rolling mills, boilers, turbo-generators, presses, machine-tools and mining equipment. The loading and dispatch took mere hours or a few days, often literally within sight of the enemy. Also shipped out was the ready stock, semi-finished and raw materials. Completing

[1] *I.V.O.V.S.S.*, Vol. 2, p. 160.

[2] N. Voznesensky, *Voyennaya ekonomika SSSR v period Otechestvennoi voiny (Soviet War Economy During the Great Patriotic War)*, Moscow, 1948, pp. 42-43.

[3] *I.V.O.V.S.S.*, Vol. 2, pp. 160-61.

[4] *Ibid.*, pp. 142-43.

the initial phase of the exploit, workers and their families followed the plant eastward to tackle the second phase — installing the equipment in new places and restarting production.

A. N. Kuzmin, director of Zaporozhstal, a big iron and steel plant, was asked during a postwar trip to the United States whether it was true all Zaporozhstal equipment was shipped out. He replied: "Yes. The workers rose to the occasion. They were defending their future."[1]

As many as 1,523 factories, including 1,360 large war plants, were removed to the East in July-November 1941. Out of this number 226 to the trans-Volga area, 667 to the Urals, 244 to Western Siberia, 78 to Eastern Siberia and 308 to Kazakhstan and Central Asia.[2]

The railways were strained to breaking point. With the outbreak of war they took troops and war materiel to the battle-lines, and did their job well. One and a half times more troop trains were brought to the front in a week as in the first two months of the 1914 war.[3] But almost simultaneously they had to evacuate industry from the western areas. It was a titanic assignment, which the Soviet railwaymen also accomplished. Nearly 1,500,000 cars of equipment were taken East in 1941 alone.[4]

And this despite fierce Luftwaffe attempts to paralyse transport. In October-December 1941 nazi bombers kept 25 railway lines, including those deep in the rear, under constant attack. The enemy flew 5,939 missions over only the tracks near the front from the beginning of the war to December 1941 alone, dropping more than 46,000 bombs.[5]

The evacuated plant was restarted in several ways. Some evacuated factories were merged with operating factories in the East. Some of the plant was installed in newly-built factories, some evacuated enterprises were split into several new specialised plants, etc.

The large tank-making plant shipped out from the Ukraine was amalgamated with other plants, forming the Urals Tank Works. And one more large tank-making plant, known as

[1] *Trud,* Oct. 3, 1947.
[2] *I.V.O.V.S.S.,* Vol. 2, p. 148.
[3] I. V. Kovalev, *Sovietskii zheleznodorozhnyi transport (Soviet Railways),* Moscow, 1947, p. 70.
[4] *I.V.O.V.S.S.,* Vol. 2, p. 148.
[5] *Ibid.,* p. 169.

Tankograd, sprang up after the merging of a Leningrad plant, the Kharkov Diesel Works and the Chelyabinsk Tractor Works.

The winter complicated matters greatly. Foundation pits had to be cut out of frozen Siberian ground. The Bolshevik Plant, evacuated from Kiev, was restarted in a Sverdlovsk suburban area in the open. Machine-tools put on foundations were provided lighting from lamps hung on the surrounding pine trees. Nearby, building elements were being cut and welded for the vault of the future factory building, and foundations laid for the walls. That was the epic birth of the new immense Uralkhimmash (Urals Chemical Engineering Plant). This was also the case with many other enterprises which began producing in the open.

To speed up matters, large temporary timber buildings were put up, some in a matter of 15-20 days. A large war plant evacuated to Novosibirsk was restarted on its new site in 14 days, and simultaneously builders put up a thermopower plant and a pontoon bridge across the Ob, joining the old and new industrial quarters of the city.

The critical low in production was passed at the end of 1941. Thenceforward output began to climb, with the flow of arms, ammunition and materiel increasing steadily.

The unfolding of Soviet war production is one of the most striking "secrets" of the Second World War. Yet it should have surprised no one—this was a logical manifestation of the strength and viability of the Soviet social and political system. Many were surprised, however, and this applies to many foreign friends of the Soviet Union, not only to the enemy. Many thought its economic victory over nazi Germany was impossible. The Soviet people proved the contrary.

Important was the fact that the Soviet Union already possessed the designs of new, sophisticated weapons, tanks and planes, and that the method of production had already been developed. The essential technical and production problems were solved in the early months of the war jointly by scientists, researchers, engineers, designers and workers.

In collaboration with the director of the Magnitogorsk Iron and Steel Combine (G. I. Nosov), engineer V. A. Smirnov, foreman M. M. Hilko, steelworker D. N. Zhukov and others developed a direct open-hearth smelting technique for high-grade armour steel, while another group of engineers, headed by the deputy senior mechanic, N. A. Ryzhenko, used the blooming mill to roll the armour. Academician Y. O. Paton's automatic welding techniques raised efficiency five times over, and were used with eminent success in making tanks. As a result tank production rose steeply. But so did that of firearms, including submachine-guns and artillery pieces of all calibres. Plane output increased somewhat more slowly, chiefly due to acute shortages of aluminium after the area of the Dnieper Hydro-Power Station fell into German hands. But soon aluminium began coming in increasing quantities from Urals plants.

A year after nazi Germany attacked, the Soviet war industry had not only recovered, but increased its capacity. By March 1942 the eastern regions produced as much as the entire country did before the war.

By mid-1942 industry had been largely reorganised, with most of the re-sited war factories back in operation. Somewhat later that year the process of wartime conversion, begun the day the war started, was complete. The Soviet economy was capable of supplying the troops uninterruptedly, with increasing abundance.

Plane production was 60 per cent up over the year before, and tank production 270 per cent.[1] The following year, 1943, aviation plants built some 35,000 planes, and armour plants made 24,000 tanks.[2] Production of firearms and artillery increased less rapidly, but the volume of output was high. Manufacture of jet mortars, popularly known as *katyushas*, climbed steadily.

The immense leverage of the Soviet socialist economic system, coupled with the mass heroism of the people, helped resolve the war's formidable organisational and economic problems and build up steadily the military-economic potential. For the first time in the history of wars the productive forces in a war-gripped country, the theatre of the main battles, continued to expand spectacularly, instead of decreasing.

Braving unspeakable difficulties and hardships, the nation forged the victory in arduous labour. Morale was high. Inspired by the Communist Party, the workers displayed a fervent patriotism, which generated a universal heroism

---

[1] *I.V.O.V.S.S.*, Vol. 2, pp. 510-11.
[2] *Soviet Armed Forces in 50 Years*, Russ. ed., p. 332.

in labour the likes of which was never seen in history. The advantage in arms which the enemy had had at the beginning of the war was soon offset by this peerless exploit.

The Soviet working class, the most revolutionary and best organised politically conscious part of the nation, stood in the front ranks of the battle for economic victory over the enemy. The services it rendered the country were a model of dedication.

There were massive patriotic movements—the all-Union socialist emulation movement among enterprises and shops, and individual workers; the movement for combining trades; the movement of two-hundreders and three-hundreders (who fulfilled their assignments 200 and 300 per cent, respectively); the movement of multiple turners (who operated several machine-tools at once), and others.

Combining several trades and simultaneously operating several lathes was necessary to make up for the depletion of manpower resulting from the high army conscription rate. Ural building worker V. F. Shalayev sparked the movement of combining several trades: he learned eight in wartime (that of stone mason, plasterer, concreter, spiderman, etc.). Lathe operator Ignatov of the Urals Heavy Engineering Plant, who began by working two lathes, then took on another two—those of a called up mate. Working four lathes, he fulfilled five to six daily assignments.

At the Krasny Proletary Engineering Works, turner V. M. Frolov worked two multi-cutter milling machines, and when a friend joined the army, he took on his job as well, fulfilling more than five assignments daily. The movement, joined by many workers, was given added impetus by Yekaterina Baryshnikova, a girl of the First Moscow Ballbearing Plant, and Yegor Agarkov, a Urals factory worker. They suggested reducing the work-teams, while increasing output. The movement they pioneered released nearly 100,000 workers, who were transferred to do other sorely-needed work.

Steelmaker Alexander Chalkov, of the Kuznetsk Iron and Steel Plant, who was one of the first to learn smelting special-grade steel in ordinary open-hearth furnaces, made enough steel in the first two years of the war to manufacture 24 heavy tanks, 36 guns, 15,000 mortars, 100,000 hand grenades and 18,000 submachine-guns. He was awarded the State Prize, which he donated to the Red Army Fund, asking that the money be used to equip the Siberian Guards Division with submachine-guns. These bore the inscription, "To the Siberians from Steelmaker Chalkov".

There was heroism, too, in the way the workers coped with breakdowns and repairs, oblivious of fatigue and danger. Cases have been recorded where repairmen overhauled furnaces that were still hot. One later said that the idea had come from a newspaper, which reported how seamen repaired a steam-boiler of a warship damaged in battle.

This is how the heroism of the factory workers blended with that of the men at the front.

The heroic labour of the collective farmers assured a steady supply of food for the army and the rear, and of raw materials for industry. And this despite the fact that for a time the Soviet Union was deprived of its main grain-producing areas, the Ukraine, the Don area and Kuban territory. This was partly compensated by expanding grain areas in other parts of the country. It is safe to say that without the collective-farm system, without the farmers' devoted patriotism, the economic victory over the enemy would have been impossible.

Agriculture, too, had its wartime shockworkers. P. S. Nazarov harvested 56 centners of wheat per hectare on the Avangard Collective Farm in Sverdlovsk Region. Collective farmer Chaganak Bersinev, of the Kurman Collective Farm in Kazakhstan, grew more than 205 centners of millet per hectare in 1943, an unheard-of yield, and I. Zhakhayev, of the Kzyl-tu Collective Farm in Kzyl-Orda Region, 156 centners of rice per hectare. In Dniepropetrovsk Region, collective farmer N. Koshik harvested 152 centners of maize per hectare in 1944, while combine operator I. P. Varanin, of Chkalov Region, brought home 3,467 hectares by coupling two combines and saving 4,654 kilograms of fuel.

But to manufacture arms, ammunition and equipment and grow food for the army, was only half the job. The supplies still had to be delivered. And Soviet railwaymen took their trains hard up to the front-lines, often under enemy fire and a hail of bombs. A few examples: engine-driver Trofimov, in charge of a munitions train, was attacked by aircraft. The driver's cabin was perforated by bomb fragments, the air duct smashed and the grease tank set alight. Trofimov and his helpers put out the fire, repaired the damage and pulled on to their destination.

A woman driver, Yelena Chukhnyuk, handled army supply trains oblivious of danger. Seventeen enemy bombers attacked the railway station where her munitions train was standing, but Yelena did not lose her head. She pulled it away from the station, away from the bombs. The locomotive and many of the cars were damaged, but the supplies were saved. During the Stalingrad Battle an enemy bomb hit the tender of her locomotive. Yelena saved the locomotive and uncoupled cars set aflame by the enemy.

Millions of tons of supplies were shipped under gunfire and air and submarine attack by the Soviet merchant marine and river fleet. The seamen assured communications and deliveries for the besieged hero-cities of Odessa, Stalingrad and Sevastopol at the height of the enemy assaults. Motor vehicles, too, were used extensively. Supplying Leningrad across Lake Ladoga ice under enemy fire and bombing is a heroic chapter in the history of the Leningrad Battle.

Soviet intellectuals performed their patriotic duty honourably. Scientists, designers and inventors solved many a wartime problem. They developed new, improved types of weapons and equipment superior to the best foreign arms. Together with engineers and technicians they found ways to steeply increase and cheapen production, developed new techniques and audacious new ways of stepping up output.

Automatic welding, developed by Academician Y. O. Paton, replaced manual welding. A group of physicists headed by S. I. Vavilov developed valuable new optical equipment for the army. A. Yakovlev, S. Lavochkin, S. Ilyushin, A. Tupolev and V. Petlyakov were prominent among designers of new aircraft; G. Kotin and A. Morozov produced new models of tanks, and V. Grabin, F. Petrov and I. Ivanov new types of artillery, while S. Simonov, G. Shpagin, V. Degtyarev and F. Tokarev produced automatic and semi-automatic firearms.

Soviet writers, poets, composers, artists, and actors popularised the exploits of Soviet people at the bench and in the trenches, cultivating patriotism and hatred of the enemy, and inspiring the millions.

Industrial executives, the captains of production, proved to be splendid organisers, among them the wartime People's Commissars I. F. Tevosyan, of the iron and steel industry, D. F. Ustinov, of armaments, A. I. Shakhurin, of the aviation industry, V. A. Malyshev, tanks, V. V. Vakhrushev, coal, etc.; factory directors I. A. Likhachev of the Moscow Car Works, I. K. Loskutov of the Gorky Car Works, B. G. Muzrukov of the Urals Heavy Engineering Plant, I. M. Zaltsman of the Kirov Works, and many others.

The morale and energy of Soviet people, their wholesale heroism in battle and on the shop-floor were inspired by the tireless work of the Communist Party. The leadership it afforded was the main factor in the economic, as well as military, victory.

2. The Economic Victory

The Soviet wartime economy was built up in a mere 12 months. It took nearly 18 months to overcome the arms shortage. By the beginning of 1943 war production was in full swing and the Red Army was getting arms and ammunition in required and continuously increasing quantities. Not only did the war plants recover lost capacity, but expanded considerably. The mammoth migration eastward was performed with amazing efficiency. By March 1942 the eastern regions alone yielded as many tools of war as the war plants of the entire Soviet Union did before the nazi attack.[1] The 1942 output of war materiel was five times as great as in 1940 in the Urals, 27-fold in Western Siberia and 9-fold in the trans-Volga area.[2] Aggregate 1944 industrial output surpassed prewar by 4 per cent, and war production was 312 per cent against 1940.[3]

At the height of the war's bitterest battles new construction was under way in the rear. Moreover, not small enterprises, but industrial giants went up. In 1943 alone three blast and 20 open-hearth furnaces, 23 electric furnaces, 8 rolling mills and 3 coking plants were put into operation, with many other industrial plants being started up and losing no time in getting into high gear.[4]

Before the war it was a hard-and-fast rule that war production should not exceed the output of raw materials. By this token, the Soviet Union, which had less fuel and metal than Germany, could never have caught up, let alone surpassed her in war production.

---

[1] *I.V.O.V.S.S.*, Vol. 2, p. 498.
[2] *Ibid.*, Vol. 6, p. 46.
[3] *Ibid.*, Vol. 4, p. 580.
[4] *Ibid.*, Vol. 3, p. 161.

But the people performed a miracle, with Soviet war production surpassing that of Germany in quantity, as well as quality. This wrought the economic victory, the material basis for military victory, though the first crushing counter-blows of the Soviet Army were delivered before the people in the rear achieved economic superiority.

In a nutshell, the advantages of the Soviet socialist economic system made it possible, despite the lesser production base, to produce more arms and ammunition than Hitler Germany and the nazi-occupied countries. War production also increased in Germany. But Soviet industry attained a rate of accretion that greatly exceeded Germany's. It was this difference in the rate of growth that finally produced the physical advantage. In 1944 the Soviet Union made 29,000 tanks and self-propelled guns against Germany's 27,300; 40,300 planes against 34,400, and 7,400 million bullets against 5,700 million.[1]

It was not until the end of 1944 that German war production began to decline, due, among other things, to the loss of occupied territory and some of the satellite countries, the loss of some German areas and the removal of industrial enterprises to the country's western regions. Germany was scraping the bottom of the barrel for manpower, while sabotage by foreign and some German workers, and general disorganisation caused by military operations on German territory, took a heavy toll.

An important factor of the Soviet war production growth was the marshalling of all available economic resources and centring them on that one aim. Consumer goods production was reduced. The motto was: "Everything for the front, everything for victory!"

Western historiographers tend to think that the decisive part in equipping the Soviet troops was played by supplies from the United States, Britain and Canada. These were undeniably of some importance, especially the supply of motor vehicles (401,400 vehicles were supplied by the United States and Britain in wartime). But US and British supplies of arms were negligibly small, as may be seen from the following table:

---

[1] For Soviet figures see *I.V.O.V.S.S.*, Vol. 4, p. 583 and for German figures *Promyshlennost Germanii v period voiny 1939-1945 (German Industry During the 1939-1945 War)*, Moscow, 1956, p. 27.

**Supplies to Soviet Armed Forces
During the Great Patriotic War (thousands)[1]**

By	Guns	Planes	Tanks
Soviet industry	489.9	136.8	102.5
USA and Britain	9.6	18.7	10.8

The figures speak for themselves. The Soviet Union defeated Hitler Germany with home-made arms and home-made equipment.

Furthermore, Soviet arms surpassed the German in quality. They were incomparably better, too, than the arms supplied to the Soviet Union by the United States and Britain. There is every reason to say, therefore, that the Soviet socialist economy went it alone, achieving the historic economic victory over fascist Germany and the nazi-occupied countries of Europe.

A tense competition was on throughout the war for superiority in the quality of arms. And Soviet designing won.

The Soviet T-34 tank, developed before the nazi attack, was the best medium tank in the war. Wehrmacht general Günther Blumentritt admitted that "in 1941 this was the most spectacular A. F. V. which could only be dealt with by other tanks.... This marked the beginning of what came to be called the 'tank terror'" among German soldiers.[2] Guderian, the German panzer theorist, says in his memoirs that attempts to copy the T-34 in German works failed due to the superior Soviet steel and inability to make a similar motor.[3] He referred to the "sinking capability of German panzer troops in face of the continuously increasing capacity of the Soviet tank forces thanks to the serial production of the excellent Russian T-34 tank".[4]

Soviet designers worked on the T-34 throughout the war. They improved its engine and transmission, and added to the strength of the armour. Instead of a 76-mm gun they were able to instal an 85-mm gun, without affecting the tank's

---

[1] *I.V.O.V.S.S.*, Vol. 6, p. 48.
[2] *The Fatal Decisions*, New York, 1956, p. 66.
[3] Heinz Guderian, *Erinnerungen eines Soldaten,* Heidelberg, 1956, S. 251.
[4] *Ibid.*, S. 256.

mobility, which became even greater by virtue of engine improvements.

In the beginning of the war Soviet plants were making a heavy tank, known as KV. By September 1943, however, the Red Army was supplied with a new heavy tank, JS, designed by the same group under G. J. Kotin. Its armour was 50 per cent superior to that of the much-vaunted German Tiger and 100 per cent to that of the Panther, and it was moreover better armed.[1] Also in 1943 Soviet plants launched quantity production of the powerful self-propelled guns, SAU-152, followed by a series of similar models. In 1943 alone Soviet designers developed 21 new types of tanks and self-propelled guns.[2]

New types of planes had only just begun to come off the production line when the war erupted. Yet a number of new ones, more up-to-date, appeared in 1942 and 1943. Designer S. A. Lavochkin's La-5 fighter surpassed the German Messerschmitt-109 and new, improved modifications of the same Lavochkin plane proved superior not only to the Messerschmitt, but even the Focke-Wulf-190, on which the German Command had pinned its hopes.

Dive-bomber Pe-2 by designer V. M. Petlyakov, after improvements in 1942 and 1943, combined unsurpassed endurance, speed and mobility.

The Il-2 Soviet attack plane, which the enemy nicknamed "black death", was the terror of the Wehrmacht throughout the war. It was improved several times, its armour thickened and fire power increased. The final model carried a 37-mm gun. No other belligerent country was able to develop as good a plane during the war.

Soviet artillery was constantly being improved. A number of new systems of different calibres and for different purposes was developed in wartime. Systems, designed for planes, tanks, self-propelled chassis and anti-tank troops were particularly good. In 1944, the Soviet Army received a 100-mm anti-tank gun which easily pierced the heaviest panzers. Soviet artillery had splendid ballistics, endurance, speed and power. New types of shells were developed, but the greatest indent was made by the new armour-piercing hard-core shells and jet shells.

---

[1] *I.V.O.V.S.S.*, Vol. 3, p. 170.
[2] *Ibid.*

Firearms, too, were greatly improved. New machine-guns were developed for planes, tanks and the infantry. And submachine-guns of several improved kinds were mass-produced.

Arms created by the genius of the Soviet working class streamed to the front in an endless flow. And the necessary abundance of arms, vehicles and ammunition enabled the Red Army to accelerate its drive to Berlin.

The food situation was difficult throughout the war. The stocks of grain, flour and cereals available at the beginning of the war (six million tons)[1] were enough only for the first several months. The loss of agricultural areas was a bitter blow. Deliveries of grain, flour and cereals from the United States and Canada were negligible (adding about to some 0.5 million tons in all the war years).[2] Food supplies had to be strictly regulated, the bulk being directed to the active army and to workers in the war industries. Local sources of food, little farms run by factories and organisations, and vegetable-growing by the population, were important. Also highly important were products grown by collective farmers on personal plots, which they sold directly to consumers.

The state and collective farms provided the country with a considerable quantity of grain, a total of 68.8 million tons, in the four years of war (1941-1944); by way of comparison it may be recalled that only 22.5 million tons were procured in the country in the four years of the First World War.[3]

Though generally coping with the food shortage, the city people suffered great hardships. Their diet shrank, and its quality deteriorated. The following figures give an idea of the state of affairs: before the war an adult in the city had an average 3,370 calories per day, which met his physiological needs. In 1942 the figure dropped to 2,555 calories, although expenditure of energy increased visibly. In the later years of the war caloricity increased somewhat, but even in 1944 the average per person was only 2,810. Consumption of fats, and especially of sugar, declined steeply, and that of proteins, too.[4]

The privations were great, but could not be compared to

[1] *Ibid.*, Vol. 1, p. 412.
[2] U. Chernyavsky, *Voina i prodovolstvieye (War and Food Supplies)*, Moscow, 1964, p. 20.
[3] N. Voznesensky, *op. cit.*, p. 175.
[4] U. Chernyavsky, *op. cit.*, p. 179.

the sacrifice in the battle-lines. Nothing could break the morale of the heroic Soviet people or diminish their determination to safeguard independence and freedom, to defend their country and its socialist gains.

It should be noted that the employment structure changed greatly during the war. The cream of the able-bodied workers, farmers and intellectuals went to the front. Women and adolescents, and older people took their places in production in town and country. Female labour in industry went up from 38 per cent in 1940 to 55 per cent in 1945.[1] In agriculture the percentage rise was still greater. More than 250,000 rural women were in executive positions—collective-farm chairmen or board members, team leaders and livestock farm managers.[2]

Young industrial workers quickly absorbed the experience and skill of the veterans. By the end of 1944 as many as one million people, comprising 150 Komsomol and youth teams, were active in industry and transport.[3] They were a model of diligence, treating their work assignments as a supreme duty. Young people and adolescents did their bit on the farms. Boys and girls of 16 and under comprised 17 per cent of the farmers in 1944.[4] And like the young workers, they performed their duties most conscientiously.

The Soviet people did not wait for the war to end to begin restoring the war-ravaged economy. This was an arduous and complicated job. Not only did the nazis carry off everything they could from territories they had overrun, but had also before withdrawing senselessly, in vandal fashion, demolished factories and dwellings, valuable monuments, blowing up and burning whatever they could. Hitler's generals boasted that their troops left a "desert zone" in their wake, in which life would be impossible for at least a decade. But the Soviet people disproved this malicious scheme, too, reviving the "desert zone" to a life of culture and humanism. An additional task faced them, that of aiding the liberated peoples in rehabilitating their economy.

This was a task which the country tackled the moment its Army liberated a region. In August 1943, the Communist Party and the Soviet Government adopted a special decision

---

[1] *I.V.O.V.S.S.*, Vol. 6, p. 97.
[2] *Ibid.*, Vol. 4, p. 598.
[3] *Ibid.*, p. 592.
[4] *Ibid.*, p. 598.

to that effect. And its implementation was successful. Factories, dwellings and public amenities rose out of the ashes and millions of hectares of land gone to waste were re-developed.

The biggest economic assignment was to rehabilitate the Donets Basin. Its mines, factories, power stations and mining towns were a heap of ruins. The mines were flooded, some of them so vastly that they had each become reservoirs of some 25 million cubic metres of water. Many of the galleries, exposed to the effects of water, had caved in.

V. V. Vakhrushev, a distinguished organiser of socialist production and the People's Commissar of the Coal Industry, was put in charge of the rehabilitation project, assisted by the heads of the biggest mining combines: A. F. Zasyadko, K. I. Pochenkov, K. K. Kartashev and A. T. Kartozia. Their leadership sparked the initiative and know-how of the miners, who submitted interesting suggestions of how to speed rehabilitation. Women who had learned the mining trade, took part in the effort. In the first 12 months after the Donets Basin was liberated, 60 million cubic metres of water was pumped out of the flooded mines and nearly 1,000 enterprises re-started.

Re-started in 1944 in territory cleared of the enemy were coal mines with an annual capacity of 29,200,000 tons, 11 blast furnaces yielding 2,100,000 tons of pig iron, 43 open-hearth furnaces yielding 1,800,000 tons of steel, 2 converters yielding 240,000 tons of steel, 22 rolling mills yielding 1,400,000 tons of rolled stock, 43 coking batteries yielding 3,800,000 tons of coke, and ore mines yielding 5,400,000 tons of iron ore.[1] Cement factories, sugar refineries, textile mills and garment factories, too, began operating.

The rehabilitation of liberated areas added to the country's economic power. The economic potential behind the Red Army's offensives kept climbing.

More than 1,800 state farms, 3,000 machine-and-tractor stations and 85,000 collective farms were rebuilt by the end of the war.[2] Towns from which the nazi invaders had been driven out were restored, re-built and newly-built dwellings adding up to a housing area of 24,800,000 sq m of living space, with 1,400,000 dwellings, put up in the countryside.[3]

---

[1] Ibid., p. 62.
[2] Ibid., Vol. 6, p. 49.
[3] Ibid.

The vigour of a nation is measured by how it copes with the hardships of war, and also by how it eliminates its ravages. Here, too, the Soviet people wrote a new chapter in world history. For the first time ever, rehabilitation began on a great scale while the war was not yet over, while battles of great magnitude were still being fought and the nazi invader still applied the greatest effort, hoping to recover the strategic initiative. This was yet another exploit of the nation of builders, whose rehabilitation effort foiled many an enemy design.

3. The Pen Is a Bayonet, the Camera a Rifle

Vladimir Mayakovsky, the Soviet poet, expressed the patriotic duty of writers and artists in the following lines:

> I want
>> that the pen
>>> be equated to the bayonet.

In the war, the pen of writers and poets, the brush of the artist, the sculptor's chisel and the cameraman's equipment were so effective a weapon that they could quite legitimately be equated to bayonet and rifle. Besides, many artists and writers were as adept with the bayonet and rifle as they were with the usual tools of their trade. They fought in the battle-lines, some of them as soldiers, some as commanders, some as political officers, and many as war correspondents and cameramen.

More than a thousand Soviet writers joined the army, including M. Bazhan, A. Bezymensky, P. Brovka, V. Vishnevsky, A. Gaidar, V. Grossman, Ye. Dolmatovsky, A. Korneichuk, V. Kozhevnikov, K. Krapiva, Yu. Krymov, M. Lynkov, S. Mikhalkov, P. Pavlenko, Ye. Petrov, A. Prokofyev, V. Sayanov, M. Svetlov, K. Simonov, L. Slavin, V. Stavsky, A. Surkov, M. Tank, A. Tvardovsky, N. Tikhonov and M. Sholokhov; also many composers, including A. Alexandrov and V. Muradeli, and artists P. Sokolov-Skalya, P. Shukhmin, B. Prorokov, and actors K. Baiseitova, Ye. Gogoleva, G. Yura, etc.[1]

---

[1] *Istoriya russkoi sovietskoi literatury (History of Russian Soviet Literature)*, Moscow, 1961, Vol. 3, p. 5.

As many as 275 men of letters gave their lives for the freedom and independence of their socialist country. Five hundred writers were decorated with war Orders and medals, ten being honoured with the title of Hero of the Soviet Union.[1]

Writers performed numerous feats of valour. The life and death of those who fell in battle is impregnated in the memory of the Soviet people. Yu. Krymov died in covering the withdrawal of his squad with a machine-gun. A. Gaidar faced nazi bullets to warn his partisan friends of danger. B. Lapin would not follow the others out of a nazi trap, staying behind with his mortally wounded friend Z. Khatsrevin, to face certain death. D. Altausen, another writer, refused a place in an airplane evacuating members of a trapped unit and, having made his decision, died fighting. A. Lebedev met his death with the rest of a submarine crew. And the fortitude of Mussah Jalil, his gallant stand in a Gestapo prison, is known the world over.

But the exploit of the Soviet writers was literary, as well as martial. When the hour of war struck, they provided the Soviet people—men at the front and workers in the rear—with what they keenly needed: the militant word. It was hard for the average Soviet men and women, peaceful by nature, to grasp the gravity of the situation, to acquire a burning hatred of the enemy. A flaming word was needed to reach the heart and bring home that the country had to be defended to the last, imbue one and all with the idea of a sacred patriotic war. And the task was splendidly accomplished by Soviet writers, poets, playwrights, journalists and cameramen.

The first wartime issue of *Pravda*, dated June 23, 1941, published verse by Alexei Surkov and Nikolai Aseyev. The following day *Izvestia* printed V. Lebedev-Kumach's "Holy War", a poem of deep wrath which, put to music by composer A. Alexandrov, became, in effect, the anthem of the Great Patriotic War. Ilya Ehrenburg made his wartime debut in *Krasnaya Zvezda* on June 26, and Alexei Tolstoy in *Pravda* on June 27. The deeply patriotic articles by Alexei Tolstoy, Mikhail Sholokhov and Alexander Fadeyev, the incisive features by Ilya Ehrenburg and the inspired reports of Nikolai Tikhonov from beleaguered Leningrad, all Soviet literature, all art, the creativity of thousands of writers,

---

[1] *Ibid.*

artists and musicians, the men and women of Soviet culture, the culture of all the peoples of the USSR, aroused in the people a hatred of the invader, inspiring courage and steeling their will.

Defence became the main theme of all literature, which turned to past history, to examples of resistance. Leonid Leonov wrote: "In a difficult hour ask them, those stern Russian people who put our country together bit by bit, and they will tell you how to comport yourself, even when alone among a multitude of enemies."[1]

Alexei Tolstoy told the Soviet soldier: "You love your wife and child; turn that love inside out, so it gives you pain, so it makes you bleed.... Kill the beast—that is your sacred commandment."[2]

Soviet literature did not depict the enemy as weak. It did not promise an easy victory. It spoke of his strength and of his weakness. He had primed for war, had prepared for aggression, his army was trained, had much experience, was malicious, greedy and cynical. His weaknesses were the absence of lofty ideals, the lowliness of aims, their contradiction with the inexorable laws of history. The spirit and morale of the Soviet man, his devotion to socialism, surpassed by far that sinister likeness to ideal nourished by fascism.

The main thing was to bring home to every Soviet man the intrinsic sense of the war. Soviet literature, hand in hand with all other forms of patriotism-inspiring ideological work, tackled the task, creating images of men fighting unto death, depicting the power and invincibility of the socialist system. It sang the ideals of the Soviet man, the theme of Soviet socialist patriotism.

Defence lines abandoned by the Red Army were gradually retaken. But if communist convictions had been similarly abandoned, they would have been irretrievable. Performing its civic and patriotic duty, Soviet literature clung to them unto death, and therein is the greatness of its exploit.

That exploit was part of the exploit of the nation. Soviet literature's bonds with the people grew stronger in those grim war years: the writers, poets and playwrights wrote and said exactly what the people wanted to hear from them. They said

---

[1] Leonid Leonov, *V nashi gody (In Our Time)*, Moscow, 1949, p. 41.
[2] Alexei Tolstoy, *Polnoye sobraniye sochinenii (Complete Works)*, Vol. 14, Moscow, 1950, p. 207.

the truth about the nation's tragedy, about its burning anger, an anger that could not but save the Soviet Union and all mankind from fascist enslavement. They used the power of the word to prove the irreversibility of world history, as manifested in socialism's victory and in the profound changes which that victory had wrought.

The people in battle, the people in the rear, the people in besieged cities—those were the main heroes. The writers showed the determinative role played by the people in the fight against fascism and in forging the victory.

The nation recognised their writers' exploit. The demand for poetry, novels and short stories, and feature articles, soared: as many as 169,500,000 copies of books of fiction were put out during the war years.[1]

Not journals alone, but also national, local and army newspapers printed the works of the Soviet men of letters. *Pravda*, *Izvestia* and *Krasnaya Zvezda* devoted pages to plays, poems and stories by Olga Bergholtz, Wanda Wasilewska, Boris Gorbatov, Vasily Grossman, P. Pavlenko, Mikhail Svetlov, Konstantin Simonov, Alexander Tvardovsky, Mikhail Sholokhov, and others.

When the guns speak, the Muses are silent. This proverb did not hold true. Thundering guns could not muffle the Muses. This is particularly true of poetry, which flowered, gaining national recognition. It linked the soldier's and workman's inner world with his patriotic duty, making heroism in the name of the country the main criterion of moral purity and strength.

Poetry proved an effective, mobile and inspiring form of art—the poems and songs of Jambul, M. Issakovsky, G. Leonidze, V. Lebedev-Kumach, Y. Kolas, Y. Kupala, M. Rylsky, K. Simonov, A. Surkov, A. Tvardovsky, and many others. In the autumn of 1941 Nikolai Tikhonov wrote a poem about beleaguered Leningrad, entitled *Kirov Is With Us*. A. Prokofiev's poem *Russia*, P. Antokolsky's *Son*, P. Tychina's *Burial of a Friend*, A. Kuleshev's *Brigade Standard*, and Margarita Aliger's *Zoya* produced heroic images of men and women who did not hesitate to accept the enemy's challenge. In Aliger's poem, Zoya says before dying: "I shall die, but the truth will win!"

---

[1] *Sovietskaya pechat v tsifrakh (The Soviet Press in Figures)*, Moscow, 1948, p. 33.

In a poem, "If Your Home Is Dear to You", popular among Soviet armymen and officers, Simonov exhorts them to kill the fascists mercilessly.

Like many other poets in close touch with the men in the armed forces, Simonov knew how keenly they wanted lyrical poetry. And he produced it for them, elevating the personal and intimate to the highest rung of civic heroism. His "Wait for Me" became one of the most popular battle-line poems, because it was so true to life. In it the soldier addresses his girl with love and faith in her loyalty. Her patient waiting, he tells her, would save and sustain him in battle. This and many other front-line poems by Simonov, Surkov and Issakovsky, imbued with an ardent patriotism, assumed the dimensions of folklore. The songs by V. Lebedev-Kumach, above all his "Holy War", which epitomised the might of the Soviet people risen in battle against the black fascist horde, inspired men going over the top.

The poets showed that hatred of the enemy was in wartime an expression of genuine humanism. Take Simonov's splendid lines:

> We have in us a severe freedom:
> abandoning Mother to her tears,
> to buy immortality for the people
> by our own death.[1]

In the autumn of 1942 Alexander Tvardovsky began publishing chapter upon chapter of his brilliant poem, *Vasily Tyorkin*. The author describes how he wrote it in the grim surroundings of the war:

> Stealthily,
> In trenches, under flimsy roofs,
> On the road, just anyhow,
> Not getting off the wheels,
> In rain beneath the trenchcoat,
> Or, pulling off a glove,
> In wind, in freezing cold,
> I put down
> Lines that lived each by itself.[2]

---

[1] Konstantin Simonov, *Izbrannyie stikhi (Selected Verse)*, 1956, p. 70.
[2] Alexander Tvardovsky, *Stikhotvoreniya i poemy v dvukh tomakh (Verse and Poems in Two Volumes)*, Vol. 2, Moscow, 1957, p. 109.

Vasily Tyorkin is the composite image of the Soviet front-line soldier who treats his wartime trade as ordinary martial business. His daily labours are illumined by a lofty patriotic idea, that of defending the great gains of socialism from a ruthless enemy. Tyorkin's image has absorbed all the energy and dynamism of the nation's fight against fascism. He is the bearer of the finest Russian features, the embodiment of an ordinary man's quickness and strength. He has a clear mind, he is hearty, vivacious, the owner of a sound sense of humour, filled with warmth and a subtle sadness. Tyorkin is a patriot in the loftiest sense of the word. There is not a shadow of doubt in his mind that victory awaits him at the end of the road.

Referring to a difficult river crossing, effected by every available, mostly makeshift, means, Tvardovsky writes:

> Crossings, crossings!
> Guns roaring in the blackest dark,
> A battle raging, right and holy,
> A mortal battle not for glory,
> But that life prevail on earth.[1]

Tyorkin, like other composite heroes, stood beside the real heroes glorified by the Soviet writers. Literature's outstanding merit was that it described the soldiers' exploits, popularised them, made them known to the entire nation. And thus, many of the exploits were repeated by others, emulated even, a thousandfold. The partisan girl Zoya Kosmodemyanskaya, pilot Alexei Maresyev, battalion commander Bourdjan Momysh-Uly and infantryman Alexander Matrosov are for all time inscribed in the epic history of the war.

Besides describing the exploits of heroes, Soviet literature described the exploits of hero-cities. Olga Bergholtz, Vera Inber, Vsevolod Vishnevsky, Vera Ketlinskaya, Nikolai Tikhonov and others dedicated their inspiration to the tragic story of beleaguered Leningrad.

Bergholtz wrote that she found her poetic happiness, the happiness of a citizen, in her involvement in the heroic story of Leningrad, in the battle for which she conceived herself as a soldier of the ranks:

---

[1] *Ibid.*, p. 113.

> *I am happy,*
> *And feel more clearly*
> *That I have always lived for this,*
> *For this embittering bloom.*
> *I make no secret of the pride I feel*
> *Of entering as a private your story,*
> *Leningrad mine,*
> *In the rank of poet.*[1]

To the garrison of Hanko Peninsula (Soviet military base in the south-west of Finland) M. Dudin dedicated his poetry, while V. Grossman, M. Lukonin, V. Nekrasov, K. Simonov, and many others, wrote about the epic of Stalingrad.

Soviet wartime prose developed somewhat later than poetry, somewhere in the summer of 1942 — such outstanding works as Sholokhov's *Science of Hatred*, Simonov's play *Russian People*, Grossman's novel *Nation Immortal*, Wanda Wasilewska's *Rainbow*, Leonid Leonov's *Invasion*, A. Korneichuk's *Front*, V. Kozhevnikov's short story *March, April*, etc. Many had elements of a popular epic. Great vitality abounded even in passages describing the death of men, whose courage defied the grave.

Grossman's *Nation Immortal* contains the following lines: "The men died. Who will tell of their brave deeds? Only the swift clouds saw how Private Ryabokon fought to the last cartridge; how Political Officer Yeretik, after filling a dozen of the enemy, blew himself up with a fast cooling hand; how Red Army man Glushko, surrounded by the Germans, fired to his last breath; how machine-gunners Glagolyev and Kordakhin, faint with loss of blood, fought as long as their weakening fingers could press the trigger, as long as their dimming eyes could see the target through the sultry haze of the battle.

"Great indeed is the people whose sons die so nobly, simply and grimly on the vast fields of battle. The sky and the stars know of them; the earth heard their last sighs; the unreaped rye and the wayside groves have seen their feats of valour."[2]

M. Sholokhov's novel, *They Fought for Their Country*, portrayed Communists imbued with a courage that vanquished death. These soldiers were deeply conscious that

---

[1] Olga Bergholtz, *Izbrannoye (Selections)*, Moscow, 1948, p. 142.
[2] V. Grossman, *The Years of War*, Moscow, 1946, pp. 87-88.

their personal fate was part of the fate of the socialist country, and in this spirit, by their own example, they inspired the men and officers around them. Even badly wounded, they stayed in the line. Communist Streltsov, a private, says to his friend Lopakhin: "Even deaf one can fight on alongside one's comrades."[1]

In the story, "Science of Hatred", Sholokhov describes Communist dedication as the strongest moral and ideological support a man can have in face of mortal danger to himself and his country.

Many other works portray war heroes: Alexei Tolstoy's *The Russian Character*, Leonid Sobolev's *A Seaman's Soul*, Sergeyev-Tsensky's *In the Snows*, and Konstantin Simonov's *The Days and the Nights*.

Alexander Bek's novel, *Volokolamsk Highway*, depicts the arduous moulding of soldiers out of men who had never handled weapons in peacetime. These men, driven by the compulsion of defending their country, hating the enemy, men who had learnt the enemy's strength and weaknesses, rapidly developed into a powerful force that crushed Hitler's war machine. Bek's book portrays the friendship of the peoples of the USSR, stressing their unity. It depicts the challenges faced by officers and political officers, showing their role in training and educating the ranks.

Many of the Soviet novels show the suffering of people fallen into nazi slavery. That is the topic to which Wanda Wasilewska dedicated her novel *Rainbow*. She shows the loyalty of people in nazi-occupied areas to Soviet power, the unbending force that fired them. Also she brings home the immeasurable superiority of Soviet morale and spirit.

Alexander Fadeyev's novel, *The Young Guard*, completed at war's end, was based on a true story—the exploits and tragic end of an underground Komsomol organisation in nazi-occupied Krasnodon, a miner's town. Forcefully, the novel reveals the sources of the heroism which moved people of different generations. Like many other novels written in wartime, *The Young Guard* shows how much the Communist Party had done to cultivate patriotism and heroism among the people.

Led by the Party, the writers dedicated their finest lines to it.

---

[1] M. Sholokhov, *Oni srazhalis za Rodinu (They Fought for Their Country)*, Moscow, 1964, p. 6.

A new topic appeared in Soviet literature at the end of the war: the soldier whom the fortune of war had taken far from his homeland, dreams of the homecoming. This is the theme of M. I. Blanter's song, with lyrics by M. V. Issakovsky, "Under the Balkan Stars":

> *Under the Balkan stars*
> *I recall with reason deep*
> *All the splendid spots of Bryansk,*
> *Yaroslavl, and places in Smolensk.*

Composers produced patriotic music of different kinds. Songs sung by millions of soldiers, cherished by them as expressive of their own feelings, were highly popular. Dmitry Shostakovich's Seventh Symphony, composed in embattled Leningrad, was an outstanding work. It was dedicated to the Hero-city and the impending victory. The music depicted the invasion, the brutality of the fascists, the struggle unto death, and the final victory over fascism, the great triumph of freedom-loving mankind. By writing the symphony in a besieged city the composer himself performed a heroic feat. Small wonder that this opus became known in all countries and was soon performed by the world's finest symphony orchestras.

Soviet artists joined in the fight against fascism. Many of them concentrated on posters and cartoons. Among these were V. Goryayev, P. Denisovsky, S. Kostin, Kukryniksy (composite name for M. V. Kupriyanov, P. N. Krylov, and N. A. Sokolov), N. Radlov, G. Savitsky, P. Sokolov-Skalya, M. Cheremnykh, D. Shmarinov, P. Shukhmin. The first war poster, "Smash and Destroy the Enemy Without Mercy!" by Kukryniksy, came off the presses on June 23, 1941, two days after the nazi assault. The poster depicted a Red Army man piercing Hitler with his bayonet. Hitler's portrait is vile and rat-like, and beside him lies the torn-up non-aggression treaty with the discarded mask of peace. N. Zhukov's poster, "Bash the Life Out of Them!", the poster "He Who Draweth the Sword Shall Perish by the Sword!" by V. Ivanov and O. Burovaya, and V. Koretsky's "Red Armyman, Help!" were known throughout the country.

In their wartime paintings, artists portrayed the brutal essence of fascism and its doom, contrasting the aggressor's cruelty with the lofty moral strength of Soviet people, their

More atrocities!

Zoya Kosmodemyanskaya, tortured to death by the hitlerites

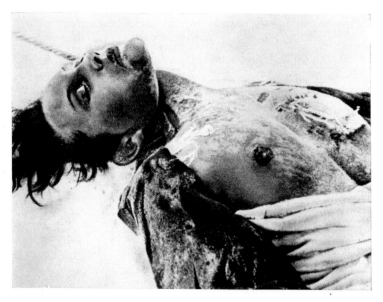

Besieged Leningrad

Soviet troops are launching an offensive near Moscow

The offensive is developing (summer 1942)

Crossing the Volga to bring relief to Stalingrad

The defence of Stalingrad

German prisoners of war taken at Stalingrad

The Kursk Battle. Soviet troops have assumed the offensive

Forcing the Dnieper

They left nazi slavery behind

After a sortie

Youngsters assembling mines

V. A. Degtyaryov, firearm designer

Girls doing their bit

The "*Tambovsky Kolkhoznik*" tank column

The battle field at Korsun-Shevchenkovsky

Soviet troops in Botoshani (Rumania)

Soviet troops in Bucharest

In one of the many nazi death camps (Kluga, Estonia)

Soviet troops in Belgrade

Field-Marshal Paulus signing the proclamation of the National Committee of Free Germany to the German people

The Yalta Summit

Soviet troops battling in Königsberg

A partisan stronghold

No rare occurrence this

Returning from a mission

A partisan detachment in the Crimea

Odessa partisans leaving the catacombs

humanism, in the name of which they had risen to a man to resist the enemy.

In A. A. Plastov's painting, "The Fascist's Been Here", is shown the tail of a German plane, whose flyer had just committed senseless murder: a little boy, a collective-farm shepherd, is shown sprawled on pale red autumn grass, his dog howling at the departing plane. The picture, profoundly humanistic, is full of scorn for the murderer. A hand to hand fight between seamen and infantrymen and the beast-like nazis is the theme of A. A. Deineka's "Defence of Sevastopol". Another painting by the same artist, "Moscow Outskirts, November 1941", depicts the firm determination of the people to defend their capital. Anti-tank "hedgehogs" are dug into the ground, the houses, ready for battle, look out with empty windows upon empty streets, along which a military truck passes, probably after delivering a supply of arms. Ye. Ye. Lansere produced a series of five paintings, "The Trophies of Russian Arms", in which, delving into history, he asserts the patriotic inevitability of Soviet victory.

S. V. Gerasimov's "A Partisan's Mother" rouses deep emotion. Fascist executioners are doing their dirty work in a village square, the corpses of people they have put to death lie on the ground, the flames of fire light the skies, while fresh victims are being brought to be executed. A plain Soviet woman stands before the fascist officer wearing an Iron Cross and holding a whip. Her visage and figure speak of fortitude, of moral superiority, of deep courage.

Kukryniksy produced a number of paintings, too. One of them, "Tanya", is dedicated to the exploit of a courageous partisan girl. In a painting called "Fascists Flee from Novgorod" fascist firebrands scurry back and forth against the setting of an old Russian cathedral church, and retribution is sure to overcome them. That, indeed, is the meaning of the raised arm of one of the figures of the monument, "Thousand Years of Russia", which the nazis had dragged off its base. T. G. Gaponenko's "After the Expulsion of the Fascist Invaders", is similar in theme and expressiveness of grief over the tragically killed. G. G. Nissky's "Hurrying to the Defence of the Moscow-Leningrad Highway", is documentary.

Soviet portrait painters produced a gallery of never-to-be-forgotten heroes—General I. V. Panfilov (by V. N. Yakovlev), partisan commander S. A. Kovpak (by A. A. Shovkunenko),

Colonel B. A. Yusupov (sculpture by V. I. Mukhina), Zoya Kosmodemyanskaya (sculpture by M. G. Manizer), Twice Hero of the Soviet Union Major M. G. Gareyev (painting by N. V. Tomsky) and General I. D. Chernyakhovsky (by the same artist), and many others. The portraits convey the lofty morality and fortitude of Soviet people defending their country.

The artists of encircled Leningrad did not lay down their arms either. In January 1942 they organised the exhibition, "Leningrad of the Time of the Patriotic War". In the hall where the paintings were shown the temperature was never above 10° C; its organisers and participants could barely move around, due to undernourishment. Yet they remained active.

Newsreel cameramen were with the army from the beginning—making their arduous way from the western frontiers of the USSR, to the banks of the Volga and then back from the Volga to Berlin and the Elbe. Many of them lost their lives. Their total performance amounted to over 3,500,000 metres of film, recording events that have gone down in history. The film is of incalculable value and is often used these days by scenario writers and film directors. All in all, 500 newsreels, 67 war documentaries and 34 feature films were put out and screened.[1]

The war was not yet over when full-length documentaries were pieced together from the materials of front-line cameramen. The film, *Defeat of German Troops at Moscow* (directors L. Varlamov and I. Kopalin) was screened soon after the historic battle, on February 18, 1942. Another documentary, *Fighting Leningrad* (directors R. Karmen, N. Komarevtsev, V. Solovtsov and Y. Uchitel) appeared soon after. On June 13, 1942, 240 cameramen in 40 rear locations and along the entire front from the White to the Black seas shot the film, *A War's Day*. The full-length documentary, *Stalingrad*, appeared in March 1943. It was shot by front-line cameramen during the battles in the Hero-city. Shown at home and abroad, the film staggered viewers by its stark reality. A US newspaper wrote: This film "is the absolute peak in documentary cinematography. No other picture could convey so

---

[1] I. G. Bolshakov, *Sovietskoye kinoiskusstvo v gody Velikoi Otechestvennoi voiny (Soviet Cinematography During the Great Patriotic War)*, Moscow, 1950, pp. 143-44.

forcefully and lucidly the destructiveness of war. The film has nothing to equal it in portraying fighting Russia."[1]

A series of films followed, showing the successive Soviet offensives, crowned by two films, the titles of which speak for themselves: *Berlin* (directors Y. Raizman and Y. Svilova) and *The Defeat of Japan* (directors A. Zarkhi and I. Kheifets). I. G. Bolshakov, head of the wartime Committee for Cinematography, commented: "Many of these films were novel in approach, and strikingly expressive. They were evidence of the high professional skill of the cameramen and had good texts and excellent musical settings. In other words all the components of a documentary—the editing, photography, text and music—were novel and of a high standard. The documentary legitimately ranked as high as a feature film for its politico-ideological and educational impact. The Soviet documentary cameramen did much to elevate the documentary cinema to the level of feature cinematography."[2]

Many documentary reels were brought back by intrepid cameramen from partisan encampments and the Resistance groups abroad. Among them was a film by Sergei Yutkevich, *Liberated France*.

It was hard to produce full length features about the war soon after it broke out. Instead, the film people resorted to short cine-novels. These, which also included comedies, were then shown together in "war programmes". In 1941 and 1942 as many as 12 such programmes were screened, their success stemming from the fact that they were based on true war episodes.

War programme No. 6 (director V. Pudovkin) contains a novel entitled *The Feast in Zhirmunka*, which tells the story of an old farm woman, Praskovya. A group of hungry nazis broke into her little house. They wanted her to feed them. Praskovya decides to do her bit in the war, to poison the two-legged animals, but the nazis are cautious. They want Praskovya to eat the food first. And she does not hesitate. Then the nazis eat, while Praskovya goes to the pantry, where, overcome by the poison, she dies. So do the fascists. When partisans come to the village they see the finale. "Quiet, there, hold your mouths," says Onisim, Praskovya's husband,

---

[1] *Ibid.*, p. 149.
[2] *Ibid.*, pp. 164-65.

to the partisans, when he finds the body of his wife. "There's a lioness here. Dead, but she defended her den to the last."[1]

Among the first wartime feature films, *Secretary of the District Party Committee* by I. Pyriev won immediate acclaim. It showed the underground in nazi-occupied territory, depicting the work of the District Party Committee Secretary and the Party branch. The same subject, that of Soviet heroism, of the gallant struggle fought in occupied territory by Soviet people, is treated in another picture — F. Ermler's *She Defends Her Country*. V. Vanin, who played the Secretary in Pyriev's picture, created the image of a Party functionary embodying the will and wisdom of the Party, whereas in *She Defends Her Country* Vera Maretskaya created the unforgettable image of a woman partisan. M. Donskoi's *Rainbow* also portrayed the life and struggle of Soviet people in the enemy rear, while L. Lukov's *Two Soldiers* was dedicated to the friendship of the fighting men.

Heroism is distinctly the dominant theme of the wartime Soviet films. The topic is treated from different angles in L. Armshtam's *Zoya*, V. Eisimont's *There Was a Girl*, M. Romm's *Human Being 217*, A. Romm's *Invasion*, L. Lukov's *It Happened in Donbas*, A. Stolper's and B. Ivanov's *Wait for Me*, Yu. Raizman's *The Sky Over Moscow*, I. Savchenko's *Ivan Nikulin, Russian Sailor*, I. Pyriev's *At 6 p.m. After the War*, and others.

There were also pictures about heroism in the rear. That particular chapter was treated in much the same vein as in wartime literature and art.

Truthfulness is the most forceful element of Soviet wartime art. This was noted by Georges Charensol, the French cinema critic, who wrote in 1945: "The Russians have done what neither the Americans nor the French had yet accomplished: they jettisoned the fake war films that inundated the cinema world. Films made in the USSR in these three past years are incontestably a distinct break from the sentimental and moralising, intellectual or vaudevillesque stereotypes that pervade the cinema.... America and Europe are making war films. Russia is farthest from the thought. What the Soviet cinema shows is the daily life of people whose thoughts and deeds are centred on one thing: to chase out the Germans

---

[1] *Soviet Cinematography During the Great Patriotic War*, p. 17.

and to avenge the suffering they have caused. These images ... express the intrinsic reality."[1]

Beyond question, the Soviet cinema, like the other arts, contributed to the victory. Like the rest of the nation, the writers, composers and artists were part of the war effort throughout the war. As the Danish writer Martin Andersen Nexö put it, they were "forces of action, militant forces.... Soviet literature and art did much to bring closer the victory of democracy throughout the world".[2]

The arts helped the Soviet people to defeat Hitler Germany and her allies in battle and economically. Their works cultivated lofty principles, a dauntless heroism, moral purity and endless loyalty to the Soviet Union.

The war effort in the Soviet rear was evidence of the unity of front and rear, of the concern shown by the Soviet people for their Red Army and of the rear's importance to victory. This joint action in the battle-lines and in the rear exemplified the decisive and creative role of the masses in making history.

The unity was expressed in the great moral fortitude of all Soviet people, in their readiness to sacrifice, their love of country, their solidarity and team spirit. The selfless labour of workers, farmers and intellectuals testified to the nation's unity, the unity of front and rear, without which victory would have been inconceivable.

The Soviet people showed their concern for the Armed Forces in many different ways. In the early months of the war, when the consumer industries had not yet gone over to wartime production, people collected warm clothes for gift parcels to soldiers in the battle-lines, millions of parcels containing *valenki* (felt boots) and sheepskins.

At the height of the battle for Stalingrad, in the autumn of 1942 members of the Krasny Dobrovolets Collective Farm, Tambov Region, called on all Soviet people to join them in collecting funds to build a tank column for the Red Army. The people in the region, who hailed this initiative, collected 43 million rubles in a fortnight.[3] In mid-December the tanks, each inscribed, "Tambovsky kolkhoznik", went into action.

Funds were collected throughout the country. Ferapont

[1] Georges Sadoul, *Histoire générale du cinéma,* Vol. VI, Paris, 1954, p. 145.
[2] *Sovietskoye iskusstvo,* Dec. 19, 1944.
[3] *I.V.O.V.S.S.,* Vol. 3, p. 201.

Golovaty, a Saratov farmer, was the first to initiate individual contributions to the Red Army Fund, donating 100,000 rubles out of his savings to build warplanes. Sakhanov, a farmer of Buryat-Mongolia, contributed 190,000 rubles, while Kubegenov, chairman of a collective farm in Omsk Region, contributed 206,000 rubles and 0.8 ton of flour. In February 1943 the men of an air regiment received a plane, bearing the legend: "From Lenochka for Father", built at the request of Lena Azarenkova, a Moscow schoolgirl who made the first contribution to the plane fund.

The patriotic initiative of the Tambov collective farmers thus grew into a powerful movement in which all towns and districts of the country, all sections of Soviet society, took part. Tanks and planes with varying inscriptions, such as "Moskovsky kolkhoznik" (Moscow Collective Farmer), "Ryazansky kolkhoznik" (Ryazan Collective Farmer), "From the Uzbek people", etc., arrived in the battle-lines and were fondly accepted by the army.

A new type of movement sprang up in February 1943. Volunteer units were fully equipped and armed on funds collected by people of a region. The first to come to the front was the Urals Volunteer Tank Corps, consisting of the best Ural workers, with equipment and arms—from shirt button to heavy tank—made in Urals factories after working hours and acquired on money collected from citizens. The corps was followed by the Special Siberian Rifle Corps, and after Krasnodar Territory was cleared of the enemy, its people helped activate the Krasnodar Infantry Division.

All in all, the people contributed as much as 94,500 million rubles for the front during the war years. Not only did this mean train replacements, first-class arms, ammunition and food supplies; it also lifted the morale of the troops. Countless letters sent to the front contained workers' accounts about their life and labour effort, inspiring the soldiers in their exploit. Soldiers, too, wrote back home, describing the battles. The front and rear were thus parts of a single whole.

In November 1967 Leonid Brezhnev, General Secretary of the CPSU Central Committee, said: "The front and rear formed a single mighty fist. The country became a single military camp. It was difficult for everybody. People were undernourished and did not get enough sleep. Women took the place of their husbands in the workshops and children took over machine-tools from their fathers. But the industrial heart of the Motherland never missed a beat. Our factories gave the Soviet Army the weapons to crush the military machine of Hitlerism which had behind it the industrial might of almost the whole of Europe. Despite the acute shortage of manpower and farm machines and despite the drastic reduction of the crop area our collective and state farms gave the country the food it needed for victory. It was a civic and patriotic feat of the people. It was a feat performed by people who saw the meaning of their life in labour for the sake of victory. And they did everything to ensure victory."[1]

[1] *Fifty Years of Great Achievements of Socialism*, Novosti Press Agency Publishing House, Moscow, 1967, pp. 28-29.

Chapter Six

Retribution

1. He Who Draweth the Sword, Shall Perish By the Sword

In 1944 and the spring of 1945 the Soviet Armed Forces carried out a series of brilliant offensive operations to complete the defeat of Hitler Germany. All Germany's satellites laid down their arms. Soviet territory was completely cleared of the enemy, and so were many adjoining countries. The long-awaited peace came to nazi-ravaged Europe.

By the beginning of 1944 the Soviet-German Front stretched from the Barents Sea along the river Svir to Lake Ilmen, then west of Velikiye Luki, east of Vitebsk and Orsha, west of Gomel and farther on from Kanev through Zhitomir, Cherkassy, Zaporozhye and Kherson to the Black Sea. The Crimea was still held by the enemy. As before, Germany's main forces were committed along the Eastern Front, consisting of 236 divisions, including 25 panzer and 8 motorised, and 18 brigades. Of this total, 38 divisions and 12 brigades were troops of the satellite countries. The total strength was 4,906,000, with 54,570 guns and mortars, 5,400 tanks and self-propelled guns, and 3,073 planes. Soviet strength was 5,568,000, with 92,650 guns and mortars, 5,357 tanks and self-propelled guns, and 8,506 planes.[1]

The advancing Red Army was only slightly superior in numbers. Success, therefore, depended chiefly on superior warcraft. Numerical superiority was achieved by skilful manoeuvres, regrouping forces and massing them in narrow sectors, with non-active sectors giving up part of their strength for this purpose.

---

[1] *I.V.O.V.S.S.*, Vol. 4, pp. 20-21.

Planning the 1944 operations, the Soviet Supreme Command took account of the existing situation and mounted the offensive with all the ten fronts (army groups) operating on a long line of more than 2,500 km, from Leningrad to the Black Sea in succession, not simultaneously. Having a single operational aim, these operations were to break up the front sector by sector in considerable depth, committing troops from other fronts to reinforce the assault group. The enemy's acute shortage of manpower was taken into account, and his transport difficulties were fully exploited.

"The realities of the war," wrote General S. M. Shtemenko[1] in his memoirs, "compelled us to abandon simultaneous offensives in favour of powerful consecutive operations or, as we used to say and write in those days, strategic blows which would be more suited to the new situation." In other words, the Soviet Command opted for a system of alternate strikes, and if the Germans had guessed the secret, it would have been in difficulties. But ingenious tactics were adopted to cover the assault preparations and assure the surprise element.

In January-February 1944 a large offensive was mounted near Leningrad and Novgorod with the purpose of fully relieving Leningrad. Though disrupted a year earlier, the enemy blockade had in a way continued, with barbarous artillery bombardments harassing the city population. The destruction of the strong enemy strategic group on the northern flank of the Soviet-German Front was to spark drives all along the line.

The Leningrad, Volkhov and 2nd Baltic Fronts were pitted against the nazi Army Group North and a Finnish operational group, "Karelian Isthmus". Running through woods and swamps, the enemy defences were well equipped, well built and well echeloned (230-260 km in depth).

With Baltic Fleet warships taking part, the offensive jumped off on January 14, 1944. The enemy resisted fanatically. Not until the fourth day did the Red Army manage to breach the German tactical defence zone, smashing its powerful fortifications. Troops of the Leningrad Front tore through the enemy armies, while Volkhov Front units surrounded and destroyed a large nazi force and took Novgorod. On January 21, the offensive got moving along the

[1] S. M. Shtemenko, *The Soviet General Staff at War (1941-1945)*, Moscow, 1970, p.199.

entire front from the Bay of Finland to Lake Ilmen. The army co-operated closely with the Navy and the local partisans, who in the first six weeks of the offensive blew up more than 58,000 rails and 300 bridges, destroying 133 nazi troop trains.[1]

The offensive did not cease until the end of February, when the German fascist armies had been flung back 220-280 km from Leningrad, with the major part of Leningrad Region cleared of the enemy. The powerful enemy fortified defences, known as the "Northern Wall", were torn down. Three enemy divisions were totally wiped out and 23 partly destroyed. This was the culmination of the Leningrad exploit, the siege that had lasted 900 days and nights. Then followed the liberation of Soviet Estonia.

Beginning with the end of December 1943 the troops of the four Ukrainian fronts, and then those of the 2nd Byelorussian Front, mounted a series of related operations in the Ukraine west of the Dnieper against a large force of 93 divisions, including 18 panzer and four motorised, and two brigades, and cleared the Crimea, smashing eight infantry and two cavalry divisions.[2]

In January and February 1944, Soviet thrusts cleared Zhitomir, Berdichev, Kirovograd, Korsun-Shevchenkovsky, Rovno, Lutsk, Nikopol and Krivoi Rog. The partisan support was highly effective, with partisans capturing towns and villages on their own. In the Korsun-Shevchenkovsky area troops of the 1st and 2nd Ukrainian fronts surrounded ten enemy divisions and one brigade. These were wiped out. Thus, the nazis were pushed away from the middle reaches of the Dnieper, which drew a line through the German plan of restoring the defence along the river bank.

The 1st Ukrainian Front routed German troops at Rovno and Lutsk, enveloping the flanks of Army Group South. In the Nikopol-Krivoi Rog operation, the 3rd and 4th Ukrainian Fronts smashed a large nazi force in heavy fighting that lasted all February, eliminating an enemy bridgehead on the east bank of the Dnieper south of Nikopol. All this favoured a Soviet drive towards the cities of Nikolayev and Odessa.

The next stage of the Soviet offensive in the Ukraine began

---

[1] P. Sheverdalkin, *Geroicheskaya borba leningradskikh partizan (The Heroic Struggle of the Leningrad Partisans)*, Leningrad, 1959, p. 274.
[2] *I.V.O.V.S.S.*, Vol. 4, p. 57.

with a simultaneous lunge by all the four fronts west of the Dnieper—the 1st, 2nd and 3rd Ukrainian, and the 2nd Byelorussian. First came the Proskurov-Chernovtsy operation, and on its heels the Uman-Botoshany and Bereznegovataya-Snigiryovka.

The nazis were pushed across the Dniester to the Carpathian foothills, the Soviet Army reaching the border of Czechoslovakia and Rumania along a more than 200-km frontage, after which the 2nd Ukrainian Front drove ahead into Rumanian territory.

The regrouping of many partisan units west of the Dnieper, effected before the operations were mounted, coupled with the quickly growing partisan movement in that part of the Ukraine, were of immense help. Co-operating closely with the Soviet troops, the partisans hit out with devastating effect behind the enemy lines.

The Soviet offensive was on a giant scale, along a 1,400-km frontage and some 500 km in depth. As a result, with the Ukraine west of the Dnieper completely cleared of the enemy, 66 nazi divisions were routed.

With the Red Army driving into Rumanian territory, the Soviet Government on April 2, 1944 issued a statement that it would pursue the enemy until total defeat and surrender. It stressed that it had no intention of acquiring any part of Rumania or of changing the existing social system, pointing out that the Soviet drive was motivated exclusively by the exigencies of the war and the enemy's continued resistance. The statement said the Red Army would continue its drive west until the aims of the just war of liberation were totally attained.[1]

The Red Army's entry into neighbouring countries was an important political and military development, dispelling the nazi hope, and that of reactionaries in other countries, that the Soviet troops would terminate their drive west on reaching the frontier and would make no effort to crush nazism. Each metre of territory taken by the Red Army as it drove forward brought closer the destruction of fascism and the liberation of the peoples from German imperialist slavery, opening up for them welcome prospects of free, independent and democratic development.

---

[1] *Soviet Foreign Policy During the Great Patriotic War*, Russ. ed., Vol. II, p. 105.

It was the first time that foreign peoples had contacts with Soviet people, the Soviet soldiers, and they displayed trust and affection. The working people in foreign countries learned from their own experience of the fair and progressive foreign policy of the Soviet Communist Party, its national programme, its war aims and its sincere desire to liberate all peoples from foreign enslavement. The masses, headed by the working class and its vanguard, the Communist and Workers' Parties, redoubled their efforts to overthrow the fascist regimes in their countries, to regain independence, carry forward radical democratic reforms and assure a close alliance and friendship with the Soviet Union. People's democratic revolutions were about to take place in the nazi-occupied East and South-East European countries.

On April 8 the 4th Ukrainian Front moved to liberate the Crimea, co-operating with the Black Sea Fleet and the Crimean partisans. The drive developed at an extraordinary pace. It took the Soviet troops only a few days to reach the approaches to Sevastopol. Preparations were begun to assault the city, which Hitler intended to hold at any cost.

The storm of Sevastopol began on May 5-7. On May 7 the enemy was expelled from the Sapun-Gora, the key to the city, and on May 9 the battle was over. Sevastopol was stormed by the enemy twice in its history—in the Crimean war of 1853-56, and again in 1942. On both occasions the battle lasted many months. Yet the Red Army expelled the enemy in a matter of days—a legendary and unparalleled exploit.

The results of the Soviet 1944 winter and spring offensive were impressive: 30 enemy divisions were wiped out and 142 badly battered, with nazi casualties exceeding one million. The enemy also lost vast quantities of arms.[1] Three-quarters of nazi-occupied Soviet territory was recaptured. Besides, the Red Army reached the Soviet frontier along a frontage of some 400 km. The Communist Party and Soviet Government worked out a plan to complete the defeat of the enemy and liberate the European peoples from the nazi occupation. For the Hitler Reich retribution was now close.

The nazi leaders dreaded the coming of the summer of 1944. They did not conceal their fears. But the facts were grimmer still than their nightmares.

The first of the Red Army summer offensives was mounted

---

[1] *I.V.O.V.S.S.*, Vol. 4, p. 102.

on the Karelian Isthmus and in South Karelia. The offensive began on June 21 and ended on August 29, with the Leningrad and Karelian Fronts aided by the Baltic Fleet and the Lake Ladoga and Lake Onega flotillas crushing the strongly fortified enemy, liberating most of the Karelo-Finnish Republic and all of the Leningrad Region. Hitler's Finnish ally was all but beaten. Soviet troops reached the Finnish frontier. The time had come to put Finland out of the war.

The Soviet operation distracted German attention from other sectors. The nazi generals expected the next Soviet stroke in the southwest. They did not think likely an assault on the powerful Army Group Centre of 63 divisions.[1] In fact, however, four Soviet fronts—the 1st, 2nd and 3rd Byelorussian and the 1st Baltic—had been priming since spring 1944 for the biggest offensive operation of the year in Byelorussia. At Stalin's suggestion it was given the code name of Bagration in tribute to the distinguished 1812 Patriotic War general.[2]

Considerable forces were deployed, totalling 166 divisions (numerically, however, the Soviet divisions were considerably smaller than the German). This produced a numerical advantage of 2:1.[3] In tanks and self-propelled artillery the advantage was 4.3:1 and in planes 4.5:1.[4] The effects of the Soviet economic victory, conclusively secured, were becoming obvious. Numerous Byelorussian partisan units co-operated closely with the advancing troops.

Success in the Byelorussian operation Bagration depended essentially on how well the jump-off could be concealed from the enemy. This was the biggest problem, for the forces involved were huge. The enemy had to be made to think that troops were being massed elsewhere along the front—in the north (the Baltic area) and the south. The commanders there were ordered to simulate arrivals of infantry divisions, backed by tanks and artillery.[5] The ruse worked: the nazi generals were convinced no offensive would be mounted in Byelorussia.

Secrecy was also secured by using the services of only a few people in the operational planning. Only five men knew the

[1] *Ibid.*, p. 157.
[2] S. M. Shtemenko, *op. cit.*, p. 235.
[3] *I.V.O.V.S.S.*, Vol. 4, pp. 163-64.
[4] *Ibid.*, p. 164.
[5] S. M. Shtemenko, *op. cit.*, pp. 231-32.

extent of the operation. All correspondence and all telephone and telegraph communications on the matter were prohibited. The strictest controls were established.

Operation Bagration went off to a start on June 23-24. In the first several days the Red Army surrounded and crushed the Vitebsk enemy group. Among the highlights of the thrust was the exploit of Engineer-Sergeant F. T. Blokhin, who, at a risk to his life, leaped on to the bridge across the Western Dvina and prevented its demolition by pulling out the detonator of an about-to-explode mine.

Simultaneously, Soviet troops lunged at and routed the Orsha group and invested a nazi force at Bobruisk. A tank crew under Lt. P. N. Rak raced across the Berezina River into Borisov during the fighting for that city, crossing a mined bridge that blew up seconds later. For 16 hours the crew battled the enemy alone in the city streets, bombarding the town *Kommandatur*, wiping out the headquarters of a German unit and throwing the fascist garrison into panic.

Minsk, the capital of Soviet Byelorussia, was liberated at dusk on July 3. East of the city 30 enemy divisions were tightly surrounded, with the mopping up taking nearly a week.

In a mere eleven days the Soviet Army smashed the main forces of Army Group Centre and liberated most of Byelorussia. The offensive was high-powered, with advances of 20 to 25 km being registered daily. Many villages, towns, even cities, were liberated by partisans—either on their own or in co-operation with the regular army.

The Lublin-Brest Operation by the 1st Byelorussian Front, July 18-August 29, 1944, was part of Bagration. On July 21 its troops arrived on the border with Poland. By then the Soviet-Polish frontier was also reached by troops of the 1st Ukrainian and 2nd Byelorussian Fronts. The Polish towns— Chelm, Lublin, and others—were liberated. The 1st Polish Army, activated in the USSR, fought splendidly beside the Soviet troops. Polish partisans, too, took part in the fighting. On July 31, 1st Byelorussian Front troops reached Praga, Warsaw's suburb across the Vistula, while more troops battle-crossed the Niemen to the frontier of Eastern Prussia.

Operation Bagration covered with new glory the hero of the 1812 War. It was titanic in scale, audacious in design and brilliant in execution. One stroke of immense force flung the enemy out of the Byelorussian Republic, driving far west and creating an immediate threat to Germany proper—a threat the German Command could no longer parry. The German defence system proved a total failure. It was clear that nothing on earth could now stem the Soviet offensive against the fascist Reich.

Army Group Centre was beaten to tatters. Seventeen divisions were completely wiped out and another 50 lost 60 to 70 per cent of their personnel.[1] Apart from Byelorussia, a large section of Soviet Lithuania was cleared. The impression in Germany was staggering. Hermann von Gackenholz, a West German war historian, writes: "The summer 1944 developments had a still greater impact (than the Stalingrad defeat—*Deborin*) on the general German war situation: the breakdown of Army Group Centre affected the entire German eastern front, enabling the Russian Command to drive the Germans back in the middle up to the Vistula and the borders of Eastern Prussia, to cut off the German forces in the Baltic countries and virtually eliminate the German positions in the Balkans militarily and politically."[2]

The nazi generals, officers and soldiers captured in the Byelorussian operation were shipped under guard via Moscow far behind the lines. German troops that had strained to enter Moscow did indeed pass through it—but under military guard. Jean-Richard Bloch, the French progressive writer, expressed the feelings of his brother Europeans on this score as follows: "I have just seen them—all 57,600 of them! The remnants of Army Group Centre—soldiers captured at Vitebsk, Bobruisk and Minsk. I, who had seen the Germans marching into our country and making themselves at home in our towns, was filled with indescribable joy.

"I was present at the crime and now relished the retribution.... Yes, my friends, these tens of thousands of Germans captured in the recent battles and marching through Moscow produced a striking, indescribable spectacle. The column of men shuffling past us in solemn silence was, in a way, a living symbol of the turning wheel of fortune that history will remember.

"But that turn of the wheel was not accidental. It was brought into motion by the mammoth energy of the Russians,

---

[1] *I.V.O.V.S.S.*, Vol. 4, p. 198.
[2] *Entscheidungsschlachten des zweiten Weltkrieges*, Frankfurt am Main, 1960, S. 474.

their marvellous perseverance, brilliant foresight and un-exampled will power."[1]

The Byelorussian Operation was timed to coincide with the opening of the second front in Europe by the Allies, showing that the Soviet people never failed to honour their international commitments. It enfeebled German strength even in the West and created a favourable situation for the Anglo-American landing in Northern France.

As for the retribution mentioned by Jean-Richard Bloch, it was hurtling down on Hitler Germany from land, sea and air.

2. Why the Second Front?

The second front in Europe was not opened when it should have been—not in 1941, and not in 1942. Nor was it opened in 1943, after the tide had been turned by the war effort of the Soviet people. Not until the war had, in effect, entered its final stage, not until it was clear that the Soviet Union could go it alone to final victory, liberating the peoples of Europe, were the British and US troops issued the order to land on the northern coast of France.

The blame for the deliberate delay may be laid at the door of British and US reactionary groups. To say the least, it was a crime against all nations that had risen to combat the fascist intruders, a crime, too, against the peoples of Britain and the United States. The nations paid heavily for it in lives and property.

Even in 1944, Winston Churchill still tried to postpone the invasion. He insisted on a large-scale offensive in Italy, though this augured few advantages from the point of view of shortening the war. Having begun in January, that offensive developed at a leisurely pace. Not until June 5 did British and US troops at last enter Rome, the Italian capital.

In the meantime, the international situation became less and less favourable for the imperialist policy-makers in the USA and Britain. To delay longer would have damaged their interests. Soviet prestige and the power of Soviet arms, bringing freedom to the European peoples, increased rapidly. The anti-fascist movement spread across most of the European

[1] Jean-Richard Bloch, *De la France trahie à la France en armes*. Commentaires à Radio-Moscou 1941-1944, Paris, 1949, pp. 430, 432, 433.

countries, including Germany. The fight in France under a progressive leadership gained in intensity as a direct consequence of the smashing Red Army victories. French patriots saw German divisions entraining eastward, never to return. The Communist Party of France called on the nation to prepare for a country-wide armed rising.

The freedom struggle of the French, gradually developing into a general armed rising against the German invader, alarmed reactionaries all over the world. The most inveterate opponents of a second front began urging haste.

Opening the front, the US and British rulers were above all pursuing their own imperialist aims, hoping to prevent Germany's total defeat, to save the reactionaries in Europe from total annihilation, to block democratisation in countries delivered from fascism and to raise a barrier to the Red Army's westward advance. Also, not forgetting their rivalry, the US and British imperialists were eager to occupy positions of advantage on the European continent.

General Omar Bradley, in command of US troops in Europe, described the aims of the Normandy landing thus: "To avoid chaos on the continent it would have been necessary for us to mount such forces as we had, cross the Channel at once, move on into Germany, disarm its troops, and seize control of the nation."[1]

There we have another of the Second World War riddles. On the one hand, the United States and Britain at last opened the second front (as part of joint action with the USSR against nazi Germany) and, on the other, the ruling groups in those two countries, scheming to turn that second front against the progressives, whose influence would certainly have been strong in Europe once fascism was flattened, strove to exploit fascism rather than destroy it. As part of this scheming, the British Government expanded its intelligence operations against the Soviet Union shortly before the Normandy landing. The job was assigned to the special British Intelligence Service Department dealing with Soviet affairs and the world communist movement, and better known as the anti-communist service. Heading that service from 1944 was Harold Adrian Russell Philby, third in line in the Intelligence Service and seen as likely to reach the top rung.[2]

---

[1] Omar N. Bradley, *A Soldier's Story*, New York, 1951, p. 199.
[2] *Izvestia*, December 18, 1967.

The true nature of Philby's work was one of the best-guarded secrets that imperialist intelligence could not break for decades. Philby, it turned out, was a convinced Communist. "You can imagine," he later said modestly, "what information I was able to send to Moscow."[1]

Never, therefore, were the true intentions and aims of the US and British rulers a total secret for the Soviet Union.

Operation Overlord, envisaging the invasion of Northern France, had long been ready. The priming for it had begun long before. The Commands did their utmost to keep it secret from the Germans until landing day in order to secure the surprise factor. But since the secret of the successive postponements of the second front between 1941 and 1943 was not well enough kept—who can tell whether deliberately or not—and the nazis knew of them through their agents, the latest date, too, leaked out.

Foreign Minister Anthony Eden briefed British diplomats abroad of the Teheran Conference decisions, including those on the second front. Hughe Knatchbull-Hugessen, the ambassador in Ankara, meanwhile, attached little importance to guarding war secrets and kept his confidential files in a black briefcase in his bedroom, where they were photographed by Elyasa Bazna, cover name Cicero, who was Knatchbull-Hugessen's butler and at the same time an agent of the nazi secret service. For his troubles, by the way, Cicero was paid in counterfeit pounds sterling. The details of the story were learned postwar from Bazna's own memoirs and those of the SS resident in Ankara, Ludwig Moyzisch. The affair was so utterly scandalous that it was raised in the House of Commons on October 18, 1950, with Foreign Minister Bevin admitting the facts, which, he begged, should not be taken too seriously, because the documents were only photographed, not stolen.[2]

There were other leaks. Shortly before the Normandy landing a parcel addressed to a woman residing in a Chicago quarter populated chiefly by Germans, was accidentally examined by the postal authorities. It was found to contain secret documents relating to Operation Overlord.[3]

But knowledge of Allied secrets no longer helped the

[1] *Izvestia*, December 18, 1967.
[2] *New Times*, No. 50, 1967, pp. 32-33.
[3] *Za rubezhom*, No. 30, 1966, pp. 18-19.

nazis when the Red Army mounted its Byelorussian operation. It kept the German forces engaged, and reinforcing garrisons in France was out of the question. Another factor favouring the Anglo-Americans was the Resistance Movement, highly active in France, Belgium and Italy. It created for the German forces no end of trouble, disrupting rear activity in the West.

German leaders had dreaded war on two fronts in Bismarck's time. And the First World War proved their fears well grounded. Hitler had gambled on the contradictions between the European powers, thinking he could divide them. But he could not escape the inevitable: the Third Reich was at last between hammer and anvil.

German troops deployed against the Allies in Northern France, Belgium and Holland comprised 45 divisions, including seven panzer and one motorised. The divisions were under-manned, with some 25 to 50 per cent numerically inferior to the Allied divisions. About half of them consisted of over-age personnel or boys of 17.[1] The German 3rd Air Fleet, stationed in Western Europe, had only 90 bombers and 70 fighters in operational condition out of a total of 500 aircraft,[2] and the nazi navy in the Atlantic, the North and Baltic seas had four battleships, seven cruisers and 419 submarines, of which 90 were training vessels.[3] Patrolling of the French coast was assigned to Naval Command West, which had a few destroyers and torpedo-boats, 30 motor torpedo-boats and 36 submarines.[4]

Allied forces standing by for the invasion consisted of 37 British and US divisions, including 10 tank divisions, and 12 brigades, plus one French and one Polish division. Allied planes totalled 11,000 combat planes, plus 2,300 transports and 2,600 gliders. The landing was supported by a fleet of 6 battleships, 2 monitors, 22 cruisers, 93 destroyers and other vessels, while the number of transport and landing vessels of all kinds exceeded 6,000.[5]

After a succession of fresh delays, this time due to objective difficulties, the invasion was at last set for June 6, 1944, jumping off at 01.30 hours under cover of darkness. Enemy

[1] *I.V.O.V.S.S.*, Vol. 4, p. 524.
[2] Hans Speidel, *Invasion 1944*, Chicago, 1950, p. 39.
[3] *Brassey's Naval Annual*, 1948, p. 376.
[4] *Weltkrieg 1939-1945*. Ehrenbuch der deutschen Wehrmacht, II. Teil, Stuttgart, 1954, S. 79.
[5] Dwight D. Eisenhower, *Crusade in Europe*, New York, 1948, p. 53.

resistance on land and in the air was negligible. In two days the US and British troops secured a bridgehead, which they methodically expanded.

When the landing began Eisenhower ordered the French population to cease fighting the Germans. But the French patriots ignored his demand. Their activity behind the nazi lines had contributed to the Anglo-American success, and even in the immediate vicinity of the landing area, partisans and franctireurs cleared the Germans out of 42 towns and hundreds of villages, helping the landing force to consolidate and develop its bridgehead.

French historian Pierre Montauban holds that if the partisans "had not sluiced off a considerable number of enemy troops, if they had not detained German reinforcements sent against the Anglo-American landing force, the Allies may have been flung back into the Sea."[1] Eisenhower, too, later admitted that the French patriots had done well. "Throughout France," he wrote, "the Free French had been of inestimable value to the campaign. They were particularly active in Brittany, but on every portion of the front we secured help from them in a multitude of ways. Without their great assistance the liberation of France and the defeat of the enemy in Western Europe would have consumed a much longer time and meant greater losses to ourselves"[2].

Despite the favourable situation, the Anglo-American forces advanced slowly—something like an average 4 km a day. This was because ruling quarters in the United States and Britain were in no hurry to build up large actions, not to impair too drastically German resistance to the Red Army offensive. Not until 90 days after the Normandy landing was the Allied bridgehead 100 km long and 30-50 km wide. On August 15 three US and seven French divisions landed in Southern France.

From their bridgehead in Northern France the Allied armies moved east on July 25, 1944, and in a month, helped by the partisans, cleared all north-western France, save a few port-towns in Brittany.

French resistance mounted. A countrywide armed rising against the occupation forces broke out. The insurrectionists relieved the cities of Lyons and Toulouse, 18 departments

---

[1] *Cahiers du communisme*, No. 8, 1950, p. 61.
[2] D. Eisenhower, *op. cit.*, p. 296.

south of the Loire and west of the Rhone, and the area from the Western Alps to the Italian and Swiss frontiers. Half a million men fought in the organised units of the French home guard, and at least another million participated in the national uprising. It was a mighty movement unmatched in French history. And it was headed by Communists.

The rising in Paris erupted on August 19 as the culmination of the struggle to liberate France. The Parisians suppressed the fairly large and well-equipped German garrison. The rising was headed by Henri Rol-Tanguy, a worker and Communist with combat experience in Spain. Actively involved was a group of Soviet war prisoners who had escaped from German concentration camps. They captured the building of the Soviet Embassy situated in the heart of the French capital and hoisted the Soviet flag.

By the evening of August 22, the insurrectionists had liberated 70 blocks of Paris. The German Command, infuriated though impotent, ordered the city's destruction. But the people frustrated the criminal plan. The main nazi forces in Paris were totally defeated in clashes on August 23 and 24. The final assault, ending in complete victory, began in the morning of August 25. A company of General Jacques Leclerc's 2nd Tank Division, operating with the Allied troops, participated. General Leclerc and Colonel Rol-Tanguy received the surrender of the remnants of the German garrison jointly—a gesture acknowledging the role played in liberating Paris by the workers and people of the capital.

US and British troops close to Paris offered no aid. General Omar Bradley notes: "We would ... enter it (Paris—Ed.) at our leisure.... I might just as well tell you we are not at all anxious to liberate Paris right now...." "It would be good if Paris could pull in its belt and live with the Germans a little longer...."[1] And another US general, George S. Patton, said: "I could have taken it had I not been told not to."[2]

The successful Paris rising spurred the Allied troops. French territory was soon cleared of the enemy and in September Anglo-American forces entered Belgium. Again, armed action by patriots, this time Belgian, was prominent. The Belgian partisans liberated a number of provinces and cities on their own, including Antwerp, enabling the Allies

[1] O. Bradley, op. cit., pp. 386-87.
[2] George S. Patton, War As I Knew It, Boston, 1947, p. 117.

to cross little Belgium without delay and approach the German frontier. The US and French forces of the 6th Allied Group of Armies reached the Rhine and in November 1944 captured the city of Strasbourg.

The second front had an unquestionably positive effect on the final outcome of the Second World War. Compressed between two fronts, Germany had not a glimmer of hope. Inexorably, retribution approached. Any other government but the gang of adventurers heading the country and ready to sacrifice millions of lives for their designs, would have recognised the futility of further resistance.

Once France was free, there arose the question of her place in the postwar world. The US and British governments held that she would not regain her great power status due to heavy war losses. The Soviet Union, on the other hand, was eager to help the French recover as an independent and sovereign power. Offering friendly aid and support, the Soviet people held that the USSR and France had the traditional common interest of preventing German aggression in Europe and safeguarding peace. To assist France, the Soviet Government invited French Government representatives to visit Moscow. A Soviet-French Treaty of Alliance and Mutual Assistance was concluded there on December 10, 1944, assuring France the friendship of the USSR in the difficult early postwar months. Thanks to this support, France regained her place among the great powers as reflected in the UN Charter and a series of Allied decisions concerning Germany.

3. Emergence of a New Poland

Nazi-occupied Poland had been made a territorial adjunct of fascist Germany. The Polish nation was doomed to annihilation. Hans Frank, Hitler's Governor-General in Poland, said so in so many words: "Henceforth, the political role of the Polish people is ended.... We shall see to it that the very concept of Poland should be eradicated once and for all. Never again will there be the Rzecz Pospolita or any other Polish state."[1] But in that, too, the nazi invaders were wide off the mark. They had not reckoned with the will of the peoples of the Soviet Union and Poland.

---

[1] *Istoriya Polshi (History of Poland)*, Moscow, Vol. III, 1958, p. 531.

As the Red Army drove closer to the Polish border, the partisan movement, especially in the Lublin area, gained in intensity. Now Frank changed his tune: "To all intents and purposes, almost one-third of the Lublin area is out of the control of the German administration. Neither the administration, nor the executive bodies are operative there—just the transport apparatus. In that territory the German police can act only in force, a force of not less than a regiment."[1] The Polish partisans fought hand in hand with Soviet partisans, who extended their field of operations to the fraternal country.

As part of the Byelorussian Operation, the Red Army entered Poland, enthusiastically welcomed by the population, which offered the Soviet troops every possible aid. The emergence of a new, people's democratic Poland impelled by the will of the Poles, was rapid.

On July 23, 1944, Chelm, a Polish town liberated by the Red Army, became the seat of the Polish Committee of National Liberation, the establishment of which, and the programme document, the Manifesto, was hailed by the masses. The Manifesto restored democratic freedoms throttled by the Pilsudski reactionaries before the war, paved the way for important social reforms, most prominently the land reform, and proclaimed close alliance and friendship with the Soviet Union. It said that with the delineation of the Soviet-Polish border Polish lands would henceforth be part of the Polish state, while Byelorussian, Ukrainian and Lithuanian areas would be incorporated in the respective Soviet Socialist Republics. Western lands, once seized by German conquerors, would be returned to Poland. The document opened a new chapter in the history of the Polish nation, raising the curtain on a new, genuinely popular state.

The 1st Polish Army activated in the USSR and the partisan Armia Ludowa merged in the Wojsko Polskie in June 1944 and by the end of the year grew into a force of 286,000 men equipped with the latest Soviet-supplied arms.[2]

The Soviet attitude to the emerging new Poland was set out in a special statement of July 26, 1944. It said that Soviet troops had entered Polish territory jointly with the Polish

---

[1] *I.V.O.V.S.S.*, Vol. 4, p. 232.
[2] *Boyevyie deistviya Voiska Polskogo 1943-1945* (*The Polish Army in Action 1943-1945*), Moscow, 1961, p. 32.

Army, thus beginning the liberation of the long-suffering fraternal nation. It stressed that the Soviet Army was determined "to smash the hostile German armies and help the Polish people to liberate itself from the yoke of the German invaders and to restore an independent, strong and democratic Poland".[1]

The Soviet Government said it regarded the military operations in Polish territory as operations in the territory of a sovereign, friendly and allied state and therefore had no intention of establishing there any of its own administrative bodies, leaving this to the Polish people. In line with this policy, the Soviet Union concluded an agreement with the Polish Committee of National Liberation governing relations between the Soviet Command and the Polish administration. A similar agreement was concluded with Czechoslovakia.

The Soviet Government said it regarded the military operations in Polish territory as operations in the territory of a sovereign, friendly and allied state and therefore had no intention of establishing there any of its own administrative bodies, leaving this to the Polish people. In line with this policy, the Soviet Union concluded an agreement with the Polish Committee of National Liberation governing relations between the Soviet Command and the Polish administration. A similar agreement was concluded with Czechoslovakia.

Referring to the joint Soviet-Polish operations during the Second World War, Wladyslaw Gomulka, First Secretary of the Polish United Workers' Party, said that "in the flames of this war, this life and death struggle, the comradeship of Polish and Soviet soldiers and of Polish and Soviet partisans cemented the Polish-Soviet alliance, spelling Poland's liberation from the bloodstained Hitler occupation".[2]

The governments of the United States and Britain looked askance at the constitution of the new People's Poland. They redoubled material and political aid to the anti-popular Mikolajczyk émigré Government and opened discussions with it of possible counter-action. "Political actions" were plotted, including the untimely Warsaw Uprising, doomed to failure before it began.

Although the uprising was against the German occupation

---

[1] *Soviet Foreign Policy During the Great, Patriotic War,* Russ. ed., Vol. II, p. 155.

[2] *Velikii Oktyabr i mirovoye revolyutsionnoye dvizheniye (The Great October and the World Revolutionary Movement),* Moscow, 1967, p. 369.

forces, its purpose was political. It was to show that the Polish émigré government was still influential in Poland, with the Polish reactionaries hoping to appear as national liberators and assume control over the national liberation movement. The reactionaries thought this would be best served by seizing control over Warsaw, if only for a few hours.

The Warsaw rising began on August 1, while the Red Army had not yet reached the Vistula anywhere close to the Polish capital, with only a minor bridgehead on the western bank south of Sandomir. Not until September 14-15 did Soviet troops, co-operating with the Polish 1st Army, liberate Praga, a Warsaw suburb on the eastern bank of the Vistula.

The uprising was started by the Armia Krajowa, which took orders from the émigré government. There were many genuine patriots among its men, thirsting to come to grips with the enemy, but unaware of the political aims of their leadership. Units of Armia Ludowa, led by the Left, were not even informed of preparations. The Armia Ludowa commanders rated the uprising as premature and reproved its organisers as people alien to the true interests of the nation. But there was no choice but to join the fighting; the city population, too, had taken up arms. The participation of the people of Warsaw in the general rising was evidence of their deep hatred of the fascist invaders and their desire to avenge the nazi atrocities.

The Soviet Government, belatedly informed of the rising, denounced it as "a reckless and fearful gamble".[1] However, it did its utmost to aid the rebellion and reduce human losses. Supplies were air-dropped regularly, with Soviet aircraft flying 2,243 supply missions between September 14 and October 1, parachuting large numbers of mortars, anti-tank guns, submachine-guns, rifles, grenades, cases of ammunition, food and medical supplies.[2]

Units of the Polish 1st Army, supported by artillery, air and engineers of the 1st Byelorussian Front, storm-crossed the Vistula during the night of September 15, with the Polish 3rd Infantry Division developing a narrow bridgehead, but failing to contact the insurrectionists and to widen its foothold due to superior enemy forces. Another reason for the failure was the reluctance of the leaders of the Warsaw rising to

[1] *Correspondence...*, Vol. I, p. 254.
[2] *I.V.O.V.S.S.*, Vol. 4, p. 246.

effect a junction and fight on jointly. After a week of costly fighting, the bridgehead had to be abandoned.

In the meantime, infuriated by the resistance of the Warsaw population, the nazis moved in large forces and began a methodical destruction of the city. They tied Polish children to their panzers as cover, or drove crowds of defence-less women before them. German engineers blew up house after house, and street after street.

More than 200,000 people, of whom the active insurrec-tionists comprised only a fragment, were killed; the entire city was all but razed to the ground. Those who escaped with their lives were shipped out.[1]

The losses could have been greater still if the Soviet troops had not rendered aid. Co-operating with Wojsko Polskie, the Red Army helped part of the insurgents and civilians to escape from embattled fire-engulfed Warsaw and cross to the eastern Vistula bank.

The Warsaw rising impaired still more the prestige of the Polish émigré. It became clear even to people ignorant of politics that the émigrés had been pursuing ends far removed from the needs and interests of the nation. The designs of Polish reaction and its protectors in the United States and Britain to re-establish a bourgeois-landlord regime, turning Poland into an anti-Soviet staging area, fell through completely. The people had the final say and made an unequivocal choice. Nothing could make them turn off the chosen road.

4. Explosion in the German General Headquarters

The disastrous 1944 defeats affected the situation inside Germany. The vast majority of Germans realised that the war had been lost, though the hitlerites tried to shore up the rear with reprisals and wholesale arrests and killings.

The Communist Party of Germany, led by a Central Committee based outside the country, conducted extensive work among the people despite the terrible losses. The main accent was on elucidating and disseminating the Manifesto of the Free Germany Committee founded on July 1-13, 1943 by German anti-fascists in the town of Krasnogorsk

---

[1] *Trybuna Ludu*, August 8, 1957.

near Moscow, with the well-known poet, Erich Weinert, elected its chairman.

A militant anti-fascist front of Communists, Social-Democrats and unaffiliated workers, farmers, intellectuals and servicemen evolved in Germany on the basis of the Manifesto. A confidential nazi journal circulated among top officials to brief them on home affairs, gave the following figures to illustrate the growth of the anti-fascist movement in Germany:

Active participants in underground anti-fascist activities detected and arrested in 1944 totalled 42,580 in January, 45,044 in February, 46,302 in March, 52,939 in April, 56,830 in May and 66,991 in June.[1]

Underground Communist groups were highly active, headed by courageous and dedicated fighters—metalworker Robert Uhrig, Albert Hössler, a veteran of the Spanish war, Anton Saefkow, former Communist Reichstag deputies Georg Schumann and Theodor Neubauer, Herbert Baum, a student, and many others. How active the groups were is illustrated by the fact that one of them, the Rote Kapelle, was found by the Gestapo to have had important contacts in the Aviation Ministry, High Command, Naval Headquarters, the ministries of economics, propaganda and foreign affairs, many educational establishments, research institutes and other organisations.[2]

Describing wartime Communist and anti-fascist activities, Wilhelm Pieck wrote: "During the darkest time of the nazi reign, too, the German Communists carried on…. The exploits of the German Communists added to the struggle of the anti-fascist and resistance fighters of many countries and saved the honour of the German working class and, at the same time, laid the first stones in the foundation for the friendly co-operation of the new, democratic Germany with other nations."[3]

Despite ferocious nazi reprisals, the Hitler dictatorship had become shaky. This the German imperialists realised clearly. The person of the Fuehrer, who had served monopoly capital assiduously for eleven years, became undesirable.

A section of the German monopolists decided that they would profit from Hitler's overthrow and thus salvage the

---

[1] *Die Lage*, July, August, September, 1944.
[2] *New Times*, No. 19, 1965, p. 30.
[3] *Pravda*, December 30, 1958.

fascist dictatorship. They plotted to kill the ringleader in the hope of saving the gang. Their aim: to set up a government less odious than that of the nazis and better able to bamboozle the masses to avert a revolutionary eruption. The new government would seek British and US protection in the event of such an eruption, while redoubling resistance to the Soviet offensive.

Since the future of German imperialism troubled certain forces in other countries, as well as its leading lights at home, the anti-Hitler conspirators who hoped to replace the dictator with some less discredited person encountered support among the rulers of the United States and Britain. A far-flung plot built up gradually. Its purpose, as the journal *Einheit*, the organ of the Socialist Unity Party of Germany, wrote shortly after the war, was nothing short of perfidious: "The conspiracy was motivated by the wish to salvage the militarist imperialist system, not by the wish to overthrow the fascist dictatorship and replace it with a democratic regime, and not by the wish to abandon the piratic war policy in favour of a policy of peace."[1]

The main organisers of Hitler's overthrow were the generals Ludwig von Beck and Erwin von Witzleben, the fascist government official Karl Goerdeler, and members of old-time Junker families, Helmuth Moltke and Fritz Schulenburg. They contacted the US and British governments through Allen Dulles, head of US intelligence in Europe, soliciting appropriate support. Briefing Washington on his negotiations with the conspirators, Dulles wrote:

"...The men who plan the proposed overthrow are of a somewhat conservative makeup, though they would work with any available leftist elements other than Communists. The principal motive for their action is the ardent desire to prevent Central Europe from coming ideologically and factually under the control of Russia."[2]

In his next coded message he pointed out that "the essence of the plan was that the anti-nazi generals would open the way for American and British troops to occupy Germany while the Russians were held on the Eastern front".[3]

Not all members of the conspiracy shared these motives of its organisers. Some were patriots sincerely moved by

[1] *Einheit*, No. 12, 1947, S. 1173.
[2] Allen Welsh Dulles, *Germany's Underground,* New York, 1947, p. 136.
[3] *Ibid.,* p. 139.

the interest of the German people; they displayed a high degree of personal courage. This applies to Colonel Klaus von Stauffenberg, the most determined and courageous of the plotters, Oberleutnant Werner von Haeften, Colonel Merz Quirnheim, and the Social-Democrats Julius Leber and Adolf Reichwein, the latter two obtaining Stauffenberg's approval to contact the leaders of underground communist groups of Anton Saefkow and Franz Jacob.

Stauffenberg undertook to execute Hitler. When fighting in Tunisia he had lost his right arm, three fingers on his left hand, and one eye. Yet according to the plan the threads of the conspiracy ran to Stauffenberg's one and only, almost fingerless, hand. On July 20, 1944, he brought a large brief-case containing a bomb into General Headquarters of Germany's Armed Forces in Rastenburg, known as Wolf-schanze, and put it under the table on the floor near Hitler's legs. Then, on the excuse of an urgent telephone call, he left the conference-room. General Heusinger, Chief of Operations, who had meanwhile begun the situation report, had time enough to say: "The Russians are moving with strong power west of the Duna toward Norden. Their forward point is already southeast of Dunaburg. If now finally the army group is not withdrawn from Peipussee, then a catas-trophe will…".[1] At this instant the bomb exploded. There were some dead and wounded, but Hitler escaped with a few bruises, and lost no time in venting his fury.

The conspiracy collapsed for reasons more profound and serious than the failure of the assassination attempt. To begin with, the conspirators had no ties with the people, while the main organisers were even hostile to the masses. This alone was enough to presage failure. Furthermore, the plan of shor-ing up the fascist regime by replacing the dictator was hard to execute against the setting of the powerful Red Army offensive. The attempt on Hitler's life was made at a time when the Fuehrer's headquarters was still in Eastern Prussia. Soon, it had to be urgently relocated. After several attempts to site it elsewhere, it was installed in the Imperial Chancel-lory in Berlin, equipped with dependable air raid shelters. The location of the German Government and General Headquarters was made a state secret.

---

[1] Louis L. Snyder, *The War. A Concise History 1939-1945*, New York, 1960, p. 376.

After the attempt on Hitler's life the terror in Germany deepened. Not only the conspirators, but many anti-fascists were executed. The Gestapo also struck at the nucleus of the Free Germany anti-fascist movement and at underground groups throughout the country. Saefkow, Bästlein, Jacob, Neubauer, Schumann, Leuschner, Leber and Reichwein were killed.

Ernst Thaelmann, leader of the Communist Party of Germany, who withstood indescribable torture unbent during the more than eleven years in nazi prisons and who, even in prison, was a model of fearlessness, his hardy spirit and political insight serving as an example for Communists and anti-fascists, his personality exercising tremendous appeal, was on August 14, 1944, ordered by Hitler to be killed. His assassination took place in Buchenwald concentration camp during the night of August 17-18. Anticipating this, Thaelmann wrote a final message, calling for unyielding resistance to fascism in the name of human freedom. He concluded his message with the following lines from Goethe's *Faust*:

> *Yes! to this thought I hold with firm persistence;*
> *The last result of wisdom stamps it true;*
> *He only earns his freedom and existence*
> *Who daily conquers them anew.*[1]

5. The Slovak Uprising

By 1944 Slovakia had become the centre of Czechoslovak resistance. Towards the end of August partisan operations began to grow into a massive guerrilla war, a national armed uprising. Sensing danger, the German Command began massing troops. There was no time to be lost, and on August 25 the partisans mounted an active offensive. In the early morning hours of August 30 they poured into the town of Banska-Bystrica, took possession of it and made it the centre of a rising that involved the population of 18 districts in central and part of eastern Slovakia.

The aim of the rising was to help liberate the country by striking against the nazi troops from the rear and thereby

---

[1] Goethe, *Faust*, Act V, Scene 6, Tr. by Bayard Taylor, *Fr. Stevenson's Book of Quotations*, 1963.

helping the Red Army cross the difficult Carpathian spurs.

The Germans flung against the Slovaks eight picked divisions, whose attacks the partisans repelled for two long months, inflicting heavy casualties. The partisan units consisting of workers and farmers proved the most dependable.

The Soviet Union rendered the Slovak resistance fighters extensive aid. Soviet partisan detachments that had penetrated into Slovakia fought shoulder to shoulder with them. Soviet aircraft landed arms, ammunition and medical supplies near Banska-Bystrica and elsewhere, and on return flights evacuated the wounded and sick, women and children. A paratroop brigade of Czechs and Slovaks, activated in Soviet territory, was also flown in.

To support the Slovak rising, the Soviet Government organised the East-Carpathian Operation, committing to it troops of the 1st, 2nd and 4th Ukrainian Fronts and the 1st Czechoslovak Army Corps. The Dukla operation opened on September 8 in extremely difficult mountain terrain which the Germans had strongly fortified. The enemy continuously sent fresh forces into the battle.

On October 6, Czechoslovak and Soviet units reached the Czechoslovak frontier, taking possession of the Dukla Pass. In the heavy fighting the new army of the future free Czechoslovakia came into being, and October 6 became Czechoslovak People's Army Day. The Dukla operation effectively aided the Slovak rising.

In view of the balance of strength, the leaders of the rising, hard-pressed by the enemy, decided to withdraw from the liberated territory and revert to guerrilla warfare, which they conducted until the final liberation of Slovakia.

The Slovak rising was a logical result of the national liberation struggle that erupted the day after Munich. It was a culmination point in the revolutionary anti-fascist struggle in that part of Europe, a stirring chapter in the glorious history of the Czechs and Slovaks, a chapter that played a prominent part in their national destiny and the popular fight for the new, people's democratic system in Czechoslovakia.

The decisive part in the uprising was played by the Czechoslovak Communist Party, the Slovak Communists. They stood at its head and their example, their lofty patriotism, had a tremendous impact. In those days, the Communists won immense prestige as men who best understood the national interest.

The Slovak uprising was internationalist. People of nearly 30 nationalities took part in it. Fighting by the side of the Slovaks, who comprised the bulk of the insurrectionists, were 3,000 Soviet partisans, 2,000 Czechs, 800 Hungarians, 400 Frenchmen, 80 German anti-fascists, 70-100 Poles, more than a hundred Yugoslavs, 50 Americans and Britons, as well as Greeks, Italians, Bulgarians, Belgians, Dutchmen, Austrians, etc.[1] This was evidence of the general expansion of the anti-fascist struggle in Europe.

The uprising was a serious setback to the nazis, disrupting an important rear zone near the battle-lines. The hitlerites lost nearly 56,000 men in fighting the partisans during and after the insurrection.[2]

The Slovak rising and the Dukla operation had a benign effect on the Soviet-Czechoslovak combat alliance, sealed with the blood of Soviet, Czech and Slovak soldiers in common struggle. Klement Gottwald said: "At Dukla was born the slogan that is firmly embedded in the hearts and the consciousness of our people: With the Soviet Union for all time! With the Soviet Union forever!"[3]

6. Liberation of Southeast Europe

The Soviet Union fought the Great Patriotic War in the name of deliverance from fascist barbarity. The fate of the peoples was decided in the battle fought on the Soviet-German Front where Soviet forces struck smashing blows at Hitler's armies. In 1944, the Soviet mission of liberation became particularly expressive.

Beginning in the latter half of August 1944, the Red Army carried out large-scale offensives against the southern wing of the German forces, clearing the enemy out of Soviet Moldavia and then Rumania and Bulgaria and, ultimately, Yugoslavia, Austria and Hungary. In Southeast Europe, the politico-military and international situation changed completely.

The mammoth Jassy-Kishinev operation, which gave the

---

[1] *Voprosy istorii*, No. 7, 1961, pp. 73-79.
[2] *I.V.O.V.S.S.*, Vol. 4, p. 334.
[3] Klement Gottwald, *1949-1950*, Prague, 1951, p. 137.

start to the developments on the southern wing of the Soviet-German Front, was the principal military event of the period.

Soviet troops deployed along the line running from the northeastern foothills of the Eastern Carpathians to the Black Sea faced 47 nazi divisions, including three panzer and one motorised, and 5 brigades of Army Group South Ukraine.[1] In addition, the Germans had a large number of separate regiments and battalions there, plus strong police forces, SS troops, anti-aircraft units and marines in the rear, in Rumania and Bulgaria.

The 2nd and 3rd Ukrainian Fronts (Generals R. Y. Malinovsky and F. I. Tolbukhin, respectively), engaged in the Jassy-Kishinev operation, comprised 90 divisions, and nine tank and mechanised corps.[2] The strength of the Soviet and German divisions differed — a Soviet infantry division consisted of 5,600-7,500 men, while a German of 10,000 to 12,000.[3] Thus, the Soviet numerical advantage was only slight (1. 4 : 1).[4] However, overwhelmingly superior strength was built up in the attack points — as much as 3.9 : 1 by the 2nd Ukrainian Front and 8 : 1 by the 3rd. This in personnel, while the advantage in tanks and self-propelled artillery amounted in both cases to nearly 6 : 1.[5]

The offensive began in the morning of August 20, 1944, with enemy defences breached the same day. On the following day Jassy was captured, and nazi fortifications wiped out in the main attack directions. The 2nd Ukrainian Front drove to Fokshani and the 3rd to Galats-Izmail. On August 24, the two fronts made a junction southwest of Kishinev, investing and destroying 18 German divisions.[6] Besides, they surrounded the Rumanian 3rd Army, which surrendered.

With the Red Army offensive getting into stride and driving into Rumania, the armed rising of the Rumanians was brought closer. The plan of the rising was adopted at a meeting of Communist Party leaders and a group of top-ranking officers on June 13-14, 1944. A Military-Revolutionary Committee was formed, and to expedite the preparing of

---

[1] *I.V.O.V.S.S.*, Vol. 4, p. 259.

[2] *Ibid.*, p. 260.

[3] M. Minasyan, *Osvobozhdeniye narodov yugovostochnoi Yevropy (Liberation of the Peoples of Southeast Europe)*, Moscow, 1967, p. 112.

[4] *I.V.O.V.S.S.*, Vol. 4, p. 262.

[5] *Ibid.*

[6] *Ibid.*, p. 273.

the rising a concentration camp escape was organised for a group of top Communists. By August 23, fifty combat groups had been formed in Bucharest, with experience of armed resistance.

These groups went into action on August 23, compelling King Mihai, eager — though somewhat belatedly — to divorce himself from Ion Antonescu, the fascist dictator, to issue an order for his arrest. A combat group headed by Emil Bodnaras brought Ion Antonescu and his deputy, Mihai Antonescu, and a few ministers, to a secret place of the Rumanian Communist Party, where they were kept under guard until transfer to the Soviet Command. Meanwhile, other groups seized important objectives and strategic points in the Rumanian capital, this assuring the victory of the anti-fascist rising and raising the curtain on a popular revolution.

On August 25, 1944, the Soviet Foreign Commissariat published a statement reaffirming absence of any intention of acquiring any part of Rumanian territory, changing the existing social system in the country or impinging in any way on her independence. "On the contrary," the Statement said, "the Soviet Government considers it necessary, jointly with the Rumanians, to restore the independence of Rumania by liberating her from the German fascist yoke…. Help by Rumanian troops to eliminate the German forces is the only way to bring closer the end of hostilities in Rumanian territory."[1]

On August 26, Rumania officially announced her acceptance of the Soviet armistice terms. The nazis retaliated by bombing Bucharest, while trying to seize it with ground troops. Proceeding with rapid liberation of the country the 2nd Ukrainian Front captured Ploesti, centre of the Rumanian oil industry, and entered Bucharest on the following day, August 31. The Soviet troops passed through the streets in perfect order, a cavalcade of thousands of lorries and cars, tanks and self-propelled guns, while hundreds of planes flew overhead. The population watched this display with amazement. The liberation army received a joyous welcome.

The 2nd Ukrainian Front developed its offensive across Transylvania, hitting the rear of the Hungarian-German

---

[1] *Soviet Foreign Policy During the Great Patriotic War,* Russ. ed., Vol. II, p. 172.

troops which defended the Carpathian passes. Meanwhile, the 3rd Ukrainian Front advanced along the Danube across Rumania southward to Dobruja and the Bulgarian border.

Rumania declared war on Germany and, later, on Hungary, fielding 13-15 divisions, which fought under Soviet command.[1]

The armistice with Rumania was signed in Moscow on September 12, 1944. Marshal of the Soviet Union R. Ya. Malinovsky, Commander of the 2nd Ukrainian Front, affixed his signature to the agreement on behalf of the United Nations on mandate of the Soviet, US and British governments.

The terms were evidence of Soviet magnanimity. In its demands on defeated Rumania, the Soviet Union confined itself to conditions essential for the successful completion of its mission of liberation and the final defeat of the fascist bloc. The armistice envisaged that Rumania, which had terminated hostilities against the USSR at 04.00 hours on August 24 and thus withdrawn from the war against the United Nations, would participate under general Soviet guidance in the war against Germany and Hungary with the purpose of recovering her independence and sovereignty. The frontier between the USSR and Rumania was restored in accordance with the June 28, 1940, agreement, with Northern Transylvania to be ultimately restored to Rumania by Hungary.

Besides, Rumania undertook to turn over to the Soviet Supreme Command as trophy all war property in her territory belonging to Germany and her satellites. Rumania was to make part of the damage caused to the Soviet Union by her armed operations and occupation of Soviet territory, the sum being set at $300 million, payable in goods in six years. Rumania also undertook to return to the Soviet Union all valuables and materials shipped out of Soviet territory during the war. The Rumanian Government accepted the obligation to co-operate with the Soviet Supreme Command in apprehending war criminals, closing down fascist organisations and preventing their revival in future. The agreement envisaged the setting up of an Allied Control Commission to supervise fulfilment of the armistice terms.

The Rumanian armistice had a reassuring effect on

---

[1] M. Minasyan, *op. cit.*, p. 206 (footnote).

Finland, the military situation of which had become hopeless in face of a Soviet drive in the Karelian Isthmus, Southern Karelia and along the Baltic shore. In the early hours of September 4, 1944, the Finnish Government declared its willingness to accept the Soviet terms. German troops in Finland were told to leave. Moving out, they maltreated the civilian population, massacring thousands of women, old men and children in the one district of Tulus alone.

The Finnish armistice was signed in Moscow on September 19 by A. A. Zhdanov, prominent leader of the Communist Party and the Soviet Government, on behalf of the United Nations and by mandate of the Soviet and British governments.

Under the armistice terms, Finland undertook to withdraw her troops behind the 1940 Soviet-Finnish border and disarm all German armed forces still in her territory, and turn over German personnel as war prisoners to the Soviet Command, with the Soviet Government agreeing to assist Finland in this operation. The Soviet-Finnish peace treaty of March 12, 1940 was reinforced.

Finland undertook to return to the Soviet Union the Petsamo (Pechenga) region, which the Soviet Union had voluntarily given to Finland under treaties concluded on October 14, 1920 and March 12, 1940. The Soviet Union, on the other hand, gave up its lease of Hanko Peninsula, while Finland granted a lease of the Porkkala-Udd area and the adjoining waters for a Soviet naval base. Reparations were set at $300 million, payable in commodities over a period of 6 years. The other armistice terms were the same as those accepted by Rumania.

The armistice was an important landmark in Finnish history, assuring the country's independence and laying lasting foundations for friendship with the Soviet Union, which the subsequent years have amply proved.

The Finnish armistice, too, thus reflected the lofty idea behind Soviet foreign policy and the deep Soviet respect for national rights and the sovereignty of other peoples.

In the meantime, troops of the 3rd Ukrainian Front rolled on to the Rumanian-Bulgarian border. The anti-popular Bulgarian Government had continued its policy of collaborating with the nazis, but deep-seated revolutionary ferment was in evidence. By the autumn of 1944 something like 30,000 active partisans supported by 200,000 helpers from among the population, had become active.[1] They operated practically all over the country. On August 26, the Central Committee of the Communist Party of Bulgaria passed a decision to start a countrywide armed uprising.

In a note to the Bulgarian Government on September 5, 1944, the Soviet Government described Bulgaria's policy as "factual prosecution of war with the German camp against the Soviet Union". For this reason, it said, "henceforth not only Bulgaria is in a state of war against the USSR, since it had earlier also, in effect, been in a state of war against the USSR, but the Soviet Union, too, is in a state of war against Bulgaria".[2]

On September 8, the Red Army crossed the Bulgarian border from Rumania along a wide frontage. There was no resistance. Bulgarian troops laid down their arms, while the population extended the Soviet Army an enthusiastic welcome. Partisan commanders released a message of welcome, the opening line of which said, "Welcome!" The message read: "We have waited for you, Red Army brothers. Every salute in honour of your victories has echoed in our hearts. While waiting for you, we have not been idle.... Your proximity and your will to fight the people's oppressors are a guarantee that Bulgaria will be free, independent and democratic".[3]

The presence of Soviet troops in Bulgaria accelerated the revolutionary eruption. In the early hours of September 9, insurrectionists in the capital rapidly seized all important objectives and arrested the government, which had worked hand in glove with the hitlerites. Power was assumed by the Fatherland Front, formed before the rising began. The new Fatherland Front Government declared war against Germany and published a declaration, spelling out what it would do to democratise the country.

The victorious Red Army offensive blended with the popular anti-fascist rising. The people made the most of the favourable situation and quickly accomplished a peoples' democratic revolution.

On September 9, 1944, the Soviet troops in Bulgaria terminated military operations, which had been quite unique

---

[1] M. Minasyan, *op. cit.*, p. 209.
[2] *Soviet Foreign Policy During the Great Patriotic War*, Russ. ed., Vol. II, p. 188.
[3] *New Times*, No. 36, 1964, p. 7.

even before, for they did not involve the use of arms. Georgi Dimitrov said: "Though the Soviet Union did declare war on Bulgaria, not a single soldier, either Soviet or Bulgarian, was killed in that 'war'.... The entry of Soviet troops into Bulgaria helped to overthrow the fascist dictatorship and assured the future of the Bulgarian people, the freedom and independence of our state."[1]

Bulgaria took an active part in the war against Germany, committing nearly 340,000 men in the subsequent operations.[2] Acting under the general guidance of the Soviet Command, Bulgarian units battled the Germans at home, in Yugoslavia, Hungary and Austria, contributing to the liberation of the Balkan countries and the final defeat of Hitler Germany.

Negotiations over the Bulgarian armistice terms between the Soviet Union, on the one hand, and the United States and Britain, on the other, were extremely sharp. The Red Army's presence in Bulgaria frustrated a plan envisaging an Anglo-American occupation. The governments of the United States and Britain were therefore determined to impose hard terms and tremendous reparations.

The Soviet Union stood up for the interests of the Bulgarians, and the United States and Britain were forced to give in. But their stand impeded a reparations settlement. The armistice terms only said that Bulgaria would pay reparations, the amount to be fixed later. Accepting these terms, the Bulgarians were confident that the Soviet Union would not allow the imperialist countries to place an insufferable burden on them. In other respects (exclusive of territorial issues), the Bulgarian armistice was much like that concluded with Rumania.

It was signed in Moscow on October 28, 1944, by Marshal F. I. Tolbukhin, Commander of the 3rd Ukrainian Front, on behalf of the United Nations and by mandate of the Soviet, US and British governments.

After liberating Rumania and Bulgaria with the co-operation of local democratic forces, in September 1944, the Red Army reached the frontiers of Hungary and Yugoslavia. There it was confronted by a considerable enemy force

---

[1] Georgi Dimitrov, *Politicheskii otchet na TsK na BRP(k) pred V Kongress na partiyata (Political Report of the Central Committee of the Communist Party of Bulgaria to the 5th Party Congress)*, Sofia, 1951, pp. 68-69.

[2] *I.V.O.V.S.S.*, Vol. 4, p. 309.

of 66 divisions, comprising Army Groups South and F.[1] The Soviet Command, however, had considerably superior forces—the 1st, 2nd, 3rd and 4th Ukrainian fronts. The frontage, however, was wide and the terrain extremely difficult, favouring the defending forces.

On October 6, the 2nd Ukrainian Front thrust into the eastern part of Hungary (the Debrecen Operation). It made good progress despite bitter resistance, liberating the city of Debrecen on October 20, and then ending the Debrecen Operation. Co-operating with troops of the 4th Ukrainian Front, the 2nd also liberated Northern Transylvania and nearly all Hungarian territory left to the Tisza, developing a bridgehead also on its right bank. In the meantime, the 4th Ukrainian Front cleared the Transcarpathian Ukraine.

The defeat of the German-Hungarian armies in the eastern and northeastern parts of Hungary crowned the first stage of Hungary's liberation. The second opened without delay. On October 29 troops of the 2nd and 3rd Ukrainian Fronts began the Budapest Operation.

Enemy defences between the Tisza and Danube were breached on the first day and at dusk on November 2 the first Soviet units approached Budapest from the south. But they failed to take the city on the march. In the ensuing battles a part of the enemy troops was cut off from Budapest, invested in a bend of the Danube and wiped out. The ring round the Hungarian capital closed towards the end of December, and after many days the city was taken on February 13, 1945, with the surrounded enemy totally routed. But western Hungary was still in enemy hands.

A Provisional National Assembly of Hungary, which formed a provisional national government, convened in Debrecen on December 21, 1944. Acting on the wishes of the people, the new government took Hungary out of the war, with Germany thus losing the last of her satellites.

On January 20, 1945, Marshal K. Y. Voroshilov signed an armistice with Hungary in Moscow on behalf of the United Nations and by mandate of the Soviet, US and British governments. It was the same in content as those concluded with Rumania, Bulgaria and Finland. Its Article 12 stipulated partial compensation of losses caused by Hungary's participation in the war on Germany's side. The total sum,

---

[1] M. Minasyan, *op. cit.*, p. 251.

which was to go to the Soviet Union, Czechoslovakia and Yugoslavia, was set at $300 million payable in commodities in the course of six years.

In Yugoslavia, a people's war had been fought from the day she was overrun. Much of her territory had been cleared of the enemy. In September 1944 the People's Army had 400,000 men.[1] But it was unable to liberate the country completely on its own, because as many as 21 German divisions, 7 brigades and some 25 separate regiments, and 10 Bulgarian and Hungarian divisions, were stationed in Yugoslavia, Albania and Greece.[2]

A new power, that of the revolutionary people, had come into being during the people's resistance. The functions of a provisional government were performed by the National Liberation Committee. The liberation of the country by a joint Yugoslav-Soviet effort had been discussed beforehand in Moscow. The Yugoslav People's Liberation Army was supplied considerable quantities of Soviet arms and equipment, and a Soviet air group of two divisions was turned over to the Yugoslav Command for support. An understanding was reached on temporary Soviet military entry into Yugoslavia.

The Belgrade Operation was launched on September 28, 1944, by troops of the 3rd and 2nd Ukrainian Fronts, the Danube Naval Flotilla and the Yugoslav People's Liberation Army. Also engaged were 13 Bulgarian divisions and brigades under Soviet command.[3] When the offensive began, a communication was published in Moscow announcing the Red Army's temporary entry into Yugoslavia with the consent of the National Liberation Committee, and that a civilian administration of the National Liberation Committee of Yugoslavia would exercise power in territory where Red Army troops were stationed.[4]

The offensive developed well. It was mounted by 19 Soviet divisions, one motorised infantry brigade, a mechanised corps, the Danube Naval Flotilla, the air arm of the 3rd Ukrainian Front and part of the air arm of the 2nd Ukrainian Front.[5] The fraternal co-operation of the Red Army, the

---

[1] *I.V.O.V.S.S.*, Vol. 4, p. 416.

[2] *Ibid.*, p. 420.

[3] *Ibid.*, p. 422.

[4] *Soviet Foreign Policy During the Great Patriotic War*, Russ. ed., Vol. II, p. 236.

[5] M. Minasyan, *op. cit.*, p. 439.

Yugoslav National Liberation Army and the Bulgarian Army proved highly effective.

On October 14, Soviet and Yugoslav troops approached Belgrade. The first to break into the city were units of the 4th Guards Mechanised Corps (General V. I. Zhdanov) and the 1st Proletarian Division of Colonel Vaso Ivanovic (People's Liberation Army of Yugoslavia). Marshal S. S. Biryuzov (then General and Chief-of-Staff of the 3rd Ukrainian Front) recalls: "What made the battle difficult was that we wanted to avoid destruction in Belgrade and casualties among the civilian population. This made us give up powerful air and artillery strikes against residential and administrative quarters. Heavy arms were used with extreme caution. The enemy was attacked chiefly with guns, hand-grenades, automatic weapons and bayonets."[1] Yet Belgrade did not escape considerable damage, caused by totally unnecessary US and British air-raids. The Soviet troops, Biryuzov recalls, were also provocatively attacked by US Air Force planes.[2]

On October 20, the city was taken. The Belgrade Operation was over. Soviet and Bulgarian troops were pulled out of Yugoslavia for an offensive in Hungary, and all further actions in Yugoslav territory were by the People's Liberation Army. Further, Soviet aid was not confined to arms and ammunition. The sustained drive of the 2nd and 3rd Ukrainian Fronts in Hungary and Austria complicated the position of the nazi troops and their Croatian menials in Yugoslavia, facilitating their final defeat by the PLA. Josip Broz Tito pointed out later that without the Soviet Union "victory over the fascist invaders would have been impossible, the liberation of Yugoslavia would have been impossible, the creation of a new Yugoslavia would have been impossible".[3]

The Soviet entry into Yugoslavia and Hungary and the speedy drive west made the position of the German divisions in Albania and Greece untenable. They were in peril of being blockaded in the south of the Balkan Peninsula and began withdrawing north towards the end of September, the Belgrade Operation adding tempo to their evacuation. Taking advantage of the major Red Army success in the Balkans, the National Liberation Army of Albania mounted a broad

[1] S. S. Biryuzov, *Surovyie gody (Hard Years)*, Moscow, 1966, p. 475.
[2] *Ibid.*, p. 476.
[3] *I.V.O.V.S.S.*, Vol. 4, p. 435.

offensive, pursuing the fleeing German divisions. Albania was totally free by November 29, that day being proclaimed a national holiday.

A similar situation arose in Greece. Germans were abandoning the country, pursued by a national liberation army of nearly 125,000 men.[1] The National Liberation Front was in the act of taking over power in the country, with hopes of independent, free and democratic development rising before the Greek people. But that did not suit the Greek monarchists, nor Anglo-American reaction. The British Government shipped in troops and mounted extensive armed operations against the people, a people fighting for national independence and freedom.

British commando landings in Albania, however, ended in total failure. According to *Polityka*, a Polish newspaper, this was the result of timely information furnished by Harold Philby.[2]

* * *

Southeast Europe was liberated by Soviet troops with the co-operation of the Balkan national liberation forces. That people's power was established in the liberated countries was a natural outcome of the mass struggle against the nazis. The people's governments of Southeast Europe, excluding that of Greece, withstood the onslaught of home and external reactionary forces. Relying on the selfless fraternal support of the Soviet Union, they moved forward to national independence and social progress.

7. Hitler's Last Trump

The German leaders saw the events approaching the inevitable end. No hope survived of a military victory. But, as they saw it, one hope remained — that of exploiting the mounting anti-democratic and anti-Soviet sentiment among the US and British rulers in the interest of German militarism. Hitler told his associates: "Never in history was there a coalition like that of our enemies, composed of such heterogeneous elements with such divergent aims.... He who, like a spider sitting in the middle of his web, can watch develop-

---

[1] *I.V.O.V.S.S.*, Vol. 4, p. 439.
[2] *Polityka*, No. 4, 1968, p. 6.

ments, observes how these antagonisms grow stronger and stronger from hour to hour."[1]

The information at Hitler's disposal was largely true. The following entry in Fieldmarshal Alanbrooke's diary, dated July 27, 1944, became known to the public after the war. Here is what the Chairman of the Committee of the Chiefs-of-Staff of British Armed Forces wrote: "Back to War Office to have an hour with Secretary of State discussing post-war policy in Europe. Should Germany be dismembered or gradually converted to an ally to meet the Russian threat of twenty years hence? I suggested the latter and feel certain that we must from now onwards regard Germany in a very different light. Germany is no longer the dominating power in Europe—Russia is…. Therefore, foster Germany, gradually build her up and bring her into a Federation of Western Europe."[2]

The nazis were also encouraged by the conduct of the British interventionists in Greece. In the early hours of October 4, 1944, British troops landed in Southern Greece without meeting resistance. The Germans had withdrawn, while the Liberation Army, in hot pursuit, had moved north. For two months, the British Government built up its armed forces in Greece, but did not betray its true intents. It acted on Churchill's order: "It is most desirable to strike out of the blue without any preliminary crisis."[3] The "strike out of the blue" came on December 3, when the British provoked a conflict in Athens. General Ronald MacKenzie Scobie, in command of the British troops, received instructions calling for extreme measures: "Do not hesitate to act."[4] And further: "We have to hold and dominate Athens. It would be a great thing for you to succeed in this without bloodshed if possible, but also with bloodshed if necessary."[5] Churchill recalled Arthur Balfour's telegram to the British authorities in Ireland in the 1880s: "Don't hesitate to shoot."[6] And General Scobie's troops did not hesitate.

Wholesale killings and arrests were complemented by brutal air and sea raids on Greek towns and villages. For 33 days

---

[1] John Ehrman, *Grand Strategy*, Vol. VI, London, 1956, p. 2.
[2] A. Bryant, *Triumph in the West*, London, 1959, p. 242.
[3] W. Churchill, *The Second World War*, Vol. VI, London, 1954, p. 248.
[4] *Ibid.*, p. 252.
[5] *Ibid.*
[6] *Ibid.*

the British interventionists waged a sanguinary war against the people of Greece, employing methods reminiscent of the nazis'. With brute force they saddled the nation with a monarcho-fascist government.

Examining the ways of exploiting this behaviour of the British and US governments, Berlin decided to mount a major counter-offensive in the West. The nazis hoped that this would encourage the tendency in Washington and London to seek a separate understanding with Germany, this disrupting the anti-fascist coalition. On the face of it, the situation was favourable. British and US troops in France and Belgium were preparing to celebrate Christmas. Officers and men were given leave and battle-preparedness dropped.

The nazi plan was to repeat the breakthrough of May 1940. Again, after breaching the front, the German armies were to hinge rapidly toward the coast with the object of cutting off and wiping out the maritime group of the Allied troops in the area. But unlike 1940, the route to the coast was to be somewhat shorter. The breach was to be in the Ardennes between Monschau and Echternach, at the junction of British and US armies. It would then develop towards Dinant-Namur-Liege, and to Antwerp, by then the main US and British supply centre. The huge depots in that part would, if Antwerp were captured, greatly ease the situation of the German Army.

The depletion in strength on the Eastern Front prevented the nazis from deploying a strong enough force for the operation. Numbers were to be compensated by quality. Three German armies—the 7th, 5th Panzer and 6th SS, including brigades of Hitler's bodyguards—were placed under the command of General-Fieldmarshal Rundstedt, but instead of the 3,000 warplanes envisaged in the plan, he was given only 700-900.[1]

The Germans struck at dawn on December 16 with the advantage of surprise. The attack was unexpected for the Allied Command, not only due to poor intelligence and reconnaissance, but chiefly to its confidence that the main German effort would continue against the Soviet Union. Lack of integrity, of the US and British governments, proved the chief reason for the German success in the Ardennes. The front was breached 80 km in width and 110 km in depth.

[1] *I.V.O.V.S.S.*, Vol. 4, p. 547.

German forward units crossed the Maas at Dinant and then reached the river west of Liege. The Anglo-American armies retreated in disorder, leaving behind vast quantities of arms, ammunition and fuel.

Before dawn on January 1, 1945, the nazis mounted another offensive, this time in Alsace, advancing 30 km in three days.

The Ardennes and Alsace offensives aggravated controversies between the US, British and French governments and the respective military commands, this adding to the difficulty of eliminating the consequences of the German breakthrough. Quite obviously, the nazis would try to deploy fresh strength to develop their initial success.

The US and British governments turned to the Soviet Union, requesting a new Red Army offensive to draw off German troops and compel them to abandon their enterprise in the West. The first to suggest this was Eisenhower in his letter to the Chiefs-of-Staff. "If...," he wrote, "it is the Russian intention to launch a major offensive in the course of this or next month, knowledge of the fact would be of the utmost importance to me and I would condition my plans accordingly. Can anything be done to effect this coordination?"[1]

Churchill sent a personal message to Stalin on January 6, laying stress on the dangers "when a very broad front has to be defended after temporary loss of the initiative."[2] He asked "whether we can count on a major Russian offensive on the Vistula front, or elsewhere, during January."[3]

Although the Soviet troops had only just completed a major autumn-winter offensive and the weather forecasts were extremely unfavourable, Stalin sent Churchill an affirmative reply the next day. It contained the opinion of the Soviet generals. Marshal of the Soviet Union Ivan Konev, then in command of the 1st Ukrainian Front, recalls in his memoirs that altering the Soviet schedule created difficulties, involving an immense organisational effort. However, the Soviet generals, officers and men "realised that the change had been dictated by general strategic considerations and, hence, had to be accepted".[4]

---

[1] Herbert Feis, *Churchill-Roosevelt-Stalin*, p. 480.
[2] *Correspondence...*, Vol. 1, Moscow, 1957, p. 294.
[3] *Ibid.*, p. 294.
[4] I. S. Konev, *Year of Victory*, Moscow, 1969, p. 15.

Less than a week after Churchill's message the Red Army launched an offensive all along the front from the Baltic to the Carpathians (on January 12, 1945). This was a striking example of faithful observance of Allied responsibility and of how coordinated actions pay off. The nazi plan in the West was thwarted, with German troops hastily pulled back to the Soviet-German front.

Soviet fidelity to the duty of ally was of fundamental significance. It shored up the coalition. And the last of Hitler's trumps was beaten. Yet he clung on with the desperation of a maniac. He still hoped for a split among the Allies.

8. The Crimea Conference

The second top-level conference of the Soviet, US and British leaders was called in the Crimea, with the Soviet delegation housed in Yusupov Palace, the British in Vorontsov Palace and the American in Livadia. Although the Crimea had been liberated only shortly, the delegates were assured the maximum possible comfort, despite the fact that negotiators and staff from abroad totalled 2,500.[1]

The conference opened at the time of a powerful Soviet offensive all along the front. "The appearance of the Red Army at the gates to Berlin," Max Walter Clauss, a West German historian, notes, "was a factor that dominated the conference."[2]

At the opening session Churchill thanked the USSR for the winter offensive that had helped the Allies squash the German Ardennes adventure. Stalin replied that he had appreciated the implications of Churchill's message and saw "that such an offensive had been necessary for the Allies. The Soviet Command had started its offensive even before the planned date. The Soviet Government had considered that to be its duty, the duty of an ally, although it was under no formal obligations on this score. He, Stalin, would like the leaders of the Allied Powers to take into account that Soviet leaders did not merely fulfil their obligations, but were also prepared to fulfil their moral duty as far as possible."[3]

---

[1] *New Times*, No. 9, 1965, p. 19.
[2] Max Walter Clauss, *Der Weg nach Jalta*, Heidelberg, 1952, S. 247.
[3] *Tehran, Yalta and Potsdam*, Progress Publishers, Moscow, 1969, p. 63.

The conference agreed Allied plans for completing Hitler's defeat. The decisive significance of the Soviet-German Front was acknowledged. In recognition, capturing Berlin was assigned to the Red Army. The Crimea Conference endorsed the European Consultative Commission proposals on occupation zones in Germany and the administration of Berlin. The question of inviting France to participate in the occupation of Germany was settled in the affirmative on the initiative of the Soviet Government.

When discussing the German occupation zones, the US and British spokesmen went back again to their partition plans. Roosevelt remarked that occupation zones "might prove to be the first step in the dismemberment of Germany". Churchill added that "he agreed in principle to the dismemberment of Germany".[1] The question remained of how it should be partitioned, he amplified. Stalin expressed strong doubts and insisted that no mention of dismemberment should be made in the surrender terms. Churchill and Roosevelt dragged through a decision that the matter be put before the Foreign Ministers for further study. Subsequently, on Soviet insistence, it was struck off the agenda.

The Soviet point of view triumphed also in relation to the political tasks of the occupation. The delegations accepted a document on this score drafted beforehand; it envisaged measures ruling out any new German aggression and securing the country's peaceful democratic development. The Big Three declared their determination to disarm and dissolve all German Armed Forces, to abolish forever the German General Staff, which had repeatedly helped German imperialism to revive, to punish all war criminals and wipe out the nazi party, nazi legislation, nazi organisations and nazi institutions.

A sharp discussion broke out over reparations. Acting on the principle of justice, the Soviet Government declared that Germany should repay her victims at least part of the damage they suffered from her aggression. Total reparations were estimated by the Soviet delegation at $20,000 million, of which half was due to the Soviet Union.

Churchill objected that reparations would cause starvation in Germany. "If one wanted to ride a horse," Churchill said, "one had to feed it with oats and hay." Stalin replied:

---

[1] *Ibid.*, p. 66.

"The horse should not charge at one,"[1] adding instantly, however, that comparisons of this kind were unacceptable. Ivan Maisky, assigned by the Soviet Government to work out a reparations plan, retorted to Churchill that $10,000 million only slightly exceeded Germany's annual arms expenditure before the war and comprised a mere 10 per cent of the US 1944-45 budget or equalled half of British wartime expenditure. He also pointed out that the problem would create no special political difficulties if "the United States and Britain would not again finance Germany after the end of the war", as they had done after the First World War.[2]

The discussion culminated in a Protocol which envisaged an Allied Reparation Commission (USSR, USA and Britain) which "should take in its initial studies as a basis for discussion the suggestion of the Soviet Government that the total sum of the reparation... should be 20 billion dollars and that 50 per cent of it should go to the Union of Soviet Socialist Republics".[3] It was noted, too, that the sum was agreed only between the Soviet and American delegations, while the British maintained their particular point of view.

The "Declaration on Liberated Europe" was high up on the list of decisions taken by the Crimea Conference. The Declaration said that the Allied powers considered it a common principle of policy towards the countries of liberated Europe to adopt an order that would enable the peoples "to destroy the last vestiges of nazism and fascism, and to create democratic institutions of their own choice".[4] By its treatment of Poland and Yugoslavia the Crimea Conference showed how the matter could be properly settled in practice.

The Soviet attitude to Poland was defined by Stalin. "The Soviet Union," he said, "had a stake in creating a powerful, free and independent Poland."[5] That was why the Soviet Union could not agree with the British and US representatives, who wished to ignore the will of the Polish people and impose upon it the mercenary émigré government. The USA and Britain could not prevail. All they managed was to obtain a decision recommending Poland and Yugoslavia to broaden their already existing governments.

---

[1] *Tehran, Yalta and Potsdam*, p. 75.
[2] *Ibid.*, p. 77.
[3] *Ibid.*, pp. 143-44.
[4] *Ibid.*, p. 136.
[5] *Ibid.*, p. 93.

Spurning the balance of class forces in those countries, the British and US governments thought representatives of the reactionary side would, once they had seats in the government, succeed in ultimately seizing power. The Soviet Union, on the other hand, trusted the intrinsic strength of the Polish and Yugoslav peoples and their ability to win, even if imperialist agents held a few government portfolios. Subsequent events proved this judgement correct.

The conference recognised Poland's eastern frontier along the Curzon line, adopted in 1919 at the Paris Peace Conference. With regard to the western frontier, the conference declared: "Poland must receive substantial accessions of territory in the north and west."[1] The size of these would be determined in due course.

The Crimea Conference also continued discussion of the idea of an international organisation for the maintenance of peace and security, later named the United Nations Organisation. The preparatory work begun at the Moscow Foreign Ministers' Conference in the autumn of 1943 was continued by the USSR, USA, and Britain in Dumbarton Oaks (Washington), August 21-September 29, 1944.

On Soviet insistence the UN structure and activity was based on the principle of the sovereignty and equality of all members. The Organisation would not interfere in their internal affairs. Maintaining peace and security was defined as its main purpose, with chief responsibility for this placed on the Security Council.

The Soviet Union advanced the unanimity principle for the five great powers, USSR, USA, Britain, France and China, all permanent members of the Security Council. Countering the wish of the imperialist powers to dominate the Organisation, this principle is expressive of the equality and unanimity of the five great powers, obliging them to seek acceptable joint solutions.

The US and British governments opposed the unanimity principle. The matter was even referred to the Crimea Conference, where the Soviet attitude was formulated by Stalin in the following words: "The unity of the three Powers was the most important requisite for the preservation of a lasting peace. If such unity was preserved, there was no need to fear the German danger. Thought should, therefore, be given

---

[1] *Ibid.*, p. 138.

to how best to ensure a united front between the three Powers, to which France and China should be added."[1]

President Roosevelt advanced a compromise solution, which was finally adopted: the work of the Security Council was based on the unanimity principle, but procedural matters were to be governed by a majority vote (of not less than 7 out of 11), while in matters related to peaceful settlement of disputes, the party involved in the conflict (even if a permanent Security Council member) should abstain from voting.

On the last day of the conference an agreement was signed that the Soviet Union would enter the war against Japan two or three months after the war in Europe ended.

The Crimea Conference showed that governments with different social systems were able to hammer out joint and effective solutions. Some participants, however, accepted international co-operation tongue in cheek. Churchill later betrayed his insincerity. He said he had accepted some of the agreements in the Crimea only to encourage the Soviet Union to make the fullest use of its giant military power against Germany and Japan. "What would have happened," he wrote, "if we have quarreled with Russia while the Germans still had two or three hundred divisions on the fighting front?"[2]

However, the perfidy of a few cannot detract from the positive significance of the Crimea Conference, the results of which appear even more important in retrospect. The conference spelled the doom of Hitler's hope of a conflict between the members of the anti-fascist coalition, producing a programme for postwar democratic arrangements.

The people of the Soviet Union and all progressives regard the Crimea Conference as an important milestone along the way to the nazi defeat and the materialisation of the legitimate liberative aims of the Second World War.

---

[1] *Tehran, Yalta and Potsdam*, p. 87.
[2] W. Churchill, *op. cit.*, Vol. VI, London, p. 352.

Chapter Seven

The Soviet Partisans

1. Invader Constantly Harassed

Long before the Second World War, the German General Staff bandied the bellicose slogan, "Attention, Panzers!" This epitomised its reckless strategy of aggression. Nazi generals expected the Wehrmacht armour to strike fear and consternation into the peoples of all countries, forcing them to their knees. What they did not reckon with was that panzers could be fought with superior armour. Neither did they reckon with the fact that panzers would not intimidate the Soviet people. A few months after the Soviet-German war began, the old slogan gave place to a panicky cry: "Attention, Partisans!" Victory chants gave place to hysterics.

Many foreign historians ascribe the appearance and growth of the Soviet partisan movement to the nazi atrocities. Quite true that the atrocities fanned the flames of resistance. But there was one reason only for the movement to spring and grow: the enemy was about to overrun the homeland, to eradicate the gains of socialism, cherished by the Soviet people.

If the iron fist were in a silk glove and German occupation policy were reversed, this would alter nothing. Goebbels, the nazi propaganda chief, was wrong when he said: "We could reduce danger from the partisans considerably if we succeeded in at least winning some of these peoples' confidence…. It might also be useful to set up sham governments in the various sectors which would then have to be responsible for unpleasant and unpopular measures."[1]

---

[1] *The Goebbels Diaries*, London, 1948, p. 169.

Indeed, Goebbels's advice was partly followed. A "Committee of Trust" was set up in Byelorussia, a "Self-Administration Committee" in Estonia and a variety of committees in the Ukraine. But all these auxiliary bodies, consisting of traitors and collaborationists, aroused bitter hatred and contempt.

The nazis committed savage outrages. They shot, hung, poisoned or buried alive hundreds of thousands of guiltless civilians, to say nothing of Red Army soldiers and officers. Forcible transportation to German labour camps was widely practised. Soviet citizens shipped to Germany were placed in concentration camps or on farms, performing hard labour, constantly insulted, ill-fed, and in most cases finally dying from exhaustion or hunger, or as a result of brutal treatment by guards.

But nothing could break the will of Soviet people. Men and women in nazi-captured towns or villages rose against them.

The patriotic struggle in enemy-occupied territory unfolded in many ways—political, economic, ideological and armed.

Political resistance took the form of distinct hostility to measures of the nazi governors, the system of plunder, coercion and abuse. The population ignored regulations of the occupation authorities, refused to believe their reports, rejected their slander of Soviet power and Soviet government bodies. All nazi attempts to subvert the people's trust in the Communist Party were in vain. That trust only increased. Underground Party bodies were stoutly supported, this serving as a dependable basis for successful action. The most striking thing was that the collective-farm system continued in the countryside despite the fascist occupation, with the nazis even trying to adapt it to their needs and interests.

Attempts to kindle distrust between workers and peasants, and between the different nationalities on occupied territory, failed dismally. What is more, as elsewhere in the country, the unity of the working class and the collective farmers only became more solid, while people of different nationalities helped each other as best they could. Many Russian, Ukrainian and Byelorussian families risked their lives hiding Jews, who were being exterminated by the nazis.

The Soviet socialist system showed its viability and endurance even in enemy-occupied territory. This struck fear into the German imperialists. They vented their fury against members of the Communist Party, government officials and shock workers who fell into their hands, and against Soviet science and culture workers.

Like many other enemies of the Soviet state, the German imperialists pretended to "liberate" the Soviet people from communism. But the moment they stepped on Soviet soil, which they bathed in the blood of guiltless victims, they discovered that communism and the life of the Soviet people were indivisible.

Economic resistance in enemy-occupied territory was centred on preventing hitlerites from exploiting the available production capacity and resources. Workers, technicians and engineers working under duress for the occupation authorities, sabotaged production on their own initiative or by assignment of underground Party bodies. As a result, the economic policy of the German invaders collapsed and, as they confessed, they gained much less from production in occupied territory than they had expected.

Probably the best showing was that of the Soviet workers, technicians and engineers in the Donets Basin, which had a strong underground Party organisation. The Germans were unable to organise coal extraction and iron and steel production there, and were compelled to ship in coal to the Ukraine, and even to the Donets Basin, from Western Europe.

Soviet railwaymen put up a tough fight. Water towers, switches and other railway accessories kept breaking down, trains were derailed and locomotives went out of order. A small group of railwaymen led by K. S. Zaslonov in Orsha performed heroic exploits, organising manufacture of special mines methodically placed in locomotives and railway cars, thus disorganising railway traffic in the rear of nazi Army Group Centre.

The nazis encountered active resistance also in the villages. Collective farmers avoided handing in food to the occupation authorities, sabotaging their orders, while supplying food to partisans and the underground. Nor did the partisans forget their loyal friends, wherever possible delivering them from the more brutal and ferocious administrators. "Many an agricultural functionary," a German newspaper admitted, "paid for his activity with his life."[1]

---

[1] *Pravda*, December 14, 1942.

War is impossible without a well-ordered and organised rear. For the Wehrmacht Germany was a distant rear. Occupied Soviet land, however, though operationally the rear of the nazi armies, was nothing of the sort in the economic sense. It worked not for, but against Germany.

Ideological Soviet resistance, guided by the Communists, made a strong impact too. The Soviet people wrathfully rejected the fascists' man-hating anti-communist ideas. Only a wretched handful of traitors and collaborators, isolated and hated, agreed to serve the occupation authorities. The people as a whole proved faithful to Marxism-Leninism and the socialist ideal.

Assassination of nazis, arson, damage to enemy communications and spreading rumours and panic among the invaders and their menials — all were part of a massive operation. Soviet people acted selflessly to preserve the nation's property, buried machinery, tools and tractors, equipment and material, to prevent them from falling into enemy hands. This was evidence of a deep faith in final victory and of loyalty to socialism.

Young men and women were hidden away to escape transportation for forced labour in Germany. On instructions of underground Party bodies, Soviet patriots agreed to be officials of labour exchanges and fascist municipalities, passport control officers, prisoners' reshipment centres, even of the police, while physicians and nurses worked in polyclinics and labour selection centres. Huge numbers of fictitious documents were issued to partisans and underground Party bodies, and certificates of disablement to young people down for transportation to Germany.

Millions took part in sabotage. This, coupled with ceaseless acts of diversion and armed partisan operations, all heroic national resistance, created an untenable situation, eroding fascist morale. Many citizens risked arrest or death, engaging Germans in conversation, proving that their aim of conquering the Soviet Union would fail.

No matter how they tried, the invaders could not gain a firm foothold on Soviet soil. They were an alien body, and hostile, and were bound to be expelled. But this required military victory over the German armada.

Soviet people remained fearless revolutionary fighters even in the frightful Gestapo prison cells and in the hell of the concentration camps. Neither torture nor execution could break them. As a symbol of unbending tenacity and will, we may cite General D. M. Karbyshev, whom the nazis turned into a block of ice, the poet Mussah Jalil, executed in a nazi prison, and many others.

In the bleak prison cells, in inhuman and terrifying conditions, Jalil wrote poetry filled with love of his country and life, with a bitter hatred and proud contempt of the fascist hangmen. Here (translated in blank verse — *Tr.*) are some of his lines:

> *I sang, sensing the freshness of spring,*
> *I sang, going to battle for my country.*
> *Now, I write my last song*
> *With the axe raised over my head.*
> *Song taught me to cherish freedom,*
> *Song orders me to die fighting.*
> *May my life be a song for my people,*
> *May my death be a song of struggle.*[1]

Fourteen million were transported to do forced labour in Germany. This includes all foreign workers and prisoners of war. Soviet people stood out by reason of their unbending will-power, fighting spirit, morale. Weakened by hunger and excessive labour, strictly guarded, stripped of all rights, they resisted with unexampled courage and tenacity, forming underground committees and preparing armed risings, while comforting and supporting those who proved weak in body or spirit. Aided by the mass of prisoners, the committees established ties with foreign workers and German anti-fascists.

A Soviet war prisoners' fraternity, an underground organisation of Soviet patriots, was formed in southern Germany, establishing lasting relations with the Communist German anti-fascist organisation, the German Anti-Nazi Popular Front. Czechoslovak and Polish patriots doing forced labour co-operated actively with the Soviet underground. This was one of the most powerful anti-fascist organisations on German soil. Several thousand men of different nationalities, organised along military lines and partly armed, prepared for a rising against the Hitler dictatorship. They failed to accomplish their plan, but the memory of their courageous bid will live forever.

---

[1] Mussah Jalil, *Moabitskaya tetrad (Moabit Notebook)*, Moscow, 1957, p. 14.

The movements among Soviet people imprisoned or doing forced labour in Germany, had a strong bearing on the general situation. From 1943 onward, the nazis lived in fear of a possible insurrection of foreign workers and prisoners throughout Germany; so they kept part of their troops on German soil. Moreover, they went to the length of drafting a special operational plan under the code name, Valkyrie, for this eventuality. Soviet resistance reached out to the den of the nazi brutes.

Soviet security agents performed feats that roused the admiration of the Soviet people. Supported by their countrymen, they sealed off the Soviet rear from enemy infiltration. The fact that only two out of the 150 spy and sabotage groups smuggled in by Abwehrkommando 104, a nazi intelligence unit, fulfilled their mission, shows how effectively Soviet security bodies operated. Archives captured by Soviet troops at the end of the war disclosed that 90 per cent of the agents sent into Soviet battle areas had been captured.[1] Several thousand enemy agents were exposed and rendered harmless during the war. Parachuted nazi agents caught, alone totalled 1,854.[2]

Hundreds of the captured fascist agents were subsequently used to transmit false reports to the Germans. In December 1942, when an offensive was being prepared in the Volkhov direction, spurious information was dispatched to the nazis from Tikhvin, Bologoye, Vologda, Yaroslavl, Rybinsk, Bezhetsk, Kalinin, Moscow and Gorky. On the eve of the Battle of Kursk the nazi command was misled by reports from nine captured German agents operating under the control of Soviet counter-intelligence.[3]

Soviet intelligence supplied invaluable information about the dislocation and deployment of nazi troops and about Hitler's operational plans. A group of intelligence officers headed by M. S. Prudnikov obtained and sent to Moscow 23 top secret German situation maps in June 1942. In spring 1943 a group known as Victors, operating behind the enemy lines, obtained early information about the move of several nazi infantry and panzer divisions to the Kursk battle area

[1] S. I. Tsybov, N. F. Chistyakov, *Front tainoi voiny (The Secret War)*, Moscow, 1968, p. 51.

[2] *I.V.O.V.S.S.*, Vol. 6, p. 137.

[3] S. Tsybov, N. Chistyakov, *op. cit.*, p. 53.

from France, Africa and the Leningrad Front.[1] V. A. Molodtsov organised a wide intelligence network from the enemy-blockaded Odessa catacombs. When captured and sentenced to death, in reply to a nazi offer of pleading for mercy, he said: "We are in our own country and do not beg enemies for mercy."[2]

Foreign intelligence experts had a high opinion of what the Soviet patriots accomplished during the war. Allen Dulles, head of US Intelligence, for one thing, noted that information obtained by Soviet officers was of a kind intelligence agencies in other countries could only dream of.

For all the impact of political, economic and ideological resistance in enemy-occupied areas, more decisive was partisan warfare. It betokened a stirring patriotism and boundless loyalty to socialism, and that the war against the invader was a people's war, testifying to the unbending will of Soviet patriots to defend the freedom and independence of their country. Naturally, in the armed struggle the main part belonged to the Soviet Armed Forces, whereas the partisan movement was the comrade-in-arms of Army, Navy and Air Force. It contributed to the victory and made a strong politico-military and international mark. It struck fear into the invaders, who could never feel safe, wherever they may have been. To use an expression of that time, the partisan movement made Soviet soil burn under the soles of the invaders, so that soon they exclaimed in panic, "Attention, Partisans!"

The country had a rich tradition of partisan warfare, going back to Ancient Rus and the partisan exploits in the Patriotic War of 1812 against the Napoleonic invasion. Partisans played a major role also in the fight against the interventionists and whiteguards in 1918-1922, when they helped defeat many an enemy of Soviet power in the Ukraine, Siberia and the Far East. But never before in Russian history was the partisan movement as sweeping as it was in the Great Patriotic War against Hitler Germany.

It had many distinctive features: rooted in the thick of the masses, it was the response to the call of the Communist Party, which rallied the population in enemy-occupied territory. That is why the partisan flames spread so quickly.

---

[1] *I.V.O.V.S.S.*, Vol. 6, p. 138.
[2] *Kommunist*, No. 18, 1967, p. 73.

Yet partisan warfare would have been inconceivable without extensive popular support. Partisans were fed, clothed, provided concealment and oriented by the people.

The other important feature was the movement's massiveness. Hundreds of thousands, with reserves reaching into the millions, took part in the partisan operations, including all segments of Soviet society: workers, farmers, office workers, intellectuals, old people, young men and women, Communists, Komsomols and non-Party people. By becoming partisans all of them displayed an equally high sense of patriotic duty, courage, heroism and dedication.

The movement was monolithic. Its members pursued the same aim. There could be no thought of differences and quarrels. Unlike many capitalist countries, the partisan movement in the Soviet Union was unaffected either by class or national differences. The wretched efforts of a handful of nationalist-minded traitors, who sold out to the nazi occupation authorities, were unable to disrupt the unity of the partisan ranks.

Many women were active in the partisan movement, staunch partisans, undergrounders, couriers, medical nurses, dynamiters and scouts coming from their midst. There are names that for Soviet people symbolise tenacity, courage and loyalty—those of A. V. Petrova, a partisan scout; Maria Melentyeva and Anna Lisitsina, message carriers; Vera Khorunzhaya, head of the Party underground in Vitebsk; Y. S. Zenkova, head of the Komsomol underground in Obol; Lyalia Ubiivovk, undergrounder in Poltava; Marite Melnikaite, a patriotic Lithuanian girl, and many others.

Rising from the thick of the nation, led and guided by the Communist Party and Soviet Government, the partisan movement swept across enemy-occupied territory and grew into an important political and military-strategic factor in the defeat of fascist Germany and her allies in Europe.

Partisan units were formed in different ways, some by local organisations of the Party, Komsomol, the Soviets or the trade unions, some by factory, collective-farm or state-farm groups, some on the initiative of the local population, servicemen separated from their units or escaped POWs, and some on the basis of groups specially sent into the enemy rear. Gradually, the units grew into larger detachments, establishing contact with each other and maintaining communications with the Red Army Command. They served as a dependable base, facilitating the work of the underground and clandestine Party organisations in the enemy rear.

The earliest units sprang up in areas first overrun by the enemy—the Baltic republics, Byelorussia, the Ukraine and Moldavia. Most prominent in Byelorussia were the units of T. P. Bumazhkov and F. I. Pavlovsky, V. Z. Korzh, M. I. Zhukovsky, M. F. Shmyryov and T. Ye. Yermakovich. Many units consisted of the population of entire villages. This was the case in the villages of Zagalye (Lyuban District) and Dromanovichi (Starobin District) where partisan detachments were headed by the chairman of the village Soviet and the chairman of the collective farm respectively. Units in the Baltic republics and the Ukraine were formed in a similar way. S. A. Kovpak, 55 years of age, formed a unit in the Ukrainian town of Putivl, growing into one of the most renowned partisan generals.

Different people became partisans. Komsomol member V. A. Zebelov, a Moscow Law Institute student, who had lost both hands in an accident, asked to be sent behind the enemy lines. Told by Komsomol officials that no one in his condition had ever jumped with a parachute, Zebelov replied: "Nowhere except in our country is there Soviet power."[1] His request was granted and he proved an excellent partisan scout. Zoya Kosmodemyanskaya, a Moscow schoolgirl, went on a partisan mission, and was apprehended and brutally killed by the nazis.

As many as 231 partisan groups were active in Byelorussia by August 1, 1941, with another 437 forming before autumn was over.[2]

At the end of June 1941, the partisans mounted active operations. In July-August they became a mighty force threatening the enemy. M. F. Shmyryov's unit alone performed 27 successful combat missions in August-September, forcing the nazis to put up signs "Partizan zone" in its area of operations.[3]

Gradually, the partisan movement gained experience and developed specific forms of combat. Partisans raided enemy garrisons and ambushed nazi troops on the march, attacked personnel and destroyed weapons, cut highways, and blew up bridges and troop trains, conducting an eminently suc-

---

[1] *Partizanskiye byli (Partisan Stories)*, Moscow, 1958, p. 248.
[2] *I.V.O.V.S.S.*, Vol. 2, p. 126.
[3] *Ibid.*, p. 131.

cessful "rail war". Clinging for months to cleared territory, the partisans wiped out fascist occupation administrations, paralysed the enemy rear and frustrated many an economic and political undertaking of the nazi authorities. Scouts were trained, who supplied valuable information to the Red Army Command.

To be sure, mistakes were made, too, in the early months of the partisan war due to inexperience and ignorance of the specifics of guerrilla warfare. Some units were overcautious, slow to unfold combat operations, while others rushed headlong against superior forces. Gradually the commanders learned that skilful well-timed moves were the key to success in their kind of war. One after the other, the groups performed daring long-distance raids across enemy-occupied territory, keeping constantly on the move. A fortnight's raid was made in September 1941 by S. P. Osechkin's Ukrainian detachment, and another unit, under I. F. Borovik, operated successfully near Kiev, then left the Malin forest in October 1941 and, after a 600-kilometre trek, established itself in the Bryansk forests. I. I. Kopeikin's detachment drove deep into the enemy rear, raiding town and village garrisons. S. A. Kovpak's operations were extraordinarily audacious. Joining forces with A. N. Saburov, he conducted a 700-kilometre raid from the Bryansk forests to the Ukraine west of the Dnieper in October and November 1942.

Facts and figures show the scale on which the partisans operated. In the first five months of the war Byelorussian partisans derailed as many as 597 troop trains, blew up or set fire to 473 railway and road bridges, destroyed 855 motor vehicles, 24 panzers and armoured cars, killing more than 2,220 German soldiers, officers and policemen.[1]

In the cities, too, partisans performed spectacular operations. City combat techniques were developed. In Minsk, for example, through the period of its occupation, partisans killed more than 1,600 military and civil officials,[2] among whom was Wilhelm Kube, Hitler's gauleiter in Byelorussia. He was executed by a girl partisan, Y. G. Mazanik, who was helped in the bold operation by other girl heroes—M. B. Osipova, N. V. Troyan and N. N. Drozd.

---

[1] *I.V.O.V.S.S.,* Vol. 2, p. 481.
[2] R. Sidelskii, *Borba Sovietskikh partizan protiv fashistskikh zakhvatchikov (Soviet Partisans' Struggle Against Fascist Invaders),* Moscow, 1944, p. 22.

Partisan co-operation with the Red Army was close. While General P. A. Belov's troops penetrated behind enemy lines towards the town of Vyazma at the end of January 1942, partisans captured Dorogobuzh, and throughout the Soviet counter-offensive at Moscow partisans hit the enemy from the rear, cutting his communications and supplying invaluable intelligence. The Red Army reciprocated, staging attacks to take the heat off the partisans and compelling the nazi command to fold up punitive operations.

Measuring the magnitude of the partisan operations, we should bear in mind the enemy strength this drew off from the battle-lines. In the summer and autumn of 1942, for example, as many as 22-24 nazi divisions were kept in the rear as protection,[1] and immediately behind the front-line troops, too, special units were held ready to repulse partisan attacks.

The mushrooming movement needed unified control to be more effective. That is why on May 30, 1942, a Central Partisan Headquarters was set up under the Supreme Command. Regional headquarters were also formed—for the Ukraine, the Bryansk area, the Western area, Kalinin Region, Leningrad Region and the Karelo-Finnish sector. These helped the movement grow and coordinated its operations with the Red Army. Through them, too, the nation extended every possible aid to the armed struggle behind the enemy lines.

The German Command was frantic. On July 25, 1941, a little over a month after the outbreak of the war, the nazis issued a special order, following up with a more specific directive on October 25, 1941. German troops were instructed to unleash wholesale terrorism against partisans and the civilian population. The later directive qualified the entire population as responsible for every act of resistance. The inhuman system of hostages was introduced, and all "suspects" were executed out of hand. On November 11, 1942, General-Fieldmarshal Wilhelm Keitel endorsed the Instructions on Combating Partisans in the East, drawn up by General Alfred Jodl. Voicing alarm over the possible effects of partisan activity on army morale, the instructions called for high-powered punitive measures.

---

[1] *I.V.O.V.S.S.*, Vol. 2, p. 485.

But the more brutally the occupation forces behaved, the more rapidly the partisan movement grew. The people's avengers, as Soviet people began to call the partisans, were a terror for the invaders. General Guderian deplored that "the guerrilla war became a veritable plague, which also affected the morale of the men at the front".[1] Werner Picht, a West German militarist ideologist, amplified: "The greater the space that the soldiers seized, the more of a hell that space became for them."[2]

Tens of thousands of more people joined in. In the first four months of 1943 partisan numbers in the Ukraine increased more than two and a half times.[3] As many as 512 units totalling 57,700 men were active in Byelorussia in January 1943, and by November the number went up to 720 with 122,600 men.[4] Partisan strength in Leningrad Region increased more than 10-fold in 1943.[5] Ties with the local population grew stronger and civilian support expanded.

Partisans were conscious of their internationalist duty and accepted people of other nationalities. In late autumn 1941 Fritz Schmenkel, corporal in the nazi army, left his unit and joined the Soviet partisan detachment, "Death to Fascism", operating in Smolensk Region. He fought for the Soviet Union and his own homeland. In the spring of 1943 a Polish partisan unit was formed in Zhitomir and Rovno regions, later growing into a large formation. In September 1943 a Polish partisan unit known as Wanda Wasilewska Brigade was activated as part of the Chernigov-Volyn partisan force.

Slovak soldiers and officers going over to the partisans formed a large unit under Jan Nalepka in May 1943. In November it participated in the fighting for the town of Ovruch, attacked jointly by Soviet troops and the partisan force. Nalepka died a hero's death in that battle and was bestowed the title of Hero of the Soviet Union posthumously.

Powerful partisan forces grew out of the earlier detachments. Some Ukrainian groups, for example, consisted of 3,000 men each by the spring of 1943: the Zhitomir force under A. N. Saburov and Z. A. Bogatyr, the Kholmy force

---

[1] *Bilanz des zweiten Weltkrieges*, S. 93.
[2] *Ibid.*, S. 45.
[3] *I.V.O.V.S.S.*, Vol. 3, p. 459.
[4] *Ibid.*, p. 460.
[5] *Ibid.*, p. 461.

under N. N. Popudrenko and S. M. Novikov, the "Motherland" force in Chernigov Region and another under N. N. Taranushchenko and K. A. Taranyuk.

With war production expanding steadily, the flow of supplies to the partisans—chiefly armaments, ammunition, explosives and communications facilities—increased. Regular radio and air communications, even with transport planes landing in partisan areas, were maintained in many places.

The nature of the operations behind enemy lines changed too. Raids featured more prominently. A partisan cavalry detachment in the Ukraine under M. I. Naumov and I. Ye. Anisimenko roamed across enemy-occupied territory a distance of 2,000 kilometres in the winter of 1943 and was the first to cross into the Southern Ukraine. The Sumy partisan force drove farther still—all the way to the Carpathian foothills, its route totalling nearly 2,000 km. And a long-distance raid by the Byelostock partisan force was also highly successful.

As before, the partisans avoided full-scale battles with large enemy forces. They repulsed the attacks of punitive troops, then disengaged themselves.

In December 1942 and January 1943 the German Command mounted a large punitive operation in Smolensk Region. Its effort proved futile. Inflicting heavy losses, the partisans moved out of reach, pitching new camps and retaining control of the Kletnya woods. In January-March 1943 the nazis went out against partisans in Kalinin Region and various parts of Byelorussia. The partisans were compelled to fight a large-scale action against superior enemy forces. The Central Partisan Headquarters concerted the operation of all partisan forces in the area, defeating the nazis. Another large-scale nazi operation, mounted from Osveya District in Byelorussia against local and Latvian partisans, was also abortive. Kalinin, Byelorussian and Latvian partisans operated jointly on orders from Central Headquarters under a unified local command. While the main force took up defensive positions, the Latvian detachment under V. P. Samson struck against the rear of the punitive troops, and at the junction of the three Soviet Republics a "mound of friendship" was erected after the war in tribute to the comradeship and unity of the Russian, Byelorussian and Latvian partisans.

One of the biggest of Hitler's operations against partisans was mounted in Western Byelorussia in the beginning of

July 1943 by 50,000 men under police Major-General von Gottberg. After 35 days of heavy fighting the punitive force was compelled to withdraw from the Ivenets-Naliboki Forest, the main partisan base.

In the second stage of the partisan movement actions against enemy communication lines, especially the railways, assumed even greater proportions. The "rail war" developed into simultaneous attacks on railways over large areas in the enemy rear. The first concentrated blow was struck in July-August 1943. In a few days tracks at more than 133,000 points were demolished, totalling some 800 km in length.[1] The second similar operation, under the code name Concert, was performed in the latter half of September 1943.

Attacks on communication lines were timed to coincide with Soviet Army operations. Besides, partisan units helped the regular troops in river crossings. During the battle for the Dnieper, the partisans built 25 pontoon bridges for the Red Army and participated in liberating towns and fortified enemy zones (Rechitsa, Yelsk, Cherkassy, Znamenka, etc.). In some cases, the partisans liberated and held towns, district centres and villages (Novoshepelichi, Ovruch, Narovlya, etc.) on their own, clearing the path for the Red Army. When regular troops came to large partisan zones, the co-ordination became closer and still more effective.

Partisans accumulated valuable combat experience, producing knowledgeable and capable commanders and fearless guerrillas. They amounted complicated operations, growing into a factor of strategic magnitude, which the Soviet Supreme Command included in its operational planning.

Unable to wipe out the partisan movement, the nazis vented their fury on captured partisans. They brutally killed the heavily wounded M. I. Guryanov, Komsomols Shura Chekalin, Liza Chaikina, and thousands of others. Yet nothing could break the will of the people's avengers or their faith in final victory.

When the last of the invaders were being driven out of Soviet territory, the partisans hit out against them effectively. The large army of Byelorussian partisans took a most active part in the final battles in Byelorussia. Three days before the Red Army began its Byelorussian Operation the partisans accomplished one of the most powerful actions of the "rail

---

[1] *I.V.O.V.S.S.*, Vol. 3, p. 467.

war", blowing up the tracks at more than 40,000 points in one night, thus paralysing enemy communications. The German Command was in distress, unable swiftly to regroup forces and bring up reserves. The partisans ruled large areas and controlled the roads, showing Soviet troops the way to the enemy rear and helping them surround large nazi formations.

Fraternal Soviet partisan aid to friends in the occupied countries expanded.

Many thousands of Soviet people whom the war had displaced, participated in the armed struggle of the peoples in the overrun countries. Most of them were soldiers and officers escaped from German concentration camps. Far away from their homeland, they saw their duty in fighting the common enemy. Their courage won them affection and respect in Poland, Czechoslovakia, Yugoslavia, France, Belgium, Italy, Norway and other countries.

The first Soviet partisan detachments on Polish soil comprised men and women who had escaped from nazi captivity. One unit was named Chapayev Detachment, and others bore the names Victory, Shchors, For Freedom, Kotovsky. They co-operated closely with Polish partisans and the Gwardia Ludowa, their help to the latter in repulsing German punitive forces in the Parczew woods being a model of co-operation. With superior numbers and armed to the teeth, the invaders were forced to flee.

In due course partisan units, earlier active in nazi-occupied Soviet territory, extended their operations to the neighbouring East and Southeast European countries. Fighting shoulder to shoulder with Polish, Czechoslovak and other patriots, they participated in liberating those countries.

More than 80 Soviet partisan units fought jointly with the Polish partisans in Poland, the joint actions increasing in scale since the spring of 1944, when the First Ukrainian partisan Division under P. P. Vershigora and the partisan detachments and units of I. N. Banov, V. P. Chepiga, V. A. Karasyov, G. V. Kovalyov, M. Ya. Nedelin, V. P. Polikh, N. A. Prokopyuk, S. A. Sankov, B. G. Shangin and I. P. Yakovlev crossed the border into Polish territory along a wide frontage.

In July-August 1944 some Soviet partisan units crossed from Eastern and Southern Poland into Slovakia, including the brigade of V. A. Karasyov, the detachments of M. M.

Shukayev and V. A. Kvitinsky and the units of S. V. Mantsev and Kurov, and the Pozharsky unit. Besides, 24 organiser groups were parachuted into Slovakia by Soviet planes.[1] These grew into large Slovak partisan formations. Captain A. S. Yegorov's group, for example, comprising but 22 men when it landed, was 850 strong a week later and then swelled into a force of 5,000 men of 22 nationalities.[2]

The Soviet partisans actively participated in the Slovak popular uprising—one of the most heroic and glorious chapters of the patriotic struggle in Czechoslovakia.

By mid-1944 as many as 32 Soviet partisan units totalling 1,440 men operated in France. Besides, according to incomplete estimates, another 900 Soviet citizens were members of French partisan units.[3] "The blood of the Soviet partisans that fell on French soil," wrote G. Laroche, a leader of the French Resistance, "is the purest and most enduring cement that has joined the French and Russian peoples in friendship for all time."[4]

Several partisan units consisting of Soviet citizens operated in Belgium. The biggest of these was known as the Homeland Brigade.

Soviet people were also active in the Italian partisan movement. According to Italian historian Roberto Battaglia, "former Soviet POWs, from the unknown soldiers who gave the signal for the rising in Santa-Maria Capua Vetere and fell in battle, to the better-known men who will be well remembered, joined the partisan movement without hesitation".[5] According to a modest estimate at least 2,000 Soviet citizens fought along with the Italian partisans,[6] the number increasing steeply during the April 1945 rising. The Russian battalion covered itself with glory in the Emilia fighting.

Fyodor Poletayev, a collective-farm blacksmith from Ryazan Region, became Italy's national hero. An official partisan document described him thus: "He was as huge

---

[1] *Kommunisticheskaya partiya Chekhoslovakii v borbe za svobodu (The Communist Party of Czechoslovakia in the Struggle for Freedom)*, Moscow, 1951, p. 212.

[2] G. Deborin, *The Second World War*, p. 387.

[3] *I.V.O.V.S.S.*, Vol. 6, p. 318.

[4] *Cahiers du communisme*, No. 3, 1960, p. 411.

[5] Roberto Battaglia, *Storia della Resistenza italiana*, Giulio Einaudi Editore, 1953, p. 324.

[6] *I.V.O.V.S.S.*, Vol. 6, p. 317.

as an oak, kind and brave, like a true Hercules. He was the best among us."[1] The inscription on the tombstone of Nikolai Buyanov, another partisan hero, erected by the Italian people on the place where he was killed, says, "Freedom knows no borders."[2]

Among the mass graves in the Ardeative Caves, sarcophagus No. 329 bears the name, "Kulishkin Alexei". But the Russian sailor, who had served on the destroyer *Silny*, and who took part in the Italian partisan movement—his name was really Alexei Afanasyevich Kubyshkin—had not been shot by the hitlerites as his Italian friends thought (failing to find his body, they put the sarcophagus symbolically) and now resides in Beryozovsk near Sverdlovsk.[3]

The heroism of the Soviet Army and partisans was an example for the entire Resistance Movement.

In the Great Patriotic War Soviet partisans killed, wounded or captured 1,500,000 nazi soldiers, occupation officials and collaborationists, and derailed more than 18,000 troop trains.[4] Not measurable in figures was the moral damage to the nazi army and the uplift and encouragement to people in enemy-occupied territory.

2. Soviet System in the Enemy Rear

If anyone had warned the nazi chiefs that they would never be the real masters in captured territory, they would have scoffed. But that was just what happened. The Byelorussians had a wartime saying: "Peasant lands, partisan forests, German roads and Soviet government." It was very close to the truth. The hitlerites found out that they were unable completely to destroy Soviet power in captured territories. Could anything be more convincing evidence of the stability and endurance of the system and its bonds with the people?

Underground Party branches were formed and were active in occupied territory from the beginning of the Great Patriotic War. They had close ties with the population and partisan units. A Party centre in Minsk guided the work of the under-

---

[1] Roberto Battaglia, *op. cit.*, p. 324.

[2] G. S. Filatov, *Italyanskiye kommunisty v dvizhenii soprotivleniya (Italian Communists in the Resistance Movement)*, Moscow, 1964, p. 113.

[3] A. Kuznetsov, *Taina rimskogo sarkofaga (Roman Sarcophagus Secret)*, Sverdlovsk, 1965.

[4] *I.V.O.V.S.S.*, Vol. 6, p. 281.

ground in the Byelorussian capital through five clandestine district committees, with the underground rural Party committee co-operating closely, along with numerous other rural anti-fascist groups. The Minsk underground was closely associated with the partisan movement.

A new form of resistance evolved: building up large nazi-free zones behind the enemy lines. Partisans in Orel and Bryansk regions and the Ukrainian partisans liberated more than 500 villages in the autumn of 1941, and an extensive partisan zone was established in the Bryansk area. It stretched 260 km north to south and 40-50 km east to west. The initiative was in the hands of the Orel Regional Party Committee.

The number of such zones increased rapidly. Enemy garrisons and the occupation administrations were driven out, with Party and government bodies taking over openly, representing the Soviet system in the enemy rear. Collective farms were put back into operation, newspapers and handbills were printed, and production of equipment and products for partisans was built up. The zones were also useful as a training ground for partisans.

People in liberated areas joined the patriotic movement, aiding the front and bringing closer the final defeat of the enemy. On the 24th anniversary of the Red Army, partisans and collective farmers in the Leningrad zone sent 223 horse-drawn carts of food to the beleaguered city. Among the carters were 30 women. The carts were accompanied by a delegation carrying a message to the defenders of Leningrad. The carts crossed the front-lines and reached their destination safely.

The German Command was aware of the danger of partisan zones. Numerous well-armed punitive expeditions were sent to wipe them out, and depending on the situation the partisans either defended their zones, with some surviving until the invader was driven out by the Red Army, or withdrew, setting up new zones elsewhere.

A large-scale nazi operation was mounted against the Bryansk partisan zone in July-August 1942. Battles raged for more than a month, with the enemy failing to accomplish his mission. In the Dorogobuzh partisan zone, Smolensk Region, however, things went differently because the terrain was hard to defend. The large partisan force moved out by decision of the underground Smolensk Regional Party Committee.

The punitive expedition did not find the partisans, whose relocation, far from reducing the scale of their activities, only facilitated more extensive operations.

The number of underground Party organisations in occupied territory increased considerably towards the end of 1942. An underground Central Committee was set up in the Ukraine to improve guidance of underground work and partisan warfare. Regional Party committees were active in most of the Ukrainian regions, with some, like the Chernigov Committee, headed by A. F. Fyodorov, also active far outside the limits of the region.

The Ukraine had 23 regional committees, 67 city committees, 564 district committees and 4,316 primary Party organisations.[1] Nine underground regional committees, 174 city and district committees, 184 territorial Party branches and 1,113 primary Party organisations in the partisan units operated in Byelorussia.[2] And it was much the same elsewhere in occupied territory.

Erich Koch, nazi Reichskommissar of the Ukraine, had his residence in Rovno, thinking the small Ukrainian town would be safer than a large industrial centre. But he did not reckon with the underground. One Rovno group, under T. F. Novak, had more than 170 members, and another, under P. M. Miryushchenko, nearly 200.[3] Also active there was N. I. Kuznetsov, a courageous undergrounder disguised as a German officer. He shot and killed Alfred Funk, fascist head judge in the Ukraine, on the premises of a German court. Then, helped by a group of partisans and undergrounders, Kuznetsov kidnapped General von Illgen, commander of special punitive forces. Kuznetsov made an attempt on the life of Paul Dargel, Koch's political deputy, the actual head of the occupation administration in the Ukraine. Finally, he executed another of Koch's deputies, General Hermann Knut, and then General Hans Hehl.

Underground Komsomol organisations and branches were active under Party leadership. The Ukraine had nine regional underground Komsomol committees and 213 city and district committees.[4] The Young Guard, an underground youth

---

[1] *I.V.O.V.S.S.*, Vol. 6, p. 275.
[2] *Ibid.*, p. 276.
[3] *Ibid.*, Vol. 3, p. 487.
[4] *Ibid.*, Vol. 6, p. 276.

organisation in Krasnodon, made things uncomfortable for the fascists and their menials in a large section of the Donets Basin. Heading the group was a headquarters comprising YCL members I. V. Turkenich (commander), V. I. Tretyakevich (commissar), Ulyana Gromova, Ivan Zemnukhov, Oleg Koshevoi, Sergei Tyulenin and Lyuba Shevtsova. The organisation issued more than 30 leaflets, each in 5,000 copies.[1] Its combat groups attacked and destroyed troopcarriers, executed traitors, helped Soviet POWs to escape and committed subversive acts in enemy-run factories.

Partisan zones multiplied towards the end of 1942, their area expanding. The biggest were in Byelorussia, with more than half its territory under partisan control by the end of 1943. A large partisan belt, stretching from north-west to south, crossed Byelorussia and the Ukraine, Kalinin, Smolensk, Orel and other regions of the Russian Federation. The zones served as operational bastions that the enemy dared not enter and from which actions were mounted. They were a dependable base for the popular struggle. An area of more than 200,000 sq km was under partisan control in the summer of 1943,[2] equal to that of Britain, Belgium and Denmark combined. Many millions of people lived there, resisting the enemy heroically.

Soviet literature, including newspapers and leaflets, was brought in across the battle-lines and widely circulated in the zones. Meetings, lectures and concerts were held, and films shown. The people observed all Soviet holidays, while the partisans hit the enemy in force to mark them. Donations were collected for tanks and planes, the money being sent to Moscow, along with conscripts for the Red Army.

But the most important fact of all was that the Soviet system existed in a large part of enemy-occupied territory either openly or clandestinely. Neither politically nor spiritually were occupied areas cut off from the rest of the Soviet land. Soviet people, even those in the occupied areas, defended Soviet power and the socialist system devotedly. Nothing the invaders did could shake the patriotism of the Soviet people and their faith in final victory over fascism.

---

[1] *I.V.O.V.S.S.*, Vol. 3, p. 484.
[2] *Ibid.*, Vol. 6, p. 254.

Chapter Eight

Victory in the Offing

1. Offensive Down the Line

Not all in nazi Germany or in Britain and America were yet able to apprehend that the country was doomed. At the beginning of 1945 Germany proper was still almost entirely unaffected by direct military action. Her armies were still immense. Their combat capacity was still of a high order. And factories in Germany were still turning out arms. Yet total defeat was but four months away. Soviet military strength had grown so that it could wipe out fascism on its own.

The Polish, Czechoslovak, Bulgarian and Rumanian armed forces participated actively in the concluding stages of the war, contributing greatly to the victory. Fighting shoulder to shoulder with Soviet soldiers, Polish, Czechoslovak, Bulgarian and Rumanian patriots displayed courage, daring and military prowess. Their meritorious conduct in battle was frequently cited in Soviet military orders.

In the meantime, the rapid succession of defeats on the Soviet-German front sapped the morale of fascist Germany in and behind the battle-lines. A new Soviet offensive would make the situation very desperate. The nazi *Kölnische Zeitung* wrote on February 24, 1945:

"We can no longer rely on the time factor. We have neither reserves nor fortifications that could inspire the hope of the enemy losing wind. Can we find the line of defence the enemy will not breach in the next 24 hours? We are compelled to commit our last strength."

The nazis resorted to their favourite "remedy", redoubling the terror and forcing the soldiers, of whom many were mere boys, to resist to the last. Many youngsters went into battle with tear-stained faces, working the trigger mechanically.

The German High Command issued a barbarous order to turn the eastern part of the country into a death zone. Special SS units forced people by the millions to evacuate. Hundreds of thousands of sick and old men, women and children filled the country roads in the bitter winter's cold. For them the retreat was a horrible and agonising trek. Villages were set afire and cattle was driven west. Roads were strewn with dead cows and horses, pigs, sheep and goats, senselessly destroyed.

The Soviet 1945 offensive was patterned differently than the one of the year before. No longer were the operations successive, but simultaneous, rolling to a start along a vast frontage. The first were the operations known as the Vistula-Oder and the East-Prussian.

In the Vistula-Oder Operation in Polish territory, the Red Army tackled Army Group "A" — 30 divisions and two brigades, not counting a great number of separate battalions and the divisions that were still in the activation stage, with many divisions at full strength, that is, of 12,000 men.

The 1st Byelorussian (Marshal G. K. Zhukov) and the 1st Ukrainian Front (Marshal I. S. Konev) co-operating with the 4th Ukrainian, totalled 163 divisions. The numerical advantage in the main direction — Warsaw and Berlin — was huge: 5.5 : 1 in men, 7.8 : 1 in guns and mortars, 5.7 : 1 in tanks and 17.6 : 1 in planes.[1] The sword of retribution was raised aloft!

The Vistula-Oder Operation began on January 12 with the Soviet troops delivering a devastating blow breaching enemy defences along a 500-km frontage to a depth of 100-160 km,[2] routing the main Army Group "A" forces and relieving a number of cities, including Warsaw, in the first four or six days.

In the second stage, the rate of the advance increased. The liberation of Poland was being completed. German troops were invested group after group, and destroyed. On January 29, the 1st Byelorussian Front crossed into Germany and early in February reached the Oder, seizing important bridgeheads on its left bank. This crowned the operation. To advance farther required appropriate preparation in face of fresh, hastily brought up enemy troops. In the course of

[1] *I.V.O.V.S.S.*, Vol. 5, p. 57.
[2] *Ibid.*, p. 80.

the operation the German Command had shifted units from other sectors, the rear and the West, totalling some 40 divisions.[1]

In the operation 35 enemy divisions were completely wiped out and another 25 almost completely. Prisoners captured totalled 147,000.[2] A huge wedge had been driven into the enemy lines, its tip crossing the Oder near Küstrin. The 1st Byelorussian Front was a mere 60 km from Berlin.

No attack on Berlin was practicable, however, before the nazi East-Prussian group, which imperilled the 1st Byelorussian and 1st Ukrainian fronts, was put out of action. The East-Prussian nazi force, Army Group Centre, comprised 41 divisions at almost full strength,[3] deployed in powerfully fortified areas built up over decades and strongly supported by naval strength.

To smash this force was the job of the 3rd and 2nd Byelorussian fronts, which surpassed the enemy 2.8:1 in men, 3.4:1 in artillery, 4.7:1 in tanks and 5.8:1 in planes.[4]

The East-Prussian Operation went off to a start on January 13, 1945. Despite frantic resistance, the formidable fortifications were crushed and the front breached. Developing the operation according to a well-laid plan, the Soviet troops cut off East Prussia from the rest of the fascist army and slashed it into three isolated sections, the Baltic Fleet, especially its air strength and submarines, taking an active part in the fighting. As a result, the fortified city of Koenigsberg, heart of East Prussia, was blockaded.

The first stage of the East-Prussian Operation ended early in February, with much of the country cleared of German troops. Nearly 52,000 were taken prisoner, and as many as 67,000 were liberated from concentration camps by the 2nd Byelorussian Front alone.[5]

In the second stage the invested nazi troops were destroyed, Koenigsberg taken by storm on April 9 and the fortress of Pilau on April 25. Army Group Centre virtually ceased to exist, East Prussia was captured and the way laid open to Berlin from the northeast.

---

[1] Ibid., p. 88.
[2] Ibid.
[3] Ibid., p. 95.
[4] Ibid., p. 97.
[5] Ibid., p. 123.

There was still a large German force in Eastern Pomerania, to which Berlin attached specific importance. Himmler was in command. Clearly, the enemy meant to use the East-Pomeranian area for a flanking move against the 1st Byelorussian Front, which had reached the Oder. To avert this, the Soviet Command ordered the 2nd Byelorussian and part of the 1st Byelorussian Front to destroy it.

The East-Pomeranian Operation began on February 10, 1945. The enemy had been reinforced, his strength increased to 42 divisions, with a well-fortified defence line and the Gdynia-Danzig fortified zone.

The enemy front was breached, cutting Army Group Vistula in two, and isolating each section. But the fighting continued for nearly three months. The men and officers of the 1st Polish "Heroes of Westerplatte" Brigade helped liberate Gdynia and Danzig, displaying dedication and valour.

The German prisoners ran to 64,000. Meanwhile, 115,000 men and women were freed from concentration camps.[1]

While part of the Soviet troops was engaged in the East-Pomeranian Operation, another part hit out in Silesia. The 1st Ukrainian Front freed nearly 114,000 people from concentration camps in that area.[2] In Upper and Lower Silesia, Soviet units drove through a powerful enemy belt along the Oder, annihilating five and routing 28 nazi divisions,[3] and taking up starting positions in the direction of Berlin, Dresden and Prague. In the meantime, the 1st Byelorussian Front captured an important operational area at the approaches to Berlin, near Küstrin, poised to deliver the final blow.

On the southern wing of the Soviet-German front, the enemy Budapest force was finally crushed and the Hungarian capital cleared of Germans in mid-February. The Red Army drove on to the Austrian border. Eager to retain Austria and at least a part of Hungary, the German Command mounted a large-scale counter-offensive. This began on March 6 near Lake Balaton, the battles assuming huge proportions.

In the first ten days of the counter-offensive, a fascist strike force, comprising chiefly SS divisions, managed to advance 20-30 km but fell short of its assignment. The enemy on-slaught was frustrated by the joint action of Soviet, Bulgarian

---

[1] *I.V.O.V.S.S.*, Vol. 5, p. 148.
[2] *Ibid.*, p. 151.
[3] *Ibid.*, p. 153.

and Yugoslav troops. Meanwhile, an offensive operation was mounted in Czechoslovakia, where the Tudor Vladimirescu 1st Rumanian Volunteer Infantry Division distinguished itself alongside the Soviet troops.

Having stemmed the nazi counter-offensive at Lake Balaton, the Soviet 3rd and 2nd Ukrainian fronts, supported by the Danube Flotilla, began the Vienna Operation on March 16, clearing the rest of Hungary and southeast Austria. On April 13, Soviet troops were in full possession of Vienna, capturing 130,000 men and officers.[1] Prisoners of concentration camps, including Mauthausen, regained their freedom.

At the height of the fighting for Vienna, the Soviet Government issued a statement emphasising that the USSR adhered to "the standpoint of the Moscow Declaration of the Allies on the independence of Austria" and would follow it to the letter.[2] An Austrian Provisional Government was formed on April 27.

The Soviet operations in Hungary and Austria facilitated the actions of the Yugoslav Liberation Army, supported by the Soviet Danube Flotilla, the ships of which were also prominent in the Vienna Operation, giving fire support to the 2nd Ukrainian Front and landing forces on both banks of the Danube.

The war in Europe was approaching its climax. The time of the decisive Berlin Operation had come.

2. In Beleaguered Berlin

In the spring of 1945 the war started by Hitler was sweeping into Germany proper. The German imperialists, who had dreaded a war on two fronts, were between the hammer and the anvil. British and US troops were some 400 km away from Berlin. Soviet troops were nearer still — a mere 60 km away. Bombs showered on Berlin and obviously the city would be stormed at any moment.

The political and military leaders of the Reich installed themselves deep underground in the subterranean vaults of the Imperial Chancellory. The imminence of retribution drove

---

[1] *Ibid.,* p. 219.
[2] *Soviet Foreign Policy During the Great Patriotic War,* Russ. ed., Vol. III, p. 171.

them deep below the surface of the earth. Hitler was there, and Bormann, and Goebbels with his family. The group of generals was headed by Hitler's relative, SS general Hermann Fegelein and Air General Robert Ritter von Greim. The Führer's entourage was fairly numerous, comprising his mistress Eva Braun, his photographer Heinrich Hoffmann, his physician Theodor Morell, who plied him with stimulants, his cook, his secretary and stenographer, his aide-de-camps Otto Günsche and Julius Schaub, the chief of his guard, his butler Heinz Linge, and Erich Kempka, head of the Führer's garage.[1] In addition, there were bodyguards, and messengers who hurried back and forth with countless orders and instructions, frantically issued to protract the resistance.

Germany's true masters, the monopoly tycoons, had long since abandoned Berlin. Some went to Switzerland, others to Sweden, others still across the ocean, while some took up temporary residence in remote country retreats. Just one thing troubled them: what part of Germany would fall to the Soviet troops. They were least bothered by possible complications with British and US occupation authorities, certain that their colleagues in the United States and Britain would give them a helping hand.

The atmosphere in the underground Chancellory was electrified by the tense waiting for the inevitable end. Its denizens appeared less and less frequently in the light of day. The evil spirits that they were, they dictated their will to the remnants of the German army and the civilian population from their subterranean hide-out. The ritual laid down by Hitler was pedantically observed. Each word he uttered was taken down conscientiously by his stenographer. And he uttered many words: he had become loquacious, irrepressibly talkative, and all he said went down in the records. Bormann saw to it, for it was part of his duties to assure that the maniac Führer's heritage should be recorded for posterity.

Hitler's thinking in the last weeks of his life was totally unimaginative: he continued to prattle about his last trump — a possible falling out among the members of the anti-fascist coalition. Here, for example, is what he said to his entourage on February 6, 1945:

"After fifty-four months of titanic struggle, waged on both sides with unexampled fury, the German people now finds

---

[1] G. Boldt, *Die letzten Tage der Reichskanzlei*, Wien, 1947.

itself alone, facing a coalition sworn to destroy it.... The situation is serious, very serious. It seems even to be desperate. We might very easily give way to fatigue, to exhaustion, we might allow ourselves to become discouraged to an extent that blinds us to the weaknesses of our enemies. But these weaknesses are there, for all that. We have facing us an incongruous coalition, drawn together by hatred and jealousy and cemented by the panic with which the National Socialist doctrine fills this Jew-ridden motley.... While we keep fighting, there is always hope, and that, surely, should be enough to forbid us to think that all is already lost."[1]

This is an illustration of the foul methods of fascist propaganda that was straining to persuade all Germans that the anti-fascist coalition would wipe them out physically. To impute its own plans of genocide on others was a typical fascist dodge. And the neo-nazis in present-day West Germany are employing it just as keenly.

According to Tippelskirch, Hitler "thought he had to hold out only until matters would reach the inevitable split among his enemies".[2] Even after the Soviet assault on Berlin began and the distance between the fighting lines and the Imperial Chancellory shrank to mere dozens of yards, Hitler kept on hoping that an armed conflict would flare up for the possession of the German capital between the Soviet Union and its Western allies.

And he did everything within his means to encourage a breach.

The German Government's refusal to surrender, even when Berlin was being stormed, caused immense and senseless losses. And this lunatic resistance was objectively encouraged by the governments of the United States and Britain, whose two-faced policies were for the nazis a source of hope, prompting them to hang on to the last.

3. Victory Flag Over the Reichstag

After the German counter-offensive in the Ardennes was neutralised, US and British troops resumed their eastward advance in February 1945. By the middle of March they

---

[1] *The Testament of Adolf Hitler*, London, 1962, pp. 46-48.
[2] Kurt von Tippelskirch, *Geschichte des zweiten Weltkrieges*, Bonn, 1951, S. 656.

crossed the frontier into Germany and reached the Rhine, capturing two bridgeheads near Remagen and Oppenheim.

The Allies were poised for a large-scale offensive with 80 divisions, including 23 tank and 5 paratroop, while the Germans had 60 divisions on the Western Front, numerically equivalent to a mere 26.[1]

The offensive began on March 23. After breaching the front near Remagen, the American 1st Army lunged east, then veered north, and on April 1 made contact with the 9th Army, which had performed a similar manoeuvre, near the city of Lippstadt. As a result, nazi Army Group "B" was trapped in the Ruhr and cut in two in the subsequent fighting, with the surviving 325,000 men surrendering.[2]

In the meantime, the main American and British forces moved east. On April 11, forward armoured units of the US 9th Army force-crossed the Elbe south of Magdeburg, capturing a bridgehead on its right bank. A second bridgehead was developed two days later southeast of Wittenberg, 100 km from Berlin. But holding these bridgeheads proved difficult. German 12th Army counter-attacks compelled the Americans to abandon the bridgehead south of Magdeburg and considerably reduce the one southeast of Wittenberg. Only some 150-200 km lay between the Red Army and the Allies.

Ever since the autumn of 1944 the Anglo-American command toyed with the idea of capturing Berlin before the Red Army. On September 15, 1944, Eisenhower wrote Fieldmarshal Montgomery: "Clearly, Berlin is the main prize. There is no doubt whatsoever, in my mind, that we should concentrate all our energies and resources on a rapid thrust to Berlin."[3]

It would appear that after the Crimea Conference, which recognised Berlin as part of the Red Army operational area, US and British plans of capturing the German capital should have been scrapped. Churchill, however, was still in favour of them. He sent urgent messages to President Roosevelt on this score, and telegraphed him on April 1: "... From a political standpoint we should march as far east into Germany

---

[1] *I.V.O.V.S.S.*, Vol. 5, p. 249.
[2] *Ibid.*, p. 250.
[3] *The Memoirs of Field-Marshal the Viscount Montgomery of Alamein*, London, 1958, p. 331.

as possible, and... should Berlin be in our grasp we should certainly take it."[1] On the following day, Churchill sent the same plea to Eisenhower: "...We should shake hands with the Russians as far to the east as possible."[2] And on April 5 he again appealed to Roosevelt in the same vein.[3]

Churchill's proposals were turned down by Eisenhower's Headquarters. To begin with, it regarded caution as essential in relations with the Soviet Union and its Red Army—a realistic view, indeed, based on a clear-sighted appraisal of the situation. The second reason flowed from the first; the setbacks with the Elbe bridgeheads showed that the Allied armies were unprepared to storm Berlin, and no time was left for priming. "We would have taken Berlin had we been able to do so," Harry Hopkins, Roosevelt's top adviser, said later. "This would have been a great feather in the army's cap."[4]

Eisenhower's Headquarters worked out an alternate plan — an assault on Dresden. That amounted to a deep Allied penetration into territory which in Yalta had been made part of the Soviet zone of occupation. However, when word of Eisenhower's plan reached the Soviet Government it did not object in the interest of joint action in consummating the defeat of Hitler's armed forces.

A new test for the anti-fascist coalition came with President Roosevelt's death on April 12, 1945. The new president — the same Harry Truman who on June 24, 1941, discoursed in the US press on the advantages that would accrue from a mutual extermination of Russians and Germans—lost no time in declaring "a strong American attitude towards the Soviet Union".[5]

Joyous excitement reigned in the underground Imperial Chancellory when word reached it of Roosevelt's demise. Goebbels congratulated Hitler, who, in turn, let the news be known to the German generals.[6] In his order on April 16, Hitler predicted a radical change in the war.

But the anti-fascist coalition withstood the test.

---

[1] W. Churchill, *op. cit.,* Vol. VI, p. 407.
[2] *Ibid.*, p. 409.
[3] *Ibid.*
[4] Robert E. Sherwood, *Roosevelt and Hopkins. An Intimate History,* New York, 1948, p. 884.
[5] W. Leahy, *I Was There,* New York, 1950, p. 351.
[6] W. Lüdde-Neurath, *Regierung Dönitz,* Göttingen, 1953, S. 22.

Soviet troops were then completing final preparations for the Berlin Operation, to be carried out by the 1st and 2nd Byelorussian and the 1st Ukrainian fronts (Marshals G. K. Zhukov, K. K. Rokossovsky and I. S. Konev, respectively), and the Baltic Fleet. The Polish Army, too, was poised for the action. The offensive was to move into gear along a sector of more than 400 km.

Red Army power was represented in force. The three fronts had 2,500,000 men, with more than 42,000 guns and mortars, more than 6,200 tanks and self-propelled guns, and 8,300 warplanes.[1] Superiority was considerable: 2.5 : 1 in men, 4 : 1 in guns, 4.1 : 1 in tanks and self-propelled artillery, and 2.3 : 1 in air strength.[2]

The enemy scraped the bottom of the barrel to build up as powerful a force as he could. Around Berlin he deployed two armies of the Army Group Vistula and two of the Army Group Centre, comprising 85 divisions and several dozen separate regiments and battalions. Besides, Berlin and the towns around it had strong garrisons, reinforced by the Volkssturm. A total of 200 Volkssturm battalions were hastily formed in the capital, the total strength of the garrison exceeding 200,000.[3] A fortified zone of powerful defence lines ran from the Oder to Berlin, manned well in advance. Fascist propaganda whipped up a fanatical resolve among the men, threatening execution for disobedience and death for surrendering. It issued assurances that the Soviet offensive could be stemmed.

The 1st Byelorussian and 1st Ukrainian fronts mounted the offensive early in the morning on April 16. As many as 143 powerful floodlights were switched on in the assault area for the 1st Byelorussian Front strike force, sending the infantry and tanks over the top. The attack was irresistible. Two hours later the first line of the enemy defences was breached. Among the many stories of bravery, was one about Lyudmila Kravets medical nurse of a company of the 63rd Guards Infantry Regiment who took her place at the head of the men when the commander had been killed and led them in the successful attack.

But when the second line of defence on the steep Zeelow Heights, barely negotiable for tanks and infantry, was reached,

[1] *Soviet Armed Forces in 50 Years*, Russ. ed., p. 434.
[2] *I.V.O.V.S.S.*, Vol. 5, p. 259.
[3] *Ibid.*, p. 253.

the advance bogged down. Costly and bitter was the fighting. Not until the morning of April 18 was the line breached at last. The delay could have slowed down the operation, and the Soviet Supreme Command ordered the 1st Ukrainian Front, advancing south of Berlin, to turn its tank armies northwest, and the 2nd Byelorussian Front, advancing north of Berlin, to turn its main forces southwest. Thus, at the height of the operation, the frontal offensive of the 1st Byelorussian Front was complemented by an enveloping move from north and south by the 1st Ukrainian and 2nd Byelorussian fronts, with part of the 1st Byelorussian Front also used to invest Berlin from the north.

The 47th Army and the 3rd and 5th Shock Armies of the 1st Byelorussian Front, and the Polish 1st Army, which flanked the city from northeast and southwest, were the first to come within firing distance of Berlin. On April 20 they began a methodical bombardment. On the following day, the autobahn ringing Berlin was cut and the fighting carried into the northern and northeastern environs of the city. On April 21 troops of the 1st Byelorussian Front approached Berlin from the east while those of the 1st Ukrainian Front closed in from the south. Investment of the Frankfurt-Guben enemy group was completed southeast of Berlin on April 24. The Berlin group was enveloped the following day, while initial contact was made with American troops near the town of Riesa and Torgau on the Elbe. A few days later Soviet and British troops met near the towns of Schwerin and Rostock. Germany and her armed forces were thus cut into several isolated segments.

The Soviet plan of encircling the enemy armies in Berlin was brilliantly carried out. The rapid advance, in complete accord with the Yalta decisions, frustrated the designs of the fascist leadership and those of certain groups in the United States and Britain. The Red Army Berlin operation was not only military, but also political. Among other things, for the fascist chiefs it closed the avenue of escape west from the German capital.

Fresh Soviet troops were to capture the capital and destroy the German troops refusing to lay down their arms. The powerful enemy force had turned the city into a strongly fortified zone. Top guidance was still in Hitler's hands, though artillery general Helmuth Weidling was put in command. General Walter Wenck's 12th Army operating against the Americans, was rapidly moved east to face the Soviet troops. The order for its deployment was published in newspapers and transmitted over the radio by Goebbels, who said: "...the German troops on the Elbe have turned their back to the Americans."[1] The battle for Berlin proper lasted seven days, from April 26 to May 2, 1945. Soviet forces encountered numerous difficulties, chiefly because the German capital was, in a way, an aggregate of several fortified zones. Marshal Ivan Konev had this to say of the Berlin defences:

"The massive stone buildings were adapted to a state of siege. The door and windows of many buildings were walled up and only firing ports were left.

"A few buildings thus fortified formed a centre of resistance. The flanks were secured by strong barricades up to 4 metres thick, which were simultaneously strong anti-tank obstacles.... In Berlin, especially in the centre, there were many special reinforced-concrete shelters. The largest of them were surface reinforced-concrete bunkers capable of sheltering garrisons of 300-1,000 soldiers.

"Some of the bunkers were six-storeyed and up to 36 metres high; their roofs were 1.5-3.5 metres thick and the walls 1-2.5 metres thick, which made them practically invulnerable to modern systems of field artillery. On the bunker platforms there were usually several anti-aircraft guns which were simultaneously used against aircraft, tanks and infantry.

"These bunkers formed part of the defences within the city limits; Berlin had about 400 of them."[2]

The Battle of Berlin was one more legendary Red Army feat.

In the meantime, the US and British governments used a variety of channels to negotiate with the nazi chiefs. One of these was the mission entrusted to Folke Bernadotte, a member of the Swedish royal family, closely connected with British monopoly tycoons. He visited Eisenhower's headquarters on November 2, 1944, after which he went to Berlin to meet Ribbentrop, Kaltenbrunner and other prominent nazis on February 16, 1945. However, he devoted himself mainly to talks with Heinrich Himmler, whom he met on several occasions. Their last conversation took place on April

---

[1] Kurt von Tippelskirch, *op. cit.*, S. 664.
[2] I. S. Konev, *Year of Victory*, Moscow, 1969, pp. 175-76.

24 in the Swedish Consulate in Luebeck, the premises spar-
ingly lit by two wax candles. Already, the lunatic fascist
world lay in darkness.

Himmler said to Bernadotte: "It is quite possible that
Hitler is already dead.... And if he isn't, he is sure to die
within the next few days. Berlin is surrounded and its fall is
a question of a few days.... I recognise that the Reich is
vanquished.... In the new situation I consider my hands free.
I am determined to spare as much territory as possible from
the Russian invasion. I am prepared to capitulate on the
Western Front. The armies of the Western powers will
thereby be enabled to advance rapidly as far as possible to
the east. In contrast, I have no intention of surrendering on
the Eastern Front."[1]

Hurrying back to Sweden, Bernadotte informed the British
and American ministers of Himmler's proposals through the
Swedish Foreign Minister. On April 25, the US leaders,
with President Truman at their head, gathered in the War
Department to discuss Himmler's terms and then consulted
Churchill by phone. The temptation to strike the deal was
great, but the military and international situation ruled out
a transaction with the most obnoxious of the nazi chiefs
after Hitler. The proposal was rejected and the Soviet
Government informed about Bernadotte's talks. Two days
later an account appeared in the British press. Learning of
Himmler's initiative, Hitler ordered him expelled from the
nazi party.

On April 23, Goering, then in South Germany, sent Hitler
a radiogram informing him of his intention to place himself
at the head of Germany, inasmuch as Hitler's government in
surrounded Berlin was incapable of functioning. Like Himmler, Goering intended to approach Eisenhower and come to
terms on terminating hostilities in the West. He ordered
General Karl Koller, Luftwaffe Chief of Staff, to draft an
appropriate manifesto. Goering said: "The Russians must
believe the manifesto when they hear it; they must believe
that we intend to continue resisting against West and East,
while the British and the Americans must interpret it as a
statement of our intention to terminate hostilities in the
West and to continue fighting the Soviets. The soldiers must
be given to understand that the war is continuing, but that

---

[1] F. Bernadotte, *La fin,* Lausanne, 1945, pp. 101, 103.

at the same time its end, a favourable one for us, is near."[1]

Learning of Goering's intentions, Hitler expelled him from his party and ordered his arrest, as well as that of Koller and others.

On April 27 the fighting had reached the centre of the German capital. The enemy force was compressed in a narrow strip running 15 km from east to west and 2-5 km from north to south. On the following day, it was cut up into three pockets. On Hitler's orders, the SS flooded the underground Friedrichstrasse station of the city railway where thousands of women, children and wounded German soldiers and officers had sought refuge on April 28.

Early in the morning of April 30 Soviet troops stormed the Reichstag building. They had to fight for every room, every corridor, every landing and the basement. In the morning of May 1 the Soviet victory banner was hoisted on the sculpture crowning the fronton, raised there by the scouts M. A. Yegorov and M. V. Kantaria of the 756th Regiment. While bitter fighting still raged for the Reichstag, other troops reached the proximity of the Imperial Chancellory.

By midday on April 30, Hitler finally understood that there was no salvation, that the hour of retribution had come. After a ceremony in which he wedded Eva Braun, he made her a gift of an ampule of calcium cyanide, then took his own life by shooting himself in the mouth. His entourage carried his corpse into the yard of the Imperial Chancellory under Soviet gunfire, poured gasoline over it and set it alight. "Hitler's funeral pyre," said Churchill, "with the din of the Russian guns growing ever louder, made a lurid end to the Third Reich."[2] Goebbels took the life of his children and wife, and committed suicide the following day. Bormann disappeared.

On May 2 the resistance of the Berlin garrison was finally crushed. Its remnants, comprising 134,000 men and officers,[3] surrendered. All in all, the Soviet troops and Polish units captured 480,000 prisoners in the Berlin Operation.[4]

The fall of Berlin and the inglorious end of the nazi chiefs was well deserved for crimes committed. It was also a serious warning to all new pretenders to world supremacy. The Red

[1] Karl Koller, *Der letzte Monat*, Mannheim, 1949, S. 39-40.
[2] W. Churchill, *op. cit.*, Vol. VI, p. 464.
[3] I. Konev, *op. cit.*, p. 191.
[4] *I.V.O.V.S.S.*, Vol. 5, p. 288.

banner over the Reichstag became the symbol of victory over fascism.

Berlin, the heart of German imperialism and the seat of German aggression, lay prostrated. The war in Europe fast neared its end.

4. Soviet Tanks Race to Prague

Soviet operations designed to liberate Czechoslovakia began in 1944 and gained in intensity at the beginning of 1945. Apart from the difficulties created by the terrain, the Red Army had to cope with a strong enemy force. At the beginning of May two enemy army groups—Army Group Centre under General Fieldmarshal Franz Schoerner and Army Group Oesterreich under Colonel-General Lothar Rendulic, were still deployed in the country, comprising 62 divisions, including 16 panzer and motorised.[1] After the Soviet troops took Berlin, the Schoerner-Rendulic group was the strongest of the remaining German fascist forces and had no intention to lay down its arms until, at worst, it had fought its way to reach the US and British armies.

Schoerner's plans were anything but unrealistic. In a telegram to Truman on April 30, Churchill said: "The liberation of Prague and as much as possible of the territory of western Czechoslovakia by your forces might make the whole difference to the postwar situation in Czechoslovakia."[2] The US and British governments wanted their troops push ahead as far as Prague. General Patton, US 3rd Army, entered Czechoslovak territory early in May 1945. Before taking Pilsen, the city was bombed by US planes, demolishing or damaging as much as two-thirds of the housing. The US Command lost no time in dissolving the national committees in Pilsen and other Czech towns, replacing them with an occupation regime.

On May 4, in a letter to the Soviet General Staff, Eisenhower revealed his intention to advance to the rivers Vltava and Elbe, meaning to capture Prague.[3] In its reply on the following day the Soviet Supreme Command insisted on

---

[1] *Ibid.*, p. 317.
[2] W. Churchill, *op. cit.*, Vol. VI, p. 442.
[3] *Izvestia*, May 5, 1968.

fidelity to the earlier agreed decision on the demarcation line between the Soviet and American troops along Czechoslovakia's western frontier.[1] On May 6, spokesmen of the US Command arrived in Schoerner's residence in Velihovka, a health resort. They came to terms with the nazi general about his suppressing the resistance movement in Czechoslovakia and continuing actions against the Red Army, with the subsequent surrender of his troops to the US Command.

In the meantime, the people of Czechoslovakia were poised for a general armed uprising. The first to rise were the workers of Kladno, a large industrial centre. On May 5 a rising flared in Prague, with the armed citizenry occupying strategic points. But the 40,000 nazis stationed in the city mounted a counter-offensive. In the order of the day, Schoerner said the rising "must be suppressed with all available means."[2] The Czechoslovak capital was attacked by the SS Panzer Reich Division, SS Panzer Wiking Division and a reinforced Reich Division regiment.[3] But the ranks of the insurrectionists swelled. They were 30,000,[4] but arms and combat experience were lacking. The nazis pressed forward steadily to the centre of the city. Unable to withstand the onslaught of the strong enemy force, the Prague patriots appealed urgently for help over the radio. And help arrived from the Soviet Army.

There was only one way to help Prague: while the months-long offensive of the 1st, 2nd and 4th Ukrainian fronts (the last-named included the Czechoslovak Corps) continued, a task force would strike from Berlin at the rear of the Schoerner group. On the way were the Krusnehory Mountains, a difficult natural barrier. "To rout Schoerner's million-strong group which had established itself in Czechoslovakia as quickly as possible, to take Prague, save the city from destruction and save the inhabitants of Prague, and not only of Prague, from annihilation, we had no alternative but to break directly through the Krusnehory Mountains."[5] Ten Soviet tank corps of the 1st Ukrainian Front, a total of 1,600 tanks, were dispatched to Prague.[6]

The Prague Operation opened on May 6 with a Soviet

---

[1] *Izvestia*, May 5, 1968.
[2] *Ibid.*
[3] *Ibid.*
[4] *I.V.O.V.S.S.*, Vol. 5, p. 315.
[5] I. Konev, *op. cit.*, p. 204.
[6] *Ibid.*, p. 207.

lunge to Dresden. On May 8, the Red Army and Polish troops captured the city. Near Dresden, across the Elbe, in the corridors of an old mine, Soviet soldiers found the priceless paintings of the famous Dresden Picture Gallery, hidden by the hitlerites.

On the night of May 8, the tank corps of the 1st Ukrainian Front traversed 80 km to literally race across the Krusnehory Mountains and at 02.30 hours of May 9 reached the outskirts of Prague. The reception they received from the people was truly enthusiastic.

On May 10, the Soviet troops closed the ring round the main Schoerner forces, preventing them from fleeing west. During May 10 and 11 most of the nazi troops, comprising 780,000 men and officers and 35 generals, were taken prisoner.[1]

The swift manoeuvre saved Prague from destruction and the insurgents from annihilation. The liberation of Czechoslovakia was complete. Furthermore, the Soviet Union frustrated the US imperialist plan of capturing Prague and occupying the country. But for this resolute action, Czechoslovak independence would not have been regained and the country's historical territory—the Sudeten region and other areas handed to Germany under the disgraceful Munich terms—would not have been returned. As many as 140,000 Soviet men and officers paid with their lives for Czechoslovak freedom.

The brilliant Soviet operation in which Prague was liberated and Schoerner's troops defeated, was legitimately the crowning event of the European war. Until the final shot the Soviet Union was a true champion of legitimate liberative aims. It lived up to its lofty mission of liberator and discharged fully its internationalist obligations to the peoples of Europe.

The military defeat of German fascism liberated the German people from the nazi yoke.

5. Intolerance of Fascism, Humane Treatment of the People

The entry of German territory by Soviet troops carried the war into the land where it had started. Red Army soldiers and officers were filled with hatred of fascism, German imperi-

---

[1] *I.V.O.V.S.S.*, Vol. 5, p. 354.

alism and the forces of war. The Communist Party taught them, however, to distinguish between war criminals and the people of Germany.

When still only driving into East Prussia, the history of which, abounding in campaigns of conquest, incensed the Soviet troops, the Military Council of the 2nd Byelorussian Front issued an order prescribing humane treatment of the population. Unlike the nazi invaders, who had sown death and destruction in territories they overran, the Red Army behaved with dignity, preserving the honour of the socialist state.

At the beginning of the Berlin Operation, General Head-quarters published a directive on changing the attitude towards Germans, prescribing humane treatment of the population and rank-and-file members of the National-Socialist Party who showed loyalty to the Red Army. Only the leaders were to be apprehended. German administrations would be set up in the districts and the town magistratures would be headed by German burgomasters.[1] The Soviet attitude was a clear manifestation of the Red Army's mission of liberation.

* * *

That the Soviet directives prescribing humane treat-ment of the German population were correct was borne out by subsequent developments. Although the democratic forces in Germany had failed to disarm the nazis before it had been too late, patriots in towns and villages braved the Gestapo and SS terror, mounting active anti-fascist operations during the last days of the Third Reich. In many localities this had facilitated the Red Army advance, saving lives and preventing destruction of towns, villages and factories; Gestapo attempts to wipe out the German anti-fascists were frustrated in many places.

In some German towns the people were happy to see the Soviet troops. This was the case in Eisleben, where a banner had been preserved which was presented before the war by Soviet miners from Krivoi Rog. More, its people put up a statue of V. I. Lenin brought by the nazis from Soviet ter-ritory for smelting. The event was later described by a journal-

---

[1] *I.V.O.V.S.S.*, Vol. 5, p. 277.

ist in the following terms: "The market-place was a sea of red flags. In the old town-hall a democratic administration, a representative body of the working class was installed under the glorious banner of the Krivoi Rog miners which Otto Brosowski, the Party veteran, would not relinquish despite torture and solitary confinement by the fascists. In the open... stood a statue of Lenin — material evidence that in this part of Germany the torch of proletarian internationalism had never gone out, that the banner of Ernst Thaelmann's Party had been held high, untainted, despite the fascist darkness."[1]

The Soviet Government and military administration extended aid to the civilian population, particularly in Berlin. Soon after the fascist garrison of the capital had surrendered, Anastas Mikoyan arrived on a special mission to assure food supplies and other material aid. Nearly six million poods of flour and grain and considerable quantities of other products, including coffee beans, were set aside for this purpose out of the army supplies; by the end of May, the Soviet Command issued ration cards to the three-million population of the city and organised the issue of food. The people were inoculated to prevent disease and life in the city began gradually returning to normal. The Berlin subway, the trams and other city transport were restarted by the beginning of June, the bridges in the city were repaired, and the supply of water, gas and electricity restored.

Soviet servicemen rendered help to the German population, assisting it as energetically as they had but recently fought the fascist armies. Intolerance of nazism blended with humane treatment of the people.

That was the beginning of the Soviet occupation of East Germany, which lasted four years. The Soviet Union helped the people in the eastern part of Germany to survive the national disaster brought about by the monopoly tycoons, lifting them back to life, helping them clear the way for progress and lay the foundation of a sovereign, independent, democratic and peace-loving state on German soil.

A credit for the Soviet occupation authorities is their help to the Germans to cast off despondence, indifference and political passiveness that gripped them after the crushing defeat. They wakened their political initiative, sense of national responsibility and democratic self-awareness. The local

---

[1] Otto Winzer, *op. cit.*, S. 259.

progressive forces co-operated. The Soviet military administration was consistently on the side of the people and the Left parties, acting as a class ally.

6. Seen and Unseen Strength of the Resistance Movement

In April and May 1945, while the Red Army was mopping up the remnants of the battered nazi war machine, armed risings swept Europe against the German occupation forces. The Prague rising was but one of many.

The resistance movement was gathering momentum in Italy. Speaking on its behalf, the Italian Communist Party issued a directive on April 10, 1945, saying in part:

"Now is the time not only to intensify the partisan war, but to prepare and spark a real uprising."[1]

The following day a partisan offensive began, and two days later the partisans cut the roads along which German troops were retreating north out of Italy.

On April 25 all Northern Italy was up in arms. Action by the people of the three biggest working-class centres—Genoa, Milan and Turin—was a signal for a general rising. The more than 30,000 German troops stationed in and around Genoa were attacked by the insurgents, and surrendered. Bitter fighting erupted in Turin, with the hitlerites resisting desperately. By April 30, however, the city was fully cleared. The workers of Milan, too, wiped out a large fascist garrison. Thus, in the north town after town were cleared of the invader. After Genoa, Milan and Turin, the nazis were expelled from Bologna, Modena, Parma, Piacenza, Verona, Padua and other cities. The partisans prevented destruction of factories and communication lines, captured depots of arms and ammunition, and took tens of thousands of prisoners. In the liberated towns and areas they established National Liberation Committees, exercising local authority. On behalf of the troops under his command in Liguria, General Meinhold surrendered in Genoa, to Remo Scappini, a worker and chairman of the local National Liberation Committee.

As many as 256,000 Italian partisans organised in 1,090 brigades participated in the liberation war against fascism.

---

[1] R. Battaglia, *op. cit.*, p. 541.

As many as 575 were named Garibaldi brigades, activated and led by Communists. Out of the 350,000 people taking part in the liberation struggle during the war, 210,000 were members of the Communist Party. And out of the 70,930 partisans killed in battle 42,558 were members of Garibaldi brigades.[1] Luigi Longo observed that "the popular resistance and national liberation war owe their scale, depth and success primarily to the activity and policy of the Communist Party, its rank-and-file, and the mass of the people".[2]

The patriotic movement in Italy was against the German occupation forces, which committed the same atrocities in Italy as they did in other occupied countries. Also, it was against the Mussolini regime, reduced to a nazi puppet and ensconced in a small northern resort, the name of which, Salo, was given to the "republic" founded by the fascist leader under German protection. A rising in that part of the country soon put an end to "La republica di Salo".

Mussolini knew the people would not spare him, and fled with the Germans. However, on April 27, 1945, a partisan detachment commanded by Pedro stopped near the border a German column consisting of an armoured car, several motorcycles with mounted machine-guns, a passenger car and 38 personnel carriers. The partisans were but 18 in all, but engaged the enemy fearlessly and finally compelled him to negotiate. In the ensuing negotiations the Germans were told they could continue on their way to the border after a thorough check.

In the armoured car was Mussolini and his entourage, many valuables and the Duce's personal archive. The fascist dictator climbed unnoticed into one of the personnel carriers, tied a handkerchief round his cheek, feigning a toothache, put on dark glasses, and wrapped a German army greatcoat round his shoulders. Masquerading as a German soldier, he lay down on the bottom of the lorry. That is where he was spotted by partisan Giuseppe Negri. The latter gave no sign of recognition, quietly approached his commander and informed him of his find. Mussolini was arrested. So were his associates, who made a desperate bid to escape in the armoured car. Sentenced by a military tribunal of the Northern Italy National Liberation Committee, Mussolini, his mistress

---

[1] *For a Lasting Peace, for People's Democracy*, May 6, 1955.
[2] *Trenta anni di vita e lotte del PCI*, Rome, p. 173.

Claretta Petacci, the ideologue of extremist fascist terror Alessandro Pavolini, and a few other close associates of the Duce, were executed by a firing squad. Their corpses were put on display in Piazza Loreto in Milan.

The workers of Trieste rose on April 28. Helped by the Yugoslav People's Liberation Army, which approached Trieste from southeast, they cleared the city of Germans in two days. The US and British rulers regarded Trieste as an important strategic point, for which reason British tanks swept into it on May 2. Churchill ordered Field-marshal Alexander to put down the insurrection. "It would be wise," he wrote, "to have a solid mass of troops in this area, with a great superiority of modern weapons and frequent demonstrations of the Air Force." He added: "Have some strong naval forces there."[1] His order was obeyed. Alexander set up a stiff occupation regime, based on Mussolini's fascist legislation.

A new series of risings erupted in nazi concentration camps. Headed by Soviet POWs, an uprising broke out in Buchenwald on April 11, culminating in victory.

Thus, all through the war and especially in 1944 and 1945, significant risings occurred in many European countries — Albania, Belgium, Bulgaria, Greece, Italy, Poland, Rumania, France, Czechoslovakia and Yugoslavia which grew into popular armed struggle. Nothing even approaching that scale had ever been seen in European history. Everywhere on the continent the risen people hit the invaders, contributing to the common anti-fascist cause.

The strength of the Resistance movement was incontestable. It was inspired by the example of the Soviet soldiers and the Soviet offensives were a major contribution to the success of Resistance fighters in all countries. The Resistance and the stand of the Soviet people against the German fascists were evidence of the enhanced role of the masses in the process of history. Last but not least, the Resistance demonstrated the peoples' craving for national independence and freedom, for deep-going social reconstruction.

It was natural that the popular movements developed. In a number of countries there emerged a people's democratic power. But even where the people failed to overcome their class adversaries for one reason or another — external rather

---

[1] W. Churchill, *op. cit.*, Vol. VI, pp. 482-83.

than internal—the Resistance bore the features of a popular revolution and left an ineradicable mark on the mass consciousness. Battaglia says the following on this score: "No matter what the adversities the future may hold for Italy, it is beyond doubt that the way to the future lies through the Resistance movement and doubtless, too, that the popular forces have deep roots in the country.... No attempt at establishing foreign or internal domination can ever rob the people of Italy of their homeland, retrieved despite all difficulties."[1]

7. The Enemy Surrenders

The pre-history of the Doenitz government is one of the unrevealed secrets of the Second World War. During the last days of the fascist Reich, Admiral Karl Doenitz was in command of the German navy, with headquarters at the extreme northern tip of the country near the German-Danish border. Unexpectedly, he received a radiogram signed by Bormann from the Imperial Chancellory on April 30 at 18.35 hours. "In place of the former Reich-Marshal Goering," it said, "the Führer appoints you, Herr Grand Admiral, as his successor. Written authority is on its way. You will immediately take all such measures as the situation requires."[2]

The telegram was sent in Hitler's name when he was already dead, though this is not mentioned in it. Yet the man who was about to commit suicide was not likely to have thought of a successor. "If I am to perish," Hitler used to say, "the German nation, too, shall perish, for then it will not have been worthy of me."[3]

What alerts one, too, is the fact that even before the telegram was sent, the British Government ordered its troops not to enter those towns in Northern Germany, where Doenitz had his headquarters. In any case, it was not Hitler who had tried to preserve the fascist regime in Germany after his death.

Doenitz, a faithful nazi and Hitler's admirer, replied to

---

[1] R. Battaglia, *op. cit.*, p. 573.
[2] H. R. Trevor-Roper, *The Last Days of Hitler*, New York, 1947, p. 207.
[3] Walter Görlitz und Herbert Quint, *Adolf Hitler, Eine Biographie*, Stuttgart, 1952, S. 627.

Bormann's telegram: "My loyalty to you, my Fuehrer, remains unshaken."[1]

A second radiogram from Bormann reached Doenitz's headquarters on May l at 10.53 hours. Curtly, it said: "Testament in force."[2] After this, Doenitz's radio stations broadcast a statement informing Germans that Hitler, who committed suicide on May 1, 1945, had appointed Admiral Doenitz as his successor. Lies that had surrounded Hitler all his life, accompanied him to his grave.

On the same day, Doenitz proclaimed himself Fuehrer of the German state and Commander-in-Chief of the Armed Forces. He quickly formed a fascist government. Some 500 prominent nazi leaders, including Himmler and General Jodl, were gathered in Flensburg, where the government was constituted. They were not daunted by the fact that the territory under Doenitz's jurisdiction was, in effect, but a small part of Schleswig-Holstein. They banked on the new government's extending its authority.

In fact, the Doenitz government was semi-officially recognised by the United States and Britain. Doenitz and Montgomery, the British Commander-in-Chief, came to terms that Flensburg and its environs would remain unoccupied.[3] Doenitz defined his policy as follows: "We must go along with the Western powers and work with them in the occupied territories in the West, for only by working with them can we have hopes of later retrieving our land from the Russians."[4]

There must certainly have been grounds for Doenitz's hope of a deal with Britain and the United States. Yet the secret behind it did not come to light until well after the war. An entry in the diary of Alanbrooke, Chief of the Imperial General Staff and Chairman of the Chiefs-of-Staff Committee, revealed that in May 1945 he had examined a report by the Planners of Chiefs-of-Staff Committee "on the possibility of taking on Russia...".[5] Field-marshal Montgomery, too, refers in his memoirs to the plan's existence.[6] And Churchill

[1] Joachim Schultz, *Die letzten 30. Tage aus dem Kriegstagebuch des OKW*, Stuttgart, 1951, S. 59-60.
[2] Walter Lüdde-Neurath, *Regierung Dönitz*, Gottingen, S. 47.
[3] *Ibid.*, S. 75.
[4] *The Times*, August 17, 1948.
[5] Arthur Bryant, *Triumph in the West 1943-1946*, London, 1959, p. 469.
[6] *The Memoirs of Field-Marshal the Viscount Montgomery of Alamein*, p. 380.

admitted in 1954 that he had telegraphed Lord Montgomery, "directing him to be careful in collecting the German arms, to stack them so that they could easily be issued again to the German soldiers whom we should have to work with if the Soviet advance continued".[1] The reference to the "Soviet advance" was pure eyewash.

American and British generals in direct command of the troops in the field, however, were opposed to a war against the Soviet Union. To begin with, they knew the USSR could not be defeated. Secondly, they knew the British soldiers would refuse to fight against the Soviet Union. Alanbrooke, for one, put down the following in his diary, referring to a war against the USSR: "The idea is, of course, fantastic and the chances of success quite impossible. There is no doubt that from now onwards Russia is all-powerful in Europe."[2]

"The British people," wrote Montgomery, "would never have been persuaded to fight the Russians in 1945." And he amplified: "The Russians had been built up as heroes during the German war, and any British government that wanted to fight them in 1945 would have been in for trouble at home."[3]

Although the plans of war against the Soviet Union, which the British and American imperialists had nourished in 1945, fell through, their governments and military commands did everything in their power to gain control of as large a part of the defeated German troops as they could.

In secret negotiations between SS General Karl Wolff and Allen Dulles back in March 1945, the two drafted the plan for Operation Crossword. The idea was that German troops would withdraw from Italy to southwest Germany, where they would stay at the disposal of the US and British governments. Vigorous Soviet protests and eruption of the armed uprising in Italy frustrated that operation.

After the Doenitz government was formed, secret negotiations on placing the surviving German armies at the disposal of the US and British commands, were continued and expanded. On Doenitz's instructions, Admiral Hans von Friedeburg, placed in command of the German navy, entered into

---

[1] *Daily Herald,* November 24, 1954.
[2] A. Bryant, *op. cit.,* p. 470.
[3] *The Memoirs of Field-Marshal the Viscount Montgomery of Alamein,* pp. 380-81.

negotiations with Montgomery. Culminating the talks, which were held behind the Soviet Union's back, an agreement was concluded in the afternoon of May 4 that all German armed forces in Holland, north-west Germany, Schleswig-Holstein and Denmark, would surrender to the British.

In the period of May 2 to 5, the Anglo-American Command accepted the surrender of German troops in Italy (Army Group "C"), Croatia and Southern Austria (Army Group "E"), Bavaria and West Austria (Army Group "G"), Vorarlberg and Tirol (German 19th Army).

Encouraged, Doenitz despatched Friedeburg to Eisenhower's headquarters in Rheims. Simultaneously, he issued the order ending the submarine war against the Western powers and prohibiting the underground fascist terrorist Werwolf groups to operate against the United States and Britain.[1]

Friedeburg arrived in Rheims on May 5. That day, General Patton, representing the American Command, assumed control of fascist Germany's military academy evacuated from Berlin. In talks with General Bedell Smith, Eisenhower's Chief of Staff, Friedeburg suggested the Allies should accept the surrender of Schoerner's and Rendulic's troops. This was tantamount to their seizing a large section of Czechoslovakia. The proposal was received favourably by Eisenhower's headquarters, but proved impracticable. Schoerner's surrender to the Allies was frustrated by the Soviet operation liberating Czechoslovakia and by the rising of the Prague patriots.

Meanwhile, Doenitz's government was preoccupied with a new plan: that of a separate surrender to the United States and Britain. Jodl was quickly bundled off to Rheims to assist Friedeburg. General Bedell Smith accepted the proposal brought by Jodl. Preparations were under way for a formal signing by Germany of an instrument of surrender to but the United States and Britain. However, aware of the firm Soviet position and the probable consequences of such unheard-of perfidy, Eisenhower turned his thumbs down. A protocol on Germany's unconditional surrender was signed in Rheims on May 7, 1945, at 02.41 hours.

In the early hours of May 7, General A. I. Antonov, Chief of the Red Army General Staff, addressed a message

---

[1] W. Lüdde-Neurath, *op. cit.*, S. 62.

to the heads of the British and American Military missions in Moscow, suggesting that the Rheims instrument be regarded as temporary and that a general unconditional surrender instrument be signed in Berlin. The governments and military commands of the United States and Britain consented.

The instrument of Germany's unconditional surrender was signed at midnight, May 8, 1945, in Karlhorst, a Berlin suburb, by representatives of Hitler's military command, Fieldmarshal Keitel, Admiral Friedeburg and Air Force Col.-Gen. Stumpff. The Soviet Supreme Command was represented by Marshal of the Soviet Union G. K. Zhukov, the Supreme Command of the Allied Expeditionary Force by British Chief Air Marshal Arthur Tedder, the US Armed Forces by General Carl Spaatz, and the French Armed Forces by their Commander-in-Chief, General Delattre de Tassigny.

The surrender instrument formalised the conclusion of the war in Europe. But for the political conclusion it was essential to dissolve Doenitz's fascist government.

That government enjoyed the increasing goodwill of the United States and Britain. On their insistence the Allied Control Commission, formed to assure fulfilment of the unconditional surrender terms, began its functions on May 13 in Flensburg—something that the Doenitz government responded to with enthusiasm. From May 13 to 16, in the absence of the Soviet representatives, the British and American members of the ACC settled many a point with Doenitz. They came to terms with him on co-operation, and on Jodl's appointment as Chief of Staff of the German High Command, with whom many military and organisational issues were settled.[1] Finally, the American and British representatives paid an official call on Doenitz, the latter assuring them of this "Western orientation" and urging joint action against the Soviet Union. "This," a German historian wrote later, "made an obviously strong impression on the two generals."[2]

On May 16, in contravention of the Crimea decisions, Churchill officially declared that the United States and Britain had "no intention of undertaking the burden of administering Germany",[3] meaning that it would be shifted

---

[1] J. Schultz, op. cit., S.112.
[2] W. Lüdde-Neurath, op. cit., S. 105.
[3] The Times, May 17, 1945.

on to the Doenitz government. The *Daily Herald*, the British Labour Party newspaper, styled this flirting with Doenitz as "monstrous", adding, "in Germany, desperate adventurers continue to pose as a Government".[1]

The situation changed when the Soviet representatives on the Allied Control Commission arrived in Flensburg on May 17. They insisted on shutting down Doenitz's "establishment". The Grand Admiral's fate was sealed. The Soviet Government took a firm stand. There was public outcry in the United States and Britain, and a total absence of support for Doenitz in Germany, whose people aptly named him and his entourage a "government of ghosts". On May 23, 1945, the Doenitz government was dissolved and its members arrested as war criminals.

On June 5 the Soviet Union, the United States, Britain and France signed in Berlin the Declaration Regarding the Defeat of Germany and the Assumption of Supreme Authority with Respect to Germany, saying that the four powers assumed "supreme authority in Germany, including all the powers possessed by the German Government, the High Command, and any state, municipal, or local government or authority".[2] The German armed forces would be disarmed and all arms and war facilities turned over to representatives of the four powers. The Declaration provided for the immediate release and repatriation of POWs and civilian nationals of the United Nations in Germany, and for the immediate arrest of all top fascist leaders and other war criminals.

Concurrently, agreements were signed on the control machinery and zones of occupation. The former envisaged that "in the period when Germany is carrying out the basic requirements of unconditional surrender, supreme authority in Germany will be exercised, on instructions from their governments, by the British, United States, Soviet, and French Commanders-in-Chief, each in his own zone of occupation, and also jointly, in matters affecting Germany as a whole. The four Commanders-in-Chief will together constitute the Control Council."[3] The Control Council was to assure agreed measures by the four C-in-Cs in their respective zones and adopt joint decisions on matters of

---

[1] *Daily Herald*, May 17, 1945.
[2] *The Times*, June 6, 1945.
[3] *Ibid.*

principle relevant to Germany as a whole. Administration of Greater Berlin was delegated to the Inter-Allied Commandatura, which functioned under the general supervision of the Control Council and consisted of four Commandants.

The Statement on Zones of Occupation defined the border between the Soviet zone and those of the Western powers, still squabbling among themselves over the borders between their zones. The agreements, concluded in Berlin, provided for the immediate withdrawal of Anglo-American troops from the Soviet occupation zone and the partition of Berlin into four sectors.

A month later, the four powers reached agreement on zones of occupation and the control machinery in Austria. Concluded thanks to Soviet diplomacy, the latter agreement recognised the right of the Austrian nation to independent national existence within an integral state. In the German question, too, the Soviet Union adhered firmly to the principle of Germany's integrity and national independence. The Soviet occupation of part of German and Austrian territory was an act of retribution against fascism, but at once selfless aid to the peoples in achieving a democratic arrangement and their national and social aspirations. Also, Soviet policy towards vanquished Germany was prompted by the long-term aim of a lasting European peace.

8. The Conference in Potsdam

The third and last war conference of the Soviet, US and British leaders took place in Potsdam's Cecilienhof, July 17-August 2, 1945. The atmosphere there was quite different from that of the two preceding conferences. The war in Europe was over. The ruling elements in the United States and Britain were eager to assure themselves of the place of dominance in the postwar world, and, if matters went so far, were prepared to make use of defeated Germany in promoting their ends. With President Roosevelt's death and Truman's assumption of the presidency, the tendency to toughen the attitude to the Soviet Union gained ascendancy in the US Administration. Work on atomic weapons was stepped up on the President's orders.

On July 16, on the eve of the conference, the US delegation, with the President at its head, received word of the first experimental bomb test in New Mexico. From then on it was preoccupied with the problem of how to demonstrate US atomic power and what advantages this would bring to the United States. State Secretary James Byrnes said: "...The bomb might well put us in a position to dictate our own terms at the end of the war."[1] The War Secretary, Henry Stimpson, expressed the same opinion. He suggested using the bomb "to win concessions from the Russian leaders as to their cherished... state".[2]

It was in Potsdam, on July 24, that Truman signed his fateful order to deliver the "first special bomb... after about 3 August 1945 on one of the targets: Hiroshima, Kokura, Niigata and Nagasaki".[3] As seen by P.M.S. Blackett, a British historian, "the dropping of the atomic bombs was not so much the last military act of the Second World War, as one of the first major operations of the cold diplomatic war with Russia".[4]

The political speculation of the US delegation, by virtue of the monopoly possession of atomic arms, began at the Potsdam Conference. President Truman told Stalin elatedly that the United States had these super-bombs.[5] While he did so, Churchill intently watched Stalin's face. But the game proved abortive. The Soviet delegation comported itself in Potsdam with calm assurance and dignity. And its behaviour secured the success of the Potsdam talks, although some points of interest to the Soviet Union, such as that of the procedure in occupying Japan, could not be settled due to the posture of the US representatives.

The Potsdam Conference set up the Council of the Foreign Ministers of the USSR, USA, Britain, France and China, authorising it to prepare peace treaties with countries of the fascist bloc. It stipulated, too, that in discussing the details of particular treaties, the Foreign Ministers' Council would include representatives of the Great Powers that had concluded

[1] Harry S. Truman, *Memoirs*, Vol. I, New York, 1955, p. 87.
[2] Henry L. Stimson and McGeorge Bundy, *On Active Service in Peace and War*, New York, 1948, p. 641.
[3] H. Truman, *op. cit.*, p. 420.
[4] P.M.S. Blackett, *Military and Political Consequences of Atomic Energy*, London, 1948, p. 127.
[5] Ralph E. Lapp, *Atoms and People*, New York, 1956, p. 68.

the armistice with the enemy state in question. Only one exception was made: it was ruled that France be regarded as a country that had signed the Italian surrender.

The German question was the main one discussed in Potsdam. The view that German dismemberment was impermissible, consistently advocated by the Soviet Union, won the day. Stalin said, "there has been a change of view on this question. Germany remains a united state."[1] The Conference decided to preserve and develop Germany as a single democratic, peace-loving state. It proclaimed the inalienable right of the German people to independent national existence and reconstruction on a democratic and peace-loving basis.

An agreement was concluded on The Political and Economic Principles to Govern the Treatment of Germany in the Initial Control Period. This set out the guidelines for denazification, democratisation and demilitarisation. The aims of the occupation were laid down as follows: total disarmament and demilitarisation, removal of all industry capable of war production, measures to convince the German people that they had suffered a total military defeat, destruction of the nazi Party and nazi institutions, prevention of all nazi and military activity or propaganda, and reconstruction of German life along democratic lines, with subsequent peaceful co-operation of Germany on the international scene.

The agreement also envisaged measures facilitating revival of German agriculture and peace industries. A decision was passed to liquidate the German monopolies and amalgamations. Measures were laid down to assure Germany's integrity despite her division into zones of occupation. The Potsdam negotiators coped with the difficult question of reparations, drawing up a just plan acceptable to all concerned. The fundamental proposition was that reparations be exacted from the respective occupation zones, with a specified share to be placed at the Soviet Union's disposal by the Western part of the country.

The Potsdam Conference re-examined the question of the major war criminals and reaffirmed the principle of swift and just trials. A decision was passed to constitute the International Military Tribunal.

---

[1] *The Tehran, Yalta and Potsdam Conferences*, p. 286.

The Potsdam decisions on the German question were prompted by concern for peace and the security of nations. That was why they were concentrated against militarism and revanchism, and consequently resented by advocates of aggression in West Germany. The savage fury of the German militarists is illustrated by the following passage: "Stalin and Truman met and sanctioned... hasty and violent solutions... forcible partition and artificial restriction of the greatest European nation and the subjugation of all East European peoples to foreign domination."[1] The style betrays its author as a follower of hitlerism.

The Conference drew the border between Germany and Poland in compliance with historical justice along the rivers Oder and Western Neisse. The decision said the frontier would be reaffirmed by the peace conference, this being regarded as a pure formality, for a decision was also passed in Potsdam on evicting the German population not only from Czechoslovakia and Hungary, but also from Poland in her new frontiers.

Prominence was given to the fulfilment of the Yalta Conference Declaration On Liberated Europe. The US President suggested that in pursuance of that declaration the democratic governments of Rumania and Bulgaria should be reorganised without delay. "We cannot resume diplomatic relations with these Governments," he said, "until they are reorganised as we consider necessary."[2] The Soviet delegation objected, countering with its own proposal: "In Rumania and Bulgaria, just as in Finland and Hungary, due order exists and lawful authority is exercised, enjoying prestige and trust among the populations of these states in the time since the signing of the armistice by their governments."[3] It stressed the absence of any rounds for interference in the internal affairs of Rumania and Bulgaria. The Soviet delegation favoured resumption of diplomatic relations in the earliest future, because further delay was unjustified. The Conference decided that each of the three Allied Governments would examine the question of establishing diplomatic relations with Bulgaria, Hungary, Rumania and Finland.

---

[1] H. Sündermann, *Potsdam 1945. Ein Kritischer Bericht*, Leoni am Starnberger See, 1963, S. 406.

[2] *The Tehran, Yalta and Potsdam Conferences*, p. 246.

[3] *I.V.O.V.S.S.*, Vol. 5, p. 456.

The Potsdam Conference examined a number of other issues and found acceptable solutions. Speaking at the closing session, British Prime Minister Clement Attlee voiced the hope that "this Conference will be an important milestone on the road which our three nations are taking together towards a stable peace, and that the friendship between the three of us who have met here will be strong and enduring".[1] Stalin and Truman joined in this wish.

"The results of the Conference," wrote *Pravda* on this score, "are evidence of a further consolidation and growth of co-operation among the three Great Powers, the war alliance of which secured military victory against the common enemy."[2]

---

[1] *The Tehran, Yalta and Potsdam Conferences,* pp. 315-16.
[2] *Pravda,* August 3, 1945.

Chapter Nine

The Victory Over Japan

1. Secret Plans of the Japanese Militarists

Conquest of the Soviet Far East, the Maritime Territory (Primorye), East and West Siberia was high up on the list of the war aims of the Japanese imperialists. Hitler Germany wanted Soviet territory west of the Urals. Japan wanted all the land to the east. That had been the raison d'être of their anti-Soviet military bloc.

Yet, for all their recklessness, Japan's rulers were somewhat more realistic than their German allies, in their estimate of Soviet strength, due probably to the object lessons at Lake Khasan and Khalkhin Gol. They were in no hurry to attack the Soviet Union, waiting until it would weaken under the German onslaught.

However, preparations for the attack, the plan for which had been nursed for many years, were continuously extended. The Kwangtung Army built up its strength to 1,100,000 by the beginning of 1942,[1] by which time the Japanese General Staff completed a new war plan. Like the nazi plan, it contained full specifications for violence in occupied territories alongside the usual strategic and operational guidelines.

Though Japan postponed the attack, her rulers extended the maximum aid to Hitler Germany in her war on the USSR, aid of every kind, and, most important of all, compelled the Soviet Command to keep a considerable force (of up to 40 divisions) in the Far East against the Japanese troop build-up in the proximity of the Soviet frontier.

The hostile attitude of Japan and action by her naval

---

[1] *I.V.O.V.S.S.*, Vol. 5, p. 525.

forces impeded Soviet shipping in the Pacific, particularly that bound from the United States. From the summer of 1941 to the end of 1944, the Japanese detained 178 Soviet merchant vessels, including three with resort to arms, while the ships *Angarstroi*, *Kola* and *Ilmen* were sunk by Japanese submarines.[1]

Her German ally profited from Japan's economic, political and military intelligence data relating to the Soviet Union gathered in many countries in various ways, including the use of diplomatic machinery. Early in Germany's war against the Soviet Union, nazi Foreign Minister Ribbentrop thanked Tokyo for providing valuable information and said he hoped Germany could count on more intelligence in the future.[2]

In the autumn of 1941 Japanese diplomats tried directing nazi raiders over Moscow. In the summer of 1942 the Japanese General Staff supplied Germans with information about the Red Army build-up near Tambov and east of Stalingrad. They also gave figures on Soviet average monthly tank production type by type.[3]

Japan shipped valuable strategic materials—tin, rubber, and the like—to Germany either by submarine or in neutral bottoms.

These and many other acts were a gross violation of the Soviet-Japanese Neutrality Treaty, which either signatory was entitled to denounce a year before its expiration.

Hitler's crushing defeat, achieved mainly by the USSR, was a cardinal premise for victory in the Far East. The moment Germany surrendered, Japan's position became all but untenable. Yet the Japanese Government opted for continuing the war, and even protested formally to Germany for capitulating whereupon it demonstratively tore up its treaties with the already non-existent nazi government.

The decision to carry on was based mainly on the assumption that the real intents of the United States and Britain would present a thousand opportunities for manoeuvre and double-dealing. Even if the Soviet Union were to enter the war, the Japanese thought, they had capacity for long resistance, which would give them time to sound out the chances of an anti-Soviet deal with their capitalist adversaries. In that sense, Tokyo's policy in the concluding months of the war

---

[1] *Ibid.*, Vol. 5, p. 529.
[2] *Ibid.*
[3] *Ibid.*

resembled that of the nazi chiefs, who continued senseless resistance even in beleaguered Berlin. It was true that the perfidious policy of the ruling element in the United States and Britain was drawing out the war, regardless of the unjustified losses. The Japanese, meanwhile, dragged on, relying on the fact that by the summer of 1945 their war-economic potential was still fairly high.

Nor did the Japanese Government sit on its hands and wait for the expected rifts in the anti-fascist coalition. Japanese agents in neutral countries sought contacts with British and American diplomats and secret agents since April 1945, trying to inveigle them in secret negotiations of a compromise "peace". The most serious were the talks in Switzerland between Ioshira Fudjimura, a Japanese naval attaché, and an operative of Allen Dulles's agency, lasting two months.

Japan's rulers also tried to initiate negotiations with the Soviet Union. The first attempt was made on March 4, 1945, when Tokyo approached the USSR semi-officially through Tanakamura, a fishing fleet owner, requesting Moscow to mediate an armistice between Japan and the United States. Tanakamura saw Yakov Malik, the Soviet Ambassador to Japan. "Neither America nor Japan can work up the courage to start talking peace," the Japanese said. "Some divine power should help them, should recommend that they stop fighting."[1] Through Tanakamura, the Japanese Government thus invoked flattery to gain its purpose, styling the Soviet Union a "divine power".

The Japanese worked doggedly to pull off the projected intricate diplomatic manoeuvre. In requesting the USSR to mediate an armistice, the Japanese did not mean peace. All they wanted was to win time and drive a wedge between their enemies. So the matter was raised once more, but at a much higher level. In June 1945 the Soviet Ambassador in Tokyo was visited several times by ex-Premier Hirota on instructions of the Togo Government. And in mid-July the Japanese embassy in Moscow put in a formal plea with the Soviet Government, asking it to mediate and announcing that Emperor Hirohito had appointed Prince Konoe as chief negotiator. The Japanese assumed that their high-ranking spokesman would be invited to Moscow.[2]

---

[1] *I.V.O.V.S.S.*, Vol. 5, p. 537.
[2] *Ibid.*, p. 538.

The USSR turned down the Japanese request and briefed US and British representatives on all details at the conference in Potsdam. Soviet sincerity and honesty in all inter-allied relations spelled the doom of Japan's hopes of a split in the anti-fascist coalition.

The conduct of the US and British governments in relation to the USSR was, in that respect, entirely different. This we know also from the proceedings in Potsdam.

Though they wanted the Soviet Union to enter the war against Japan, the United States and Britain intended to deny it a say in postwar Far East solutions. That the two powers were eager for the Soviet Union to become involved against Japan is borne out by the fact that at Yalta they recognised the status of the Mongolian People's Republic, consented to the restoration of the legitimate Soviet right to South Sakhalin and the Kuriles and to the lease of Port Arthur, also accepting Soviet pre-eminence in Dairen and joint Sino-Soviet exploitation of the Chinese Eastern and South Manchurian railways.[1]

Their wish to deny the Soviet Union a say in postwar Far East arrangements, meanwhile, was betrayed by the fact that one of the most important Potsdam documents—the Declaration on Japan—was framed by them separately, without Soviet participation. The USSR was confronted with a fait accompli after its appearance in print.

However, the public outcry at home and the prestige of the Soviet Union, champion of the just liberative aims of the Second World War, blocked the US and British governments from laying down the terms of an imperialist peace. By and large, the programme set out in the Declaration was consistent with the idea of a democratic peace. It called for Japan's immediate and unconditional surrender and outlined in the form of an ultimatum the general political principles to be applied to defeated Japan: removal from power and influence of the culprits of the Japanese aggression, punishment of war criminals, democratic guidelines in Japan's national development, economic and military disarmament, and constitution of a peace-loving government doing the will of the people. Once this was achieved, the Declaration said, Allied occupation troops would withdraw.

---

[1] *Soviet Foreign Policy During the Great Patriotic War*, Russ. ed., Vol. III, p. 111.

However, the matter of Japan's frontiers was so worded as to leave unclear the fate of some Japanese islands, seizure of which was contemplated by the US Government. This applies to the Ryukyu islands, Okinawa included, Iwojima, the Bonin and Volcano islands, and others. Nor did the content of the other items in the Declaration accord with the true US intentions. The Declaration referred to Japan's occupation by Allied troops, whereas the US Government was resolved not to let any troops but its own discharge that mission. The Declaration referred to Japan's democratisation and removal from power of the war culprits, while Secretary of War Henry Stimson explained that in the US opinion a "monarchy under her present dynasty" should be preserved in Japan.[1]

The Japanese Government rejected the Potsdam Declaration and refused to surrender, set firmly on the course of drawing out the war.

A unique political situation arose in Southeast Asia and the Pacific. There was a distinct parting of the roads between the exponents of a temporising policy, including the ruling clique in Japan and quarters in the United States and Britain, and the protagonists of a swift victorious conclusion of the war, including the Soviet Union and the Mongolian People's Republic, the Resistance fighters in Southeast Asia and Pacific, and people throughout the world.

The Soviet entry into the war against Japan was of extraordinary international importance. None but the Soviet Union could secure for the peoples of Asia genuine liberation from the Japanese imperialist yoke and the right of forging their own future.

2. The Atomic Crime

The Soviet victory over Germany had a decisive bearing on the strategic situation in the Pacific. Germany had massed all her resources against the USSR, especially after Stalingrad, which enabled the US and British commands, who were not involved in any active engagement in Europe, to concentrate part of their forces in the Pacific and, from November 1943 onward, to assume the offensive. Throughout 1942 and 1943

---

[1] Henry L. Stimson, "The Decision to Use the Atomic Bomb", *Harper's Magazine*, February 1947, p. 104.

the United States had a mere 13 divisions in that theatre, complemented by 6 Australian divisions and an insignificant British force. That speaks of the scale of the operations, listless and half-hearted, amounting, in effect, to but the one Guadalcanal Operation. Not until September 1943 did US troops mount an action in New Guinea, dragging it out to September 1944. Simultaneously, engagements were fought to oust the Japanese from the Gilbert and Marshall islands. The lull on the Burma front lasted until January 1944, when the British took the offensive with extremely limited resources.

In autumn 1944 operations began on a grander scale, when the Americans landed in the Philippines. The Japanese navy attempted an attack on US naval forces covering the operation, but was badly defeated, losing four battleships, three aircraft carriers, three light carriers, one carrier escort, 14 cruisers, 32 destroyers and 11 submarines. US losses amounted to one light aircraft carrier, three carrier escorts, six destroyers, three destroyer escorts, one transport and seven submarines.[1] The naval victory enabled the United States to complete the Philippines operation at the end of April 1945, whereupon an Anglo-American operation was launched in Indonesia. There, as in the Philippines, the Allied action was distinctly colonialist in complexion.

An offensive by American, British and Chinese troops, supported by local guerrillas, unfolded in Burma, with the Japanese accepting defeat in May-August 1945.

The last of the operations in the Pacific war theatre was the US landing on Okinawa in the morning of April 1, 1945, under covering fire from ten battleships, thirteen cruisers and 23 destroyers.[2] The Japanese garrison of 72,000 resisted the 450,000-strong landing force until June 21.[3] On capturing the island, the United States virtually ceased hostilities against Japan, excluding air assaults on Japanese cities.

In autumn 1944 the bombing of Japan became methodical. Out of Japan's 206 large cities as many as 81 were substantially damaged. Forty-nine per cent of the buildings in Tokyo, Kawasaki and Yokohama were destroyed, 32.6 per cent in Kobe and Osaka and 31 per cent in Nagoya (those are six

---

[1] *Kampanii voiny na Tikhom okeane (War Campaigns in the Pacific)*, Moscow, 1956, pp. 402-03.

[2] *I.V.O.V.S.S.*, Vol. 5, p. 502.

[3] *Ibid.*, p. 501.

biggest Japanese cities). Nearly three-quarters of the damage was to dwellings, schools and hospitals. Meanwhile, factories, transport facilities and railways suffered insignificantly.[1] More than four million homeless in the bombed Japanese capital and nearly 22 million in the rest of the country camped among the rubble or migrated to the country.[2]

Nothing the allies did affected Japan's military backbone — her land army, which at the beginning of 1945 was an effective force of 4,100,000 men, with another 1,265,000 in the navy.[3] So long as the Japanese Government had this force it would obviously not surrender. The decisive battles were still ahead. The Allied Combined Chiefs of Staff drew up Plan Olympic, scheduling the seaborne invasion of Kyushu for November 1945, with action developing under Plan Coronet in February of the following year. The war was not expected to end before 1947.

Military and political leaders in the United States and Britain were not certain, however, that their troops would grind down the Japanese will to resist even within those liberal terms. Churchill said as much quite frankly. "These operations," he said, "involved an effort not surpassed in Europe, and no one could measure the cost in British and American life and treasure they would require. Still less could it be known how long the stamping out of the resistance of Japan in many territories she had conquered, and especially in her homeland, would last."[4]

So much the greater was the importance the US and British ruling element attached to the Soviet Union's entering the war in the Pacific. At Big Three summit conferences the subject was raised with much insistence. There was, of course, another side to it: reactionary groups in the USA and Britain did not expect a quick Soviet victory and hoped a war of attrition would sap the strength of the USSR, enabling them to re-establish their influence in Asia, as well as in Europe. That was what lay behind the strange US leisureliness after capturing Okinawa, while the bombing of residential quarters in the Japanese cities from air and sea was redoubled in order,

[1] *Istoriya voiny na Tikhom okeane (History of the War in the Pacific)*, Vol. 4, p. 169.
[2] *I.V.O.V.S.S.*, Vol. 5, p. 490.
[3] *Ibid.*, p. 493.
[4] *Parliamentary Debates. House of Commons*, Vol. 413, August 16, London, 1945, p. 77.

as the US military thought, to hammer into the Japanese and other Asian nations a "healthy" respect for US superiority and convince them of the US "predestination" of dominating other lands.

Not content, the US imperialists weighed various schemes to reduce the impact of the impending Soviet entry into the war against Japan so as to prevent the relation of world forces tipping in favour of the national and social emancipation of the peoples. That was what prompted them to use the newly-developed atomic bomb, which, they figured, would face the nations with the dilemma of either being reduced to atomic dust or accepting US diktat.

The US President ordered the atomic bombs dropped not on military targets, but peaceful citizens. In the epicentre of the bomb released over Hiroshima on August 6 were hostels for children evacuated from Tokyo. This was no pilot's error: the target, picked in advance, was a large concrete bridge in the immediate proximity of the hostels. The bomb exploded at an altitude of less than 600 metres, destroying 60,000 houses in an area of 14 square kilometres.[1] The same fate befell Nagasaki on August 9. Casualties in Hiroshima totalled over 306,000 out of a population of 430,000 and in Nagasaki nearly 137,000 out of 200,000.[2] And a quarter of a century later the radiation disease is still reaping a harvest among the survivors.

The act was a blatant crime against humanity, the guilt for which falls squarely on the US imperialists, who showed a callous disregard for elementary, universally accepted standards of international law and for the customs of war and humane principles. The bombings amounted to a deliberate extermination of civilians. "Hair-raising pictures arise in the memory of staggering devastation," Japanese authors recall. "Few escaped; people perished in explosions and fires, and from atomic radiation. On March 10, 1945, as many as 100,000 people died in the big US night raid on the eastern section of Tokyo. Those who saw the streets piled high with bodies, who saw Sumida River filled with corpses, will never forget that night."[3]

---

[1] *I.V.O.V.S.S.*, Vol. 5, p. 540.
[2] *International Affairs*, No. 8, 1965, Moscow.
[3] M. Kiyesi, O. Sindzaburio, S. Sesi, *History of Modern Japan*, Russ. ed., Moscow, 1955, p. 259.

The anger that swept the world betokened a moral and political defeat for the US imperialists. Hanson Baldwin, the *New York Times* military observer, wrote: "The use of the atomic bomb cost us dearly; we are now branded with the mark of the beast."[1]

An advocate of aggression and a prominent participant in the US Government's fateful atomic bomb decision, Admiral William D. Leahy, the President's adviser, said: "In being the first to use it, we have adopted an ethical standard common to the barbarians of the Dark Ages.... These new and terrible instruments of uncivilised warfare represent a modern type of barbarism not worthy of Christian man."[2]

The US ruling element, however, was anything but conscience-stricken. It was thrown into wild jubilation by the lowering clouds of the atomic explosions. The sycophant press averred euphorically the new weapon would bend the world to the will of the United States. It devised elaborate arguments to prove that in the new atomic age the concept of national sovereignty was outdated and the nations were preordained to submit to a world government dominated by the United States.

The atomic bombs made no immediate military impact on the course of the war. US war historian Morton, for one, holds that neither the Hiroshima nor the Nagasaki tragedies had inclined the Japanese to surrender.[3] Churchill, too, says in his war memoirs: "It would be a mistake to suppose that the fate of Japan was settled by the atomic bomb."[4]

These and other anteceding developments added importance and weight to the entry of the Soviet Union into the war against Japan.

3. Asian Peoples Fight for Liberation

Under the impression of Red Army victories and the collapse of Hitler's Reich, Japan's number one war ally, the national liberation struggle expanded swiftly in Southeast Asia and the Pacific.

In Vietnam, guerrilla units merged into armies of liberation

[1] H. Baldwin, *Great Mistakes of the War*, London, 1949, p. 99.
[2] W. Leahy, *I Was There*, pp. 441-42.
[3] L. Morton, *The Atomic Bomb and Japanese Surrender*, p. 27.
[4] W. Churchill, *op. cit.*, Vol. 6, p. 559.

Byelorussian partisans in Minsk

Soviet bombers over Berlin

The nazi eagle in the dust

For these members of the Volkssturm the war is over

Soviet soldiers dispensing food to Berliners

The Soviet flag over Berlin

Front commanders meeting in the final stages of the war

The Potsdam Summit

Tokyo following a US raid

Yet another Tokyo street after a US raid

Hiroshima after the A-bomb blast

The Red Army enters Dairen

Homewards-bound victorious

and national salvation, which mounted extensive operations against the Japanese occupation forces in the end of 1944 and the early months of 1945. A Provisional People's Committee, the nominal government of the rapidly expanding liberated areas, was formed on June 4, 1945, with control over six of the country's provinces with a population of more than one million.[1]

In Burma, the prominent liberation fighter, Aung San, became chairman of the Anti-Fascist People's Freedom League in August 1944. On March 27, 1945, the League headed a popular armed uprising — a decisive factor that aided the British troops, jointly with the insurgents, to clear the country of the Japanese. In the Philippines the guerrilla liberation army, Hukbalahap, fought with eminent success, easing the US landing and defeat of the Japanese occupation forces. Major-General Decker, US 6th Army Chief-of-Staff, heaped praise on the Hukbalahap for being "one of the best fighting units" he had ever known.[2] Extensive guerrilla fighting erupted in Malaya in 1944, led by the Anti-Japanese Union, which formed an Anti-Japanese Army of Malaya. The three nationalities — Malayans, Chinese and Indians — fought shoulder to shoulder in its ranks. The three stars on the flag of that army of peasants, workers and men of the national bourgeoisie, symbolised the wartime unity of these nationalities.

People in Indonesia and Korea also rose up against the occupation forces.

The Chinese people fought on heroically against the imperialist invader. The Eighth and New Fourth armies, and the partisans, were highly active. Regular troops operated in the first half of 1945 chiefly in the Shansi-Chahar-Hopei area, but the main form of combat was guerrilla warfare, which spread to most parts of the country.

In 1944 and 1945 the Kuomintang armies were still suffering heavy losses, conceding to the enemy much territory and many important strategic points. A large-scale Japanese offensive in the summer of 1944 in Hunan and along the Canton-Hankow railway rolled across all Hunan Province and extended Japan's control over Central China.

---

[1] *Le Viet-Nam en lutte contre le fascisme*, Paris, 1948, pp. 8, 14.
[2] George Phillips, *What Price Philippine Independence?*, New York, 1946, p. 17.

From Peking to Canton the Japanese were in control, with the seaboard and its at least 100,000,000 population totally in their hands. The Kuomintang Government was denied a considerable portion of the nation's food sources, raw materials, the manufacturing industry, railways and motor-roads, and inland waterways. By the summer of 1945, out of the country's 11,000 kilometres of railway track (figure for 1937) the Kuomintang was in control of but 1,100.[1] Casualties climbed to over 1,100,000 dead, wounded and captured with the heavy loss in lives traceable to mass desertions of the demoralised Kuomintang troops in face of the Japanese.[2] Many Kuomintang generals went over to serve the invaders.

Yet, despite the sweeping Japanese advances, Kuomintang China was deterred from surrendering by the Red Army victories in Europe, which had pushed the fascist bloc to the brink. Besides, the US and British governments objected strongly to Chiang Kai-shek's toying with the idea of surrender. The US imperialists made the most of the Kuomintang's difficulties: American monopolies became highly active in China in 1944. US Vice-President Henry Wallace, who visited China that year, and a special mission headed by Donald Nelson, Chairman of the War Production Board, which came in the autumn, studied "opportunities" for US capital.

Washington asked the Kuomintang regime to grant US monopolies the key heights in the economy. A series of agreements was drafted in 1944, and soon signed, granting US interests extensive room for colonial-style exploitation.

The turning of the scales in the Second World War, effected by the Red Army, was, however, utilised by the Chinese People's Liberation Army. While Chiang Kai-shek's troops conceded the country's most important regions to the enemy, suffering ignoble defeats and heavy losses, the People's Army made significant advances, although Japan's main forces in China were massed against it. Much territory was cleared in the course of 1944. At the beginning of the following year there were 19 liberated areas, stretching from Inner Mongolia in the north to Hainan in the south, with a population of some 95,500,000. Against them operated 56 per cent of the enemy troops and 95 per cent of the Nanking puppet

---

[1] *I.V.O.V.S.S.*, Vol. 5, p. 508.
[2] *Ibid.*

government's armies, totalling over 800,000, of which a large portion consisted of former Kuomintang troops who had gone over to the enemy with their generals.[1]

Nothing but Soviet aid could save China from colonial enslavement — if not by Japan, then by some other imperialist power.

4. The Victorious End

The Soviet entry into the war against Japan was prompted by a vital and objective necessity. A swift, powerful and active operation in the Far East could cut the knot, crush the Japanese invader and eliminate the seat of war and aggression in the East, deliver the Asian peoples from the Japanese imperialist yoke and help them attain political independence and freedom, secure the sovereign interests of the USSR in the Far East, prevent any dragging out of the Second World War and bring closer the day of peace.

With the US imperialists trying their hand at atomic black-mail, it was of the utmost importance to show the world there was a force uncowed by the intimidation. Besides, the action was in complete accord with the responsibility of the USSR as an ally meeting commitments.

The Japanese Command received advance information of the imminent Soviet campaign due to the loquaciousness of US and British military and political leaders. But it did not think the term of two or three months (from the day of Germany's surrender) sufficient for the Soviet Union to move troops and arms and deploy for combat in the East. At best, it held, this would take 10 to 12 months, and planned to strike first.

But under Communist Party guidance, the Soviet people accomplished what all foreign military experts — not just the Japanese — thought impossible. In a matter of three months (May-July) the railwaymen of the world's longest, Trans-Siberian track shuttled 136,000 troop and freight cars[2] to the Far East and Transbaikal. (The need to carry certain freights was obviated by the Party's concentrated effort in building up the Soviet Far East economy.) The railwaymen and soldiers displayed unexampled endurance. Despite the heat,

---

[1] *I.V.O.V.S.S.*, Vol. 5, p. 510.
[2] *Ibid.*, p. 551.

desert sand and water shortage, infantry units marched 40 kilometres daily, and tanks and motorised troops as much as 150.[1]

Hostilities were to be unfolded mainly in Northwest China (Manchuria) where the main Kwantung Army forces were deployed. The Japanese militarists had been preparing methodically in Manchuria for aggression against the Soviet Union since 1931, had strongly fortified zones in the most important sectors, especially along the border with the Soviet Maritime Territory. The terrain, too, was favourable for defence, with powerful mountain ranges, partly covered by dense forests, many large and lesser rivers, and large stretches of swampland. The battlefront would be over 5,000 km long and more than 800 km in depth.[2]

Considering the strength of the Kwangtung Army and characteristics of the war theatre, British and American military observers held the Soviet Union could not count on a rapid success. Hanson Baldwin, the *New York Times* observer, wrote that any swift advance was out of the question in face of the overwhelming odds.[3] The British *Daily Telegraph* commentator, Lt.-Gen. Henry Martin, maintained there was little hope of serious progress in less than 6 months.[4] These and other articles to the same effect, obviously written in advance, appeared on the first day of the operation, reflecting the secret hopes of the US and British ruling element, as well as the opinion of their writers.

On August 8, 1945, the Soviet Government addressed a statement to Japan, saying that "after the crushing defeat and surrender of Hitler Germany, Japan is the only great power still desiring to continue the war". The USSR, therefore, the statement said, was bent on "bringing closer the day of peace, delivering the peoples from further sacrifice and suffering, and enabling the people of Japan to escape the danger and destruction suffered by Germany after she had rejected unconditional surrender".[5] Acting on these considerations, and thereby fulfilling its duty as ally, the Soviet Union declared war on Japan as of August 9.

---

[1] *I.V.O.V.S.S.*, Vol. 5, p. 551.
[2] *Ibid.*, p. 549.
[3] *The New York Times*, August 10, 1945.
[4] *The Daily Telegraph and Morning Post*, August 10, 1945.
[5] *Soviet Foreign Policy During the Great Patriotic War*, Russ. ed., Vol. 3, pp. 362-63.

The lofty Soviet war aims were reflected in the strategic
plan, based on the conviction that a rapid and crushing
stroke against the Kwantung Army would compel the Japanese Government to accept the unconditional surrender, saving
the Japanese islands from direct involvement in the hostilities. The Soviet action was aimed exclusively against Japan's
armed forces, unlike that of the British and, especially,
American commands. No intention existed of making war on
civilians.

Three fronts were formed under Marshal A. M. Vasilevsky—the Transbaikal and the 1st and 2nd Far Eastern—to
destroy the Kwantung Army. A prominent part was assigned
to the Soviet Pacific Fleet.

The main blow, by the Transbaikal Front, was delivered
from the Mongolian People's Republic in a straight line at
Changchun and Mukden across desert terrain and the Great
Khingan Mountains. In the meantime, the two Far Eastern
Fronts thrust forward from north and southeast towards
Harbin, which was also to be sidewiped by the left flank of
the Transbaikal Front. The lacerating drives from three
directions converged towards the heart of Northeast China.
This was a mammoth strategic operation, also involving
the Amur Naval Flotilla.

Apart from co-operating with the ground forces, the navy
was ordered to capture Japanese ports and naval bases in
North Korea, South Sakhalin and the Kuriles.

The Soviet Armed Forces were amply primed for their
assignment. Their superiority in numbers was 1.3 : 1, tanks
4.8 : 1 and planes 1.9 : 1.[1] The Soviet force consisted of 80
divisions, 4 tank and motorised corps and 64 brigades.[2] But
superior ordnance was not enough to overcome enemy fortifications in the perplexingly difficult terrain. Superior morale
was also essential. The Soviet soldiers had been properly prepared for their mission of liberation. Once more, just as in
the war against Hitler Germany, they displayed fervent
patriotism, a deep sense of their internationalist duty and a
high degree of morale. Hence their tenacity and willingness
to contend with all but insuperable difficulties, their wholesale
heroism. The superior quality of the Soviet system over the
capitalist was the decisive factor.

---

[1] *I.V.O.V.S.S.*, Vol. 5, p. 551.
[2] *Ibid.*

The soldiers were inspired by the justice of their cause and mission. The internationalist duty of the Soviet Union and its national interests required that the Far Eastern aggressor should be crushed and hundreds of millions of people delivered from Japanese oppression.

The armed forces of the Mongolian People's Republic, which declared war on Japan on August 10, fought shoulder to shoulder with the Soviet troops. The people's armies and partisans of other Asian countries — China, Korea, Vietnam, Indonesia, Malaya, etc. — also assumed the offensive, and the population of Manchuria, too, extended aid and comfort to the Soviet Army.

The offensive began in the early hours of August 9, 1945 despite heavy rains which made the roads all but impassable, especially in the Great Khingan area. The Japanese resisted desperately. But the courage and stamina of the Soviet troops, their high morale, guaranteed success. Many soldiers — I. Batorov, A. Firsov, G. Popov and V. Kolesnik, to mention a few — displayed courage beyond compare. Pilot M. Yankov, whose plane was hit, steered his flaming aircraft into military installations in the North Korean port of Rashin, causing an explosion that demolished the installations. Examples of this kind were many.

In the first six days the Soviet troops made major strategic advances. The Transbaikal Front crossed the Great Khingan Mountains and drove forward 250-400 km, thrusting deep into the enemy's rear and moving towards the large industrial centres of Kalgan, Jehol, Mukden, Changchun and Tsitsihar. The 1st Far Eastern Front suppressed enemy resistance in the east of Manchuria, progressed 170 km and cut off the Kwantung Army from Korea. The 2nd Far Eastern Front, meanwhile, breached Japanese long-term defences and crossed the Amur and Ussuri rivers with the co-operation of the Amur Flotilla, advancing 120 km and nearing Harbin and Tsitsihar. Part of its troops were diverted for an operation liberating South Sakhalin.

On August 14 the Japanese Government became conscious of the disastrous plight of the Kwantung Army. The Supreme War Council, the government and the Emperor decided to proclaim surrender, while continuing armed resistance. And since no real capitulation ensued, the Red Army carried on with the offensive.

The US Government, meanwhile, chose to betray its

duty as ally, proclaiming August 14 as Victory Day. Addressing a press-conference, President Harry Truman declared he
was satisfied with the Japanese Government's decision and
that cease-fire orders were being issued to the Allied Armed
Forces.[1]

On the following day, General Douglas MacArthur,
nominally Allied Supreme Commander in the Far East,
issued a directive terminating the hostilities. The US Military
Mission in Moscow forwarded it to the Supreme Soviet
Command "for execution". This US attempt to prevent the
final elimination of the Kwantung Army, to prevent the
Soviet Army from moving ahead, was another bit of evidence
of the expansionist designs of the US monopolists. And it
was clumsy in the extreme, because neither operationally
nor in any other respect could the Soviet Armed Forces be
subject to MacArthur's commands. The directive was rejected,
whereupon the Military Mission said a mistake had occurred
and the directive had been forwarded not "for execution",
but "for information".[2]

However, there were additional facts testifying to the
intents of the US rulers. Acting unilaterally, in defiance of
the principles of international co-operation, President Truman
announced on August 16 that Japan would be placed under
the control of the US Command.[3] He ordered Admiral
Chester Nimitz to capture Dairen. But the order was abortive,
because Soviet troops came there first.[4] An American paratroop unit landed northwest of Mukden, but also missed the
bus, for Soviet troops were there before it.[5]

On August 18, in a message to the Soviet Government,
Truman insisted on US air bases on the Kuriles. Two days
later the matter was raised in US Congress, which declared
its desire to have US bases in the area.[6] Also, negotiations
began between MacArthur's headquarters and Chiang Kai-
shek, on the one hand, and the Japanese Command, on the
other, for Japanese troops to help combat the national liberation movements in China and other Asian countries.

---

[1] *Pravda*, August 16, 1945.
[2] John R. Deane, *The Strange Alliance*, New York, 1947, pp. 179-80.
[3] *The New York Herald Tribune*, August 17, 1945.
[4] Frederick C. Sherman, *Combat Command. The American Aircraft Carriers in the Pacific War*, New York, 1950, p. 376.
[5] *The New York Herald Tribune*, August 20, 21, 22, 23, 1945.
[6] *The New York Times*, August 19, 1945.

Meanwhile, the Soviet offensive continued, repulsing frantic Japanese counter-attacks. From different directions the Soviet troops converged on central Manchuria, to which the remnants of the Kwantung Army were fast retreating. Although the Japanese were still in command of extensive territory, their plight deteriorated rapidly. No longer did they have their fortifications. Moreover, they were cut off from Japan and from the Japanese troops in China.

Red Army operations grew in scale and, co-operating with the Pacific Fleet, moves were made to clear Korea and the Kuriles.

The Kwantung Army Command had no choice but to order its troops to lay down arms on August 17. In Japan proper, an extremist fascist group, meanwhile, attempted a coup d'état to prevent the surrender. It was poised to capture the Imperial Palace, but was denied army support, and failed.[1]

The surrender order was disobeyed by many Kwantung Army units, and the Soviet Command redoubled the pressure. The offensive was speeded by paratroop landings in the biggest Manchurian cities, one of them in Changchun, seat of Kwantung Army Headquarters. A Soviet officer suddenly appeared on the threshold of General Otosoo Yamada's quarters, handing him a demand to effect the surrender without further delays. The Commander and his staff were taken prisoner.[2]

As of August 19 the remnants of the Kwantung Army began surrendering en masse, but some seats of resistance were not wiped out until early September. Liberation of South Sakhalin was completed on August 25, and that of the Kuriles on September 1.

Japanese prisoners taken in the Soviet campaign totalled nearly 600,000.[3]

The Kwantung Army defeat was a decisive factor in Japan's capitulation. General Claire Chennault, Commander of US air forces in China, told *The New York Times* correspondent that "Russia's entry into the Japanese war was the decisive factor in speeding its end and would have been so even if no atomic bombs had been dropped.... Their (of

---

[1] *Za rubezhom*, No. 14, 1968, p. 25.
[2] S. M. Shtemenko, *The Soviet General Staff at War*, Moscow, 1969, p. 356.
[3] *I.V.O.V.S.S.*, Vol. 5, p. 581.

Soviet armies — *Ed.*) swift stroke completed the circle round Japan that brought the nation to its knees."[1]

The instrument of unconditional surrender was signed by representatives of the Allied Powers and of vanquished Japan on board the battleship *Missouri* in Tokyo Bay on September 2, 1945. The Second World War was over. The anti-Hitler coalition had won.

US and British armed forces contributed substantially to the victory over Japan. However, their success in the Pacific rested upon the Soviet victories in the main war theatre, the Soviet-German. Germany was the most powerful of the fascist allies, and Japan's condition depended on Hitler's. Regardless, it was the defeat of the Kwantung Army by the Soviet Armed Forces that was the immediate factor that compelled Japan to lay down her arms.

Swift and determined action covering Soviet arms with fresh glory, considerably reduced the duration of the Second World War, preventing more casualties. Also important was the fact that the Japanese aggressors were crushed before the pretenders to their role of Far Eastern imperialist gendarme succeeded in taking over. The Red Army victory over Japan was an effective aid to the peoples of Korea, China, Vietnam and many other Asian countries — those under Japanese occupation and those, which, though they had escaped its horrors, had by their own experience known the horrors of foreign imperialist oppression.

The victory of the Soviet Union and all other freedom-loving nations over the Japanese militarists opened a new chapter in world history, highlighted by liberation from colonialism of the peoples of Asia and then of Africa.

---

[1] *The New York Times*, August 15, 1945.

Conclusion

It is a quarter of a century since the victorious end of the war against fascism. Many Second World War secrets have come to light. But no less necessary than before is it to weigh its lessons and results.

Though the war years are receding farther into the past and fewer people are left who had participated in World War II, the magnificence of the exploit of the freedom-loving peoples has not faded. On the contrary, it is better known today, and its historic significance better understood. The victory over fascism is past history—one of the most important and decisive of its chapters. And the lessons derived are of immense value.

The most consequential outcome of the war is that socialism, represented by the Soviet Union, wrested the victory from the most aggressive and most reactionary force of world imperialism, represented by the fascist bloc, in mammoth battles of unseen dimensions. Socialism's victory over fascism is the decisive and natural outcome of the war. It proved that socialism cannot be defeated, that it is vastly superior to imperialism.

The crushing defeat of the fascist aggressors—the shock force of world imperialism—has weakened capitalism, deepened its general crisis, giving impetus to the socialist, democratic and national liberation movements.

The Soviet Union safeguarded its socialist gains, its advanced social and political system, its freedom and independence. It delivered the peoples of Europe and Asia from the fascist plague, from enslavement and extinction. The countries of

East and Southeast Europe and Southeast Asia were liberated by the Red Army; other countries, though it never set foot on their soil—as a result of its martial success.

The Soviet victory created favourable conditions in many of the liberated countries for popular democratic revolutions, which in due course, in the postwar, developed into socialist revolutions. Socialism emerged beyond the confines of one country and grew into a world system. And on this, too, the victories of the freedom-loving nations, most prominently those of Soviet arms, had a bearing.

The Soviet victory gave impetus to national liberation movements in Asia, Africa and Latin America. The crisis of the imperialist colonial system sparked by the October Socialist Revolution became more acute. Colonialism crumbled in the postwar years. Independent national states arose in place of most of the former colonies and semi-colonies.

The heroic Soviet war effort was an inspiring example for the champions of freedom, democracy and socialism in other lands. The Communist and Workers' Parties that stood in the van of the anti-fascist movement in their respective countries, proved to be the staunchest fighters for the national independence and freedom of their peoples. The influence of Communists increased visibly. Communist Parties in many countries emerged from the war as a leading influential political force. Their ranks multiplied. Prewar (1939), the Communist Parties of the world counted in their ranks 4 million members, and postwar, in 1945, as many as 20 million.[1] And this despite the fact that Communists had suffered the heaviest casualties in the fight against fascism.

At the time the war broke out the situation was highly unfavourable for the freedom-loving nations. Many European countries collapsed under the war's impact in a matter of days or, at most, weeks. Looking back today, one may say with assurance that no other country could have survived the plight of the Soviet Union at the beginning of the war. None but the Soviet people, a people that had coped with the difficulties of building socialism in a capitalist encirclement, could have performed the feat, unprecedented in magnitude,

---

[1] *Ocherki istorii KPSS (Essays on the History of the CPSU)*, Moscow, 1967, p. 351.

of turning the tide of a war that had begun so adversely. None but the Soviet people could have surmounted the incredible hardships and trials of the war, stemmed the invasion and turned the tables on the nazis.

It is farthest from our mind to belittle thereby the exploit of other nations. During and after the war the Soviet people paid due tribute to the exploit of the Englishmen, who did not bend under the impact of the air "blitz", admired the exploit of the Resistance fighters and the courage of the men who had fought shoulder to shoulder with the Red Army — the French airmen, the men and officers of the people's armies of Poland, Czechoslovakia, Bulgaria and Rumania. The Soviet people applauded the opening of the second front in Western Europe. But we should remember that the second front against Hitler Germany came into being when the outcome of the war had become a foregone conclusion thanks to the victories of Soviet arms, that Hitler's armoured armadas had been stemmed by Soviet armies, armies equipped with Soviet-made weapons. The grandeur of the exploit performed by the Soviet people will never fade.

The Soviet people stood like an insuperable barrier in the way of the nazi's drive for world supremacy. It displayed courage and tenacity beyond compare. Its heroism was the heroism of all, the day-to-day business not of individuals, not even of thousands of individuals, but of many millions — of men who had but the 'day before been teachers, bookkeepers, factory hands or miners, farmers or timbermen. This mass heroism was the most striking feature of the Great Patriotic War of the Soviet Union. Never in man's history had any nation been as closely united and as firmly determined in its dedication to the war effort.

Before the war was over 5,300,000 Soviet soldiers were decorated with Orders and more than 7,500,000 with medals. And as many as 11,525 were honoured with the highest title of all, that of Hero of the Soviet Union.[1] Among the decorated were over 100,000 women,[2] with 86 awarded the title of Hero of the Soviet Union.[3]

The Soviet war effort had been decisive. The nazi war machine was smashed, suffering crippling defeats in battles

---

[1] *I.V.O.V.S.S.*, Vol. 6, p. 156.
[2] *Ibid.*, p. 117.
[3] *Voyenno-istorichesky zhurnal*, No. 2, 1968, p. 54.

on the Soviet-German Front. The Armed Forces of the USSR destroyed 507 of Hitler's best divisions and nearly 100 divisions of his allies. And this compared to the 176 divisions that the nazi Reich lost on all the other Second World War fronts combined.[1] Three out of every four Luftwaffe planes were destroyed on the Soviet-German Front. So was the bulk of Hitler's artillery and panzers, and out of the total of 13,600,000 killed, wounded or captured German soldiers and officers, Germany lost 10,000,000 in the East.[2] Destruction of the main nazi strength on the Soviet-German Front brought about the collapse of Hitler's military and political machine. "The fact remains," wrote British historians Ernest J. Knapton and Thomas K. Derry, "that it was Soviet manpower that stemmed the tide of German conquest while Europe was still helpless in the German grip."[3] Incontestable, too, is the decisive contribution of the Soviet Armed Forces to the defeat of imperialist Japan. It was the swift drive that crushed the Kwantung Army which compelled the Japanese Government to surrender.

Victory was wrested from the enemy by the concerted effort of the Soviet people, of its Armed Forces. A galaxy of outstanding generals appeared from its midst, brought up and trained by the Communist Party. Among the most renowned are I. Kh. Bagramyan, I. D. Chernyakhovsky, V. I. Chuikov, A. G. Golovko, S. G. Gorshkov, L. A. Govorov, A. A. Grechko, I. S. Isakov, I. S. Konev, N. I. Krylov, N. G. Kuznetsov, R. Y. Malinovsky, K. A. Meretskov, K. S. Moskalenko, A. A. Novikov, F. S. Oktyabrsky, I. Ye. Petrov, M. M. Popov, K. K. Rokossovsky, B. M. Shaposhnikov, V. D. Sokolovsky, F. I. Tolbukhin, V. F. Tributs, A. M. Vasilevsky, N. F. Vatutin, K. A. Vershinin, N. N. Voronov, A. I. Yeremenko, I. S. Yumashev, M. V. Zakharov and G. K. Zhukov. Men of the Old Guard, too, helped organise the resistance, men known since Civil War times, such as S. M. Budyonny, K. Y. Voroshilov and S. K. Timoshenko.[4]

---

[1] *I.V.O.V.S.S.*, Vol. 6, p. 28.
[2] *Soviet Armed Forces in 50 Years*, Russ. ed., p. 454.
[3] E. Knapton, T. Derry, *Europe and the World Since 1914*, London, 1957, p. 271.
[4] L. I. Brezhnev, *Velikaya pobyeda sovietskogo naroda (The Great Victory of the Soviet People)*, p. 19.

The outstanding Soviet role in forging the victory was noted by many top Allied Statesmen. "On behalf of the people of the United States," wrote President Franklin D. Roosevelt on February 23, 1943, "I want to express to the Red Army on its 25th anniversary our profound admiration for its magnificent achievements unsurpassed in all history.... Such achievements can only be accomplished by an army that has skilful leadership, sound organisation, adequate training and above all determination to defeat the enemy no matter what the cost in self-sacrifice.... The Red Army and the Russian people have surely started the Hitler forces on the road to ultimate defeat and have earned the lasting admiration of the people of the United States."[1] And Winston Churchill wrote in a message two years later: "The Red Army celebrates its twenty-seventh anniversary amid triumphs which have won the unstinted applause of their allies and have sealed the doom of German militarists."[2]

The Second World War was an imperialist war when it began, a war unjust whichever way you looked at it, a war of two capitalist coalitions—Germany and her allies, on the one hand, and Britain and France, on the other. But with millions of people becoming involved in the struggle it grew gradually into a just war of liberation. This process was culminated by the Soviet Union's entry into the war. It defended the gains of socialism, championed just liberative aims, progressive ideas, and the most advanced social and political system of the times. Not only did its involvement in the war change the war's complexion; it was also the earnest of victory against fascism. The Soviet example rallied the peoples of all countries to the fight against fascism, consolidating the anti-fascist coalition.

It was the socialist system that defeated fascism in the mammoth collision with imperialism and fascism, its most monstrous progeny. The socialist economic system, the socio-political and ideological unity of the people, Soviet patriotism and the friendship of the peoples of the USSR, the unity of the people and the Communist Party, the stamina and incomparable heroism of the Soviet soldier—those were the sources of Soviet strength.

---

[1] *Correspondence...*, Vol. 2, Moscow, 1957, pp. 57-58.
[2] *Ibid.*, Vol. I, p. 305.

The victory was a natural result of the economic and political advantages implicit in the socialist system. It was a victory for the Communist Party, which had concentrated the prewar effort of the Soviet people on socialist industrialisation, on collectivising agriculture, on the cultural revolution, on firming up the socialist brotherhood of all nationalities inhabiting the country. By doing so it acted on V. I. Lenin's behests, building up the powerful material and politico-moral foundation that enabled the Soviet people to stand up to the enemy and finally crush him.

This superiority of the Soviet system, coupled with the politico-ideological unity of Soviet society, exercised a direct and decisive influence on the outcome of the war. The might and endurance of the socialist state, based on the fraternal friendship of workers, farmers and intellectuals, on the friendship of the peoples of the USSR, enabled the nation to put its economy swiftly and effectively on a war-time footing. The Soviet war industry, though plunged into highly unfavourable circumstances at the beginning of the war, excelled the German towards the end of the war in quality and quantity of production. Soviet agriculture, too, coped with its basic task, supplying the nation with the essential foods and industry with raw material.

US and British deliveries to the Soviet Union doubtless played a certain role, but amounted to but a fraction of the stream of supplies flowing from the Soviet rear during the years of war. The deliveries were miserably small also in relation to the magnitude of what the US and British war industries produced. For example, the United States manufactured 297,000 planes and 86,000 tanks in wartime alone, out of which only 14,500 planes and 7,000 tanks were sent to the Soviet Union.[1] Besides, the US and British governments would not reveal important scientific and technical information to the USSR, although it was supplied to American corporations with close cartel links with German trusts.

It will be only proper to say, therefore, that the Soviet economy went it alone in scoring its historic victory over the economies of fascist Germany and nazi-occupied Europe. Soviet strength was built up month by month in the war

---

[1] *I.V.O.V.S.S.*, Vol. 6, p. 48; *International Affairs*, No. 3, 1967, Moscow.

years, tilting the balance of strength, as illustrated by the following table:

Change in Alignment of Forces on Soviet-German Front[1]

	Active Army of the USSR			Active Forces of Germany and her Allies		
	Person-nel (thous.)	Heavy and medium tanks.*	Warplanes	Person-nel (thous.)	Heavy and medium tanks**	War-planes
June 22, 1941	2,900	1,800***	1,540****	5,500	3,712	4,950
December 1, 1941	4,200	517	2,495	5,093	1,453	2,465
May 1, 1942	5,500	2,070	3,164	6,200	3,230	3,400
November 1, 1942	6,124	2,745	3,088	6,144	6,600	3,500
July 1, 1943	6,442	6,232	8,293	5,165	5,850	2,980
January 1, 1944	6,100	3,146	8,500	6,906	5,400	3,073
January 1, 1945	6,000	7,494	14,570	3,100	3,950	1,960

* Including self-propelled artillery
** Including siege guns
*** Including new types of tanks: 1,475
**** New types of warplanes only.

The Second World War proved that the Soviet social and political system is genuinely democratic, originating from the people, responding to the people's will and resting on popular support. During the war the entire nation participated actively in discharging tasks set by the state in forging the victory, tasks often suggested and organised by the people themselves.

Directives and orders would never have elicited the initiative, dedication and heroism of the masses. The working class, the farmers and the intelligentsia were undeterred by difficulties and the sacrifice. They suffered the war's hardships and deprivations stoutly, fought heroically and worked no less heroically in defence of their socialist land.

The socialist ideology proved its superiority over the bourgeois fascist ideology. The Communist cause and Soviet patriotism, combining with internationalist ideas and the friendship of peoples, inspired the Soviet soldier in the battle

[1] Taken from *Soviet Armed Forces in 50 Years*, Russ. ed., p. 459.

against the fascist ideology, an ideology of stark nationalism, of "higher" races dominating the "lower", denying the right of existence to the bulk of the world's population, of extremism reduced to sadism, cruelty, barbarity and vandalism.

In its daily ideological and educational work, the Communist Party imparted to the people awareness of the great socialist cause, in the name of which victory over the enemy was imperative.

The lofty morale and energy of Soviet people, their mass heroism in battle and in the rear, were wrought by the tireless work of the Communist Party, and so its leadership was the chief factor in the Soviet victory.

The Communist Party led the people of Russia to victory in the Great October Socialist Revolution and rallied them for the defeat of the foreign intervention and of the whiteguards. The workers, peasants and the intelligentsia built socialist society under the guidance of the Party, producing the essential material and moral resources for the country's defence.

In the Great Patriotic War, the Party inspired and organised the struggle against the fascist invaders. Its organisational effort concerted and directed the work and strength of Soviet people in assuring the enemy's defeat. The Party rallied the entire nation for the sacred patriotic war.

The best men of the Party were sent to the most dangerous and most responsible sectors. One in every three members of the Party's Central Committee was in the battle-lines. By the end of 1941 the Red Army counted as many as 1,300,000 Communists. During the war 3 million Communists laid down their lives for the freedom and independence of the socialist land. Five million Soviet people—at the front and in the rear—joined the Party's ranks in wartime.[1]

Army Communists cemented the fighting forces, firmed up the fighting spirit of the troops. Their courage and bravery, their readiness to fight to the last breath, won them the respect and affection of their mates in army, navy and air force.

Being the guiding and leading force of Soviet society, the Communist Party also secured the fulfilment of the tasks behind the battle-lines. It mobilised workers, peasants and the intelligentsia in overcoming the difficulties, it organised

---

[1] L. I. Brezhnev, *The Great Victory of the Soviet People*, Russ. ed., p. 17.

them in a mighty upsurge of labour, it put the economy on a wartime footing and saw to it that the country became a smithy of victory.

While resolving the military and economic problems, the Communist Party also conducted extensive politico-educational work among the masses. It helped the people understand the just character of the Great Patriotic War, better to understand the advantages of the Soviet social and political system, the importance of the worker-peasant alliance, of the friendship of the peoples of the USSR, of Soviet patriotism.

The Party cultivated love of country and burning hatred of the enemy who impinged on the honour, freedom and independence of the socialist fatherland. It worked tirelessly to elevate the morale and warcraft of the Soviet soldier. It directed the political and military training of personnel in army, navy and air force. It elucidated the origins and aims of the war, tempered the soldier's fighting spirit and cultivated fearlessness and discipline. The effect of this immense ideological effort was that every Soviet soldier was aware of the war aims and of the imperative of defeating the enemy. The organisational, political and educational work of the Party among the troops, coupled with the model of heroism and fearlessness displayed by its members, were largely instrumental in mobilising the men of the Armed Forces in defeating the enemy and achieving victory.

The collective experience and collective wisdom of the Party's Central Committee, resting on the scientific basis of the Marxist-Leninist doctrine and the creative initiative of the people, assured correct leadership in the war. The Soviet victory over Hitler Germany was a triumph for the Communist Party, for its policy.

The international situation in wartime was highlighted by the emergence and vigorous action of the anti-fascist coalition which, starting in the summer of 1944, went over to coordinated military operations.

The emergence and action of the anti-fascist coalition had an extremely beneficial effect. To begin with it stood for co-operation among states with different social systems, showing that the ideas of peaceful coexistence were viable and correct.

The anti-fascist coalition defeated Hitler's policy of destroying opponents one by one. The coalition confronted Germany with the prospect of a war on two fronts, finally compelling it to fight such a war. Allied deliveries to the Soviet Union helped it to some extent in the selfless struggle. Last but not least, the existence of the anti-fascist coalition created a favourable setting for the Resistance movement in the nazi-occupied countries.

Among the war objectives pursued by the ruling element in the United States and Britain was that of maintaining and consolidating class rule. Its true aims and intents had nothing in common with the actual nature of the war, deriving from the involvement in it of the Soviet Union and the masses in other countries. This contradiction—between the nature of the war and the war aims of the US and British rulers—left a mark on the home affairs, foreign policy and war strategy of the Western members of the anti-fascist coalition. Hence the delays of the second front by the US and British governments. In a certain sense this policy was a continuation of the Munich policy and the "phoney war" because its basic aim was to weaken and exhaust the USSR in the hope of establishing Anglo-American supremacy in the post-war world. In the final count, however, it boomeranged against its makers. By the beginning of 1944 it was obvious that the Soviet Union could complete the defeat of Hitler Germany on its own. That was what prompted the US and British governments to open the second front.

When the war was over its veterans in the United States and Britain became involved in a discussion—still in train—as to who was guilty of the long delays in opening the second front. With facts in hand, American political leaders, generals and many of the historians blame their British friends, but overlook the role played by the second front opponents in the United States.

Here, for example, is how General Albert C. Wedemeyer described British behaviour at second front negotiations:

"The British were masters in negotiations—particularly were they adept in the use of phrases or words which were capable of more than one meaning or interpretation. Here was the setting, with all the trappings of a classical Machiavellian scene. I am not suggesting that the will to deceive was a personal characteristic of any of the participants. But when matters of the state were involved, our British opposite numbers had elastic scruples.... What I witnessed was the British power of diplomatic finesse in its finest hour, a power that had been developed over centuries of successful interna-

tional intrigue, cajolery, and tacit compulsions."[1] Might
we add that what Wedemeyer describes as "elastic scruples"
and "intrigue, cajolery and tacit compulsions" was all
that and much more when directed against the socialist
state.

The anti-fascist coalition moved quite distinctly towards
a democratic postwar arrangement. This was an area where
it could have displayed its positive side to the fullest. But US
and British ruling element preferred to end the co-operation
as soon as the war ended. More, they went back on the decisions adopted in Yalta and Potsdam. In place of co-operation
came the cold war.

The Resistance Movement in the nazi-occupied European
countries acquired great importance in the Second World
War. Its eruption and powerful growth was an unexpected
and highly undesirable impediment for Hitler. The movement
drew inspiration from the resistance and successes of the
Red Army and from the partisan movement of Soviet patriots.
Underscoring this, L. M. Chassin, the French war historian,
wrote: "This magnificent resistance of the Russians, which
shrank from no sacrifice, was the signal for the immense
wave of revolt that swept across all the countries occupied
by Germany."[2] We might mention other important points:
the freedom fighters of the Resistance movement benefited
greatly from the experience of the Soviet partisans and their
methods; they displayed a deep sense of communion with the
Soviet patriots and were eager, in the absence of the second
front in Europe, to help the Soviet Union in every way they
could.

The support—moral, military and, in some cases, material—extended to the Resistance movement by the Soviet
Union was of great importance for its growth. First and
foremost, it was the crushing blows delivered to the nazis on
the Soviet-German Front that helped the Resistance movement grow.

The exploit of the Soviet people wakened the national and
internationalist feelings of millions of people all over the
globe. It epitomised the unity of national and international
war aims, prompting many people whose patriotism had

---

[1] A. Wedemeyer, *Wedemeyer Reports!*, New York, 1958, pp. 105-06.
[2] L. Chassin, *Histoire militaire de la seconde guerre mondiale 1939-1945*,
Paris, 1947, p. 132.

been overlaid with self-interest and egoism to regain their integrity and join the Resistance.

The Resistance movement contributed to smashing the fascist bloc and the various reactionary ruling cliques associated with it.

The Second World War showed that all imperialist aspirations for world supremacy have no chance to succeed in the modern world. That Germany went down in defeat was no accident. And that was why her defeat was so crushing. The main outcome of the war was that the defeat was visited on fascism and imperialism in that most mammoth of all conflagrations, while democracy, progress and socialism proved victorious.

The history of the war against fascism is first and foremost the history of peoples fighting for liberation and achieving a conclusive victory. The lessons of the war showed once more that the masses play an immense and growing role in the process of history and that growth of their political involvement and awareness is an incontestable law of the age.

The victory over fascism was gained through the heroic efforts of tens of millions of Soviet people, blending with the efforts of Resistance fighters and the struggle of the peoples of the United States and Britain on the front and in the rear. The price of victory was dearly paid in life and blood, and the victory belongs to all humanity, the supreme duty of which is to cherish it and to safeguard peace.

REQUEST TO READERS

Progress Publishers would be glad to have your opinion of this book, its translation and design and any suggestions you may have for future publications.

Please send all your comments to 21, Zubovsky Boulevard, Moscow, U.S.S.R.